LEARNING AND UNDERSTANDING

IMPROVING ADVANCED STUDY OF MATHEMATICS AND SCIENCE IN U.S. HIGH SCHOOLS

Committee on Programs for Advanced Study of Mathematics and Science in American High Schools

Jerry P. Gollub, Meryl W. Bertenthal, Jay B. Labov, and Philip C. Curtis, Editors

Center for Education

Division of Behavioral and Social Sciences and Education

National Research Council

NATIONAL ACADEMY PRESS
Washington, DC

NATIONAL ACADEMY PRESS • 2101 Constitution Avenue N.W. • Washington, DC 20418

NOTICE: The project that is the subject of this report was approved by the Governing Board of the National Research Council, whose members are drawn from the councils of the National Academy of Sciences, the National Academy of Engineering, and the Institute of Medicine. The members of the committee responsible for the report were chosen for their special competences and with regard for appropriate balance.

This study was conducted under an award from the National Science Foundation and the United States Department of Education (Award # ESI-9817042). Any opinions, findings, conclusions, or recommendations expressed in this report are those of the members of the committee and do not necessarily reflect the views of the sponsors.

Library of Congress Cataloging-in-Publication Data

Learning and understanding : improving advanced study of mathematics and science in U.S. high schools / Committee on Programs for Advanced Study of Mathematics and Science in American High Schools, Center for Education, Division of Behavioral and Social Sciences and Education ; Jerry P. Gollub ... [et al.], editors.
   p. cm.
Includes bibliographical references and index.
  ISBN 0-309-07440-1
  1. Mathematics--Study and teaching (Secondary)—United States. 2. Science—Study and teaching (Secondary)—United States. 3. Advanced placement programs (Education) I. Gollub, J. P., 1944- II. National Research Council (U.S.). Committee on Programs for Advanced Study of Mathematics and Science in American High Schools.
  QA13 .L38 2002
  507.1'073--dc21

                 2002006487

Additional copies of this report are available from

National Academy Press
2101 Constitution Avenue, NW
Box 285
Washington, DC 20055
800/624-6242
202/334-3313 (in the Washington Metropolitan Area)
<http://www.nap.edu>

Printed in the United States of America.

Suggested citation:

National Research Council. (2002). *Learning and understanding: Improving advanced study of mathematics and science in U.S. high schools*. Committee on Programs for Advanced Study of Mathematics and Science in American High Schools. J.P. Gollub, M.W. Bertenthal, J.B. Labov, and P.C. Curtis, Editors. Center for Education, Division of Behavioral and Social Sciences and Education. Washington, DC: National Academy Press.

THE NATIONAL ACADEMIES

National Academy of Sciences
National Academy of Engineering
Institute of Medicine
National Research Council

The **National Academy of Sciences** is a private, nonprofit, self-perpetuating society of distinguished scholars engaged in scientific and engineering research, dedicated to the furtherance of science and technology and to their use for the general welfare. Upon the authority of the charter granted to it by the Congress in 1863, the Academy has a mandate that requires it to advise the federal government on scientific and technical matters. Dr. Bruce M. Alberts is president of the National Academy of Sciences.

The **National Academy of Engineering** was established in 1964, under the charter of the National Academy of Sciences, as a parallel organization of outstanding engineers. It is autonomous in its administration and in the selection of its members, sharing with the National Academy of Sciences the responsibility for advising the federal government. The National Academy of Engineering also sponsors engineering programs aimed at meeting national needs, encourages education and research, and recognizes the superior achievements of engineers. Dr. Wm. A. Wulf is president of the National Academy of Engineering.

The **Institute of Medicine** was established in 1970 by the National Academy of Sciences to secure the services of eminent members of appropriate professions in the examination of policy matters pertaining to the health of the public. The Institute acts under the responsibility given to the National Academy of Sciences by its congressional charter to be an adviser to the federal government and, upon its own initiative, to identify issues of medical care, research, and education. Dr. Harvey V. Fineberg is president of the Institute of Medicine.

The **National Research Council** was organized by the National Academy of Sciences in 1916 to associate the broad community of science and technology with the Academy's purposes of furthering knowledge and advising the federal government. Functioning in accordance with general policies determined by the Academy, the Council has become the principal operating agency of both the National Academy of Sciences and the National Academy of Engineering in providing services to the government, the public, and the scientific and engineering communities. The Council is administered jointly by both Academies and the Institute of Medicine. Dr. Bruce M. Alberts and Dr. Wm. A. Wulf are chairman and vice chairman, respectively, of the National Research Council.

COMMITTEE ON PROGRAMS FOR ADVANCED STUDY OF MATHEMATICS AND SCIENCE IN AMERICAN HIGH SHOOLS

JERRY P. GOLLUB, *Cochair*, Department of Physics, Haverford College
PHILIP C. CURTIS, Jr., *Cochair*, Department of Mathematics, University of California, Los Angeles
CAMILLA BENBOW, Peabody College of Education and Human Development, Vanderbilt University
HILDA BORKO, School of Education, University of Colorado, Boulder
WANDA BUSSEY, Department of Mathematics, Rufus King High School, Milwaukee, WI
GLENN A. CROSBY, Department of Chemistry, Washington State University
JOHN A. DOSSEY, Department of Mathematics (retired), Illinois State University
DAVID ELY, Department of Biology, Champlain Valley Union High School, Hinesburg, VT
DEBORAH HUGHES HALLETT, Department of Mathematics, University of Arizona
JOHN K. HAYNES, Department of Biology, Morehouse College
VALERIE E. LEE, School of Education, University of Michigan
STEPHANIE PACE MARSHALL, President, Illinois Mathematics and Science Academy
MICHAEL E. MARTINEZ,* Department of Education, University of California, Irvine
PATSY W. MUELLER, Department of Chemistry, Highland Park High School, IL and Regina Dominican High School, Wilmette, IL
JOSEPH NOVAK, Department of Education (Emeritus), Cornell University; Institute for Human and Machine Cognition, University of West Florida
JEANNIE OAKES, Graduate School of Information Studies, University of California, Los Angeles
VERA C. RUBIN, Department of Terrestrial Magnetism, Carnegie Foundation of Washington (through November 2, 2000)
ROBIN SPITAL, Science Department, The Bolles School, Jacksonville, FL
CONRAD L. STANITSKI, Department of Chemistry, University of Central Arkansas
WILLIAM B. WOOD, Department of Molecular, Cellular, and Developmental Biology, University of Colorado, Boulder

---

*Michael Martinez was an active member of the committee from its inception until August 1, 2001, when he began a position as program officer in the Directorate for Human Resources at the National Science Foundation. National Research Council rules prevented Dr. Martinez from contributing to the final preparation of the report after assuming this position.

JAY B. LABOV, *Study Director*, Center for Education
MERYL W. BERTENTHAL, *Senior Program Officer*
JOHN SHEPHARD, *Research Assistant*
ANDREW E. TOMPKINS, *Senior Project Assistant*
ALEXANDRA BEATTY, *Senior Program Officer* (until November 1999)
RICHARD J. NOETH (until January 2000)
MARILEE SHELTON, *Program Officer*, Board on Life Sciences (until November 2000)

MEMBERS OF THE DISCIPLINARY CONTENT PANELS*

Biology

WILLIAM B. WOOD, *Committee Liaison and Chair*, Department of Molecular, Cellular, and Developmental Biology, University of Colorado, Boulder

ROBERT A. BLOODGOOD, Department of Cell Biology, University of Virginia

MARY P. COLVARD, Department of Biology, Cobleskill-Richmond High School, NY

PATRICK G. EHRMAN, Department of Molecular Biotechnology, University of Washington

JOHN JUNGCK, Department of Biology, Beloit College

JAMES H. WANDERSEE, Department of Curriculum and Instruction, Louisiana State University

Chemistry

CONRAD L. STANITSKI, *Committee Liaison and Chair*, Department of Chemistry, University of Central Arkansas

ARTHUR B. ELLIS, Department of Chemistry, University of Wisconsin, Madison

PATRICIA METZ, Department of Chemistry, United States Naval Academy

JOHN C. OLIVER, Department of Chemistry, Lindbergh High School, St. Louis, MO

DAVID PYSNIK, Chemistry Department, Sydney High School, Sydney, NY

A. TRUMAN SCHWARTZ, Department of Chemistry, Macalester College

GLENDA M. TORRANCE, Chemistry Department, Montgomery Blair High School, Silver Spring, MD

Physics

ROBIN SPITAL, *Committee Liaison and Chair*, Science Department, The Bolles School, Jacksonville, FL

S. JAMES GATES, JR., Physics Department, University of Maryland, College Park

DAVID M. HAMMER, Physics Department, University of Maryland, College Park

---

*Biographical sketches for members of the four disciplinary content panels are included as an appendix with each panel report.

ROBERT C. HILBORN, Department of Physics, Amherst College

ERIC MAZUR, Department of Applied Physics, Harvard University

PENNY MOORE, College of Mathematical and Physical Sciences, Ohio State University

ROBERT A. MORSE, Physics Department, St. Albans School, Washington, DC

Mathematics

DEBORAH HUGHES HALLETT, *Committee Liaison and Chair*, Department of Mathematics, University of Arizona

HAROLD BOGER, Department of Mathematics, Crenshaw High School, Los Angeles, CA

MARILYN P. CARLSON, Department of Mathematics, Arizona State University

ROGER HOWE, Department of Mathematics, Yale University

DANIEL J. TEAGUE, Department of Mathematics, North Carolina School of Science and Mathematics, Durham, NC

ALAN C. TUCKER, Department of Applied Mathematics and Statistics, State University of New York, Stony Brook

Preface

The United States has compiled a remarkable record of excellence and leadership in science, mathematics, and technology over the past half century. Effective mathematics and science education at the advanced high school level is critical if this record is to continue. In addition, quality science and mathematics education is important in preparing students to succeed in higher education and to be informed citizens.

This report is the product of a 2-year study of programs for advanced science and mathematics education in U.S. high schools. Recent research on learning and program design served as the basis for the analysis. This emerging knowledge was used to evaluate the Advanced Placement (AP) and International Baccalaureate (IB) programs and to examine specific ways in which these and other programs of advanced study can be made more effective and more accessible to all students who might benefit from them.

The study committee comprised professional educators, teachers with experience in the AP and IB programs, university scientists and mathematicians, experts in learning and talent development, and authorities on access and equity in education. Their diverse perspectives resulted in an interdisciplinary approach to the analysis and assessment of programs for advanced study. We appreciate the cooperative efforts of the study committee to achieve a balance among these different perspectives.

This study was particularly complex for several reasons. First, the committee was charged by the National Research Council (NRC) to consider advanced study in depth in four disciplines: biology, chemistry, physics, and mathematics (with an emphasis on calculus). The committee therefore convened diverse panels of experts in each of these fields, and their extensive reports form an important part of the study results, grounding the analysis in the classroom practice of advanced study programs.[1] A second source of complexity in the study was the fact that the AP and IB programs must be

---

[1]The four panel reports are available online as pdf files at www.nap.edu/catalog/10129.html.

examined in the context of the entire system of education in the United States. These programs have important effects on school curricula and staffing starting in the middle-school years, and they also influence and are shaped by trends in higher education. A third source of complexity was the dilemma of how to deal with extensive disparities in access to advanced study that have the effect of excluding many students, especially minorities and residents of impoverished communities, while continuing to ensure that traditionally advantaged students are served effectively.

All members of the committee contributed generously to the study, both to discussions held during and between meetings, and, by providing draft text or comments, to the process of preparing this report. Four committee members also served as panel chairs, drafted the respective panel reports, and responded to reviews: William Wood, biology panel; Conrad Stanitski, chemistry panel; Robin Spital, physics panel; and Deborah Hughes Hallett, mathematics panel. Their exceptional efforts contributed substantially to the success of this project. We also acknowledge important scholarly work on access and equity by Valerie Lee and Jeannie Oakes. In addition, we note the central contributions of Camilla Benbow, Hilda Borko, John Dossey, Stephanie Pace Marshall, Michael Martinez, and Joseph Novak, who as a group developed the material presented in Chapters 6 and 7 and guided the analyses of Chapters 8 and 9. We thank David Ely, Patsy Mueller, Robin Spital, and Wanda Bussey, the members of the committee who are teachers of the AP and IB programs, for helping the committee understand today's high school settings. Finally, we acknowledge Glenn Crosby's contributions to our discussions of teacher education and professional development.

The NRC's Center for Education provided exceptional support for this project. Project director Jay Labov and senior program officer Meryl Bertenthal worked tirelessly to seek out the extensive information required by the study committee and to help overcome obstacles to achieving consensus. They also contributed substantially to the process of drafting this report and guiding the panel reports successfully through the stringent NRC review process. We appreciate as well the capable efforts of John Shephard and Andrew Tompkins, our research and project assistants. Leslie Ann Pierce, an experienced AP and IB teacher, served as consultant to the committee and contributed to the report. Program officer Marilee Shelton and consultant Billy Goodman assisted in the early phases of the project.

We acknowledge the helpfulness of the staff of the AP and IB, who provided the committee with extensive information. Their commitment to the long-term improvement of these programs and their receptiveness to the committee's ideas were evident. Although this report constitutes a strong critique in many respects, its recommendations should not be regarded either as questioning the importance of these programs or as conflicting with improvement efforts already in progress. The active collaboration of many different groups will be required to implement the recommendations of this study.

This study is part of a major commitment by the NRC to use its expertise in the service of science and mathematics education. The committee anticipates that the report will be useful to all those concerned with improving educational quality and equity, including program developers, science and mathematics teachers, university scientists, policymakers, school administrators, and parents.

Jerry W. Gollub and Philip C. Curtis, *Cochairs*

Acknowledgments

The committee and staff thank the many individuals and organizations that gave generously of their time and expertise to help with this study.

First, we acknowledge the support of the National Science Foundation and the U.S. Department of Education, Office of Educational Research and Improvement. We particularly thank Janice Earle of the National Science Foundation and Patricia Ross of the Office of Educational Research and Improvement of the Department of Education for the support and encouragement they provided to this committee during the past 36 months.

We acknowledge the important contributions of the 22 individuals who, as members of four disciplinary content panels, conducted in-depth analyses of the Advanced Placement (AP) and International Baccalaureate (IB) programs in mathematics, chemistry, biology, and physics. Our sincerest thanks go to Robert A. Bloodgood, University of Virginia; Harold Boger, Crenshaw High School, Los Angeles, California; Marilyn P. Carlson, Arizona State University; Mary P. Colvard, Cobleskill-Richmond High School, NY; Patrick G. Ehrman, University of Washington; Arthur B. Ellis, University of Wisconsin, Madison; S. James Gates, Jr., University of Maryland, College Park; David M. Hammer, University of Maryland, College Park; Robert C. Hilborn, Amherst College; Roger Howe, Yale University; John Jungck, Beloit College; Eric Mazur, Harvard University; Patricia Metz, United States Naval Academy; Robert A. Morse, St. Albans School, Washington, DC; Penny Moore, Ohio State University; John C. Oliver, Lindbergh High School, St. Louis, Missouri; David Pysnik, Sydney High School, Sydney, New York; Truman Schwartz, Macalester College; Daniel J. Teague, North Carolina School of Science and Mathematics, Durham, North Carolina; Glenda M. Torrance, Montgomery Blair High School, Silver Spring, Maryland; Alan C. Tucker, State University of New York, Stony Brook; and James H. Wandersee, Louisiana State University.

We are grateful to Lee Jones, director of the AP program, and Paul Campbell, associate director of the International Baccalaureate Organisation of North America (IBNA), for providing program materials and data throughout the study. They attended several committee meetings and workshops as invited guests, organized presentations to the committee, and answered ongoing questions about their respective programs. Their cooperation was critical to our efforts.

When this study began, the IB program was less familiar than the AP program to most committee members. We thank the many individuals who provided the committee with in-depth information about the IB program. David Roylance, IB coordinator, Jeb Stuart High School in Fairfax, Virginia, presented an overview of the IB program model. The committee obtained insight into the structure, organization, and goals of IB science and mathematics curricula, instructional models, assessment, and professional development opportunities from Jonathan Knopp, Rufus King High School, Milwaukee, Wisconsin; Ken Fox, Smoky Hill High School, Aurora, Colorado; Arden Zipp, State University of New York at Courtland; and IBNA associate director Paul Campbell. We acknowledge as well the ongoing help received from IBNA staff members George Pook, Roger Brown, Jeff Thompson, and Helen Drennen.

Individually and collectively, members of the committee benefited from discussions with experts in a variety of fields. We especially thank James Pellegrino, University of Illinois at Chicago, and José Mestre, University of Massachusetts at Amherst, who helped expand our understanding of the relevance of research on human cognition to the design and evaluation of advanced study programs. Their advice helped the committee conceptualize the model presented in this report for the design and evaluation of advanced study programs.

Results from the *Third International Mathematics and Science Study (TIMMS)* contributed to the motivation for this study. We wish to thank Michael Martin, TIMSS international deputy study director, and Patrick Gonzales, National Center for Education Statistics, U.S. Department of Education, for helping the committee understand the *TIMMS* results.

Many individuals aided the committee's work by participating in a series of information-gathering workshops that were held in conjunction with several of the committee's meetings. The following individuals participated in a committee workshop addressing the design and development of AP programs and assessments in mathematics and science: Dr. John Smarrelli, chair, AP Biology Committee, Loyola University, Chicago; Dr. Robert Cannon, chief faculty consultant, AP Biology, University of North Carolina at Chapel Hill; Dr. Thomas P. Dick, chair, AP Calculus Committee, Oregon State University; Dr. Larry Riddle, chief faculty consultant, AP Calculus, Agnes Scott College; Dr. William H. Ingham, chair, AP Physics Committee, James Madison University; Patrick Polley, chief faculty consultant, AP Physics, Beloit College; Beth Nichols, assessment specialist, Educational Testing Service; Chancey Jones, assessment specialist, Educational Testing Service; Ann Marie Zolandz, assessment specialist, Educational Testing Service; and Rick Morgan, measurement statistician, Educational Testing Service. Howard Everson, The College Board vice-president for Teaching and Learning, was also instrumental in helping the committee understand the mission and goals of the AP program.

Bernard L. Madison, professor of mathematics, University of Arkansas, Fayetteville, and a member of the College Board's Commission on the Future of the Advanced Placement Program, provided the committee with an overview of the commission's findings and recommendations.

Three individuals—Peter O'Donnell, president of the O'Donnell Foundation in Dallas, Texas; Carolyn Bacon, executive director of the Foundation; and Gregg Fleisher, president, Advanced Placement Strategies—spoke with the committee about an innovative program that engages students, teachers, and schools in an effort to increase the number of traditionally underrepresented Texas students who take AP courses and succeed on AP examinations.

We also acknowledge several consultants who contributed significantly to the project. Carolyn Callahan, University of Virginia, helped the committee understand the roles of AP and IB in meeting the needs of gifted and talented students. Karen Boeschenstein, Office of Undergraduate Admission at the University of Virginia, assisted the committee in interpreting data that was gathered through an informal survey of deans of admission (see Chapters 2 and 10). Bert Green, The Johns Hopkins University, helped the committee with an independent evaluation and interpretation of the College Board's AP validity studies (see Chapter 10). Julie Heifetz, Moss Rehabilitation Center in Philadelphia, Pennsylvania, interviewed AP and IB students from different schools.

Many individuals within the National Research Council (NRC) assisted the committee. We are grateful for the support of Bruce Alberts, president of the National Academy of Sciences, who took a particular interest in this study and provided support and encouragement along the way. Alexandra Beatty drafted the original proposal for the project, and Richard Noeth was study director in the early months of the project. We thank Michael Feuer, director of the Center for Education, for his support and encouragement, and Kirsten Sampson Snyder, who shepherded the four panel reports and the main committee report through the NRC review process, and Yvonne Wise for processing the report through final production. Genie Grohman gave valuable assistance in thinking about the organization of this report, and Judy Koenig contributed to the assessment sections of the report. Rona Briere capably edited the final version. Naomi Chudowsky, study director of the Cognitive Foundations of Assessment Committee, shared with us early drafts of her committee's report and consulted with us about our conceptual model for the design and evaluation of advanced study programs. Brenda

Buchbinder managed the finances of the project, and Viola Horek, administrative officer for the Center for Education, provided important assistance.

This report has been reviewed in draft form by individuals chosen for their diverse perspectives and technical expertise, in accordance with procedures approved by the NRC's Report Review Committee. The purpose of this independent review is to provide candid and critical comments that will assist the institution in making the published report as sound as possible and to ensure that the report meets institutional standards for objectivity, evidence, and responsiveness to the study charge. The review comments and draft manuscript remain confidential to protect the integrity of the deliberative process. We wish to thank the following individuals for their participation in the review of this report:

Jo Boaler, Stanford University
Stephen B. Dunbar, University of Iowa
Martin L. Johnson, University of Maryland
Joel J. Mintzes, University of North Carolina at Wilmington
Carolyn J. Morse, University of North Carolina at Chapel Hill
Harris Sokoloff, University of Pennsylvania
Patsy Wang-Iverson, Research for Better Schools
James A. Watts, Southern Regional Education Board

Although the reviewers listed above have provided many constructive comments and suggestions, they were not asked to endorse the conclusions or recommendations nor did they see the final draft of the report before its release. The review of this report was overseen by Royce W. Murray and Melvin C. George. Appointed by the NRC, they were responsible for making certain that an independent examination of this report was carried out in accordance with institutional procedures and that all review comments were carefully considered. Responsibility for the final content of this report rests entirely with the authoring committee and the institution.

In addition, the following individuals served as reviewers for the four panel reports included as supporting documentation in this volume:

Biology:
Neil A. Campbell, University of California, Riverside
Warren Hunnicutt, St. Petersburg Junior College, FL
Charles Lytle, North Carolina State University
Randy McGonegal, Palm Harbor University High School, Palm Harbor, FL
Duncan MacQuarrie, Tacoma Public Schools, Tacoma, Washington

Chemistry:
William R. Robinson, Purdue University
Keith Sheppard, Columbia University
Myra Thayer, Fairfax County Public Schools, Virginia
David Thissen, University of North Carolina at Chapel Hill

Physics:
Susan A. Agruso, Charlotte-Mecklenburg School District, North Carolina
Arthur Eisenkraft, Foxlane High School, Bedford, NY
Mark Headlee, United World College, Montezuma, NM
William H. Ingham, James Madison University
Kris Whelan, Plano Independent School District, Plano, TX

Mathematics:
John R. Brunsting, Hinsdale Central High School, Hinsdale, IL
Miriam Clifford, Caroll College, Waukesha, WI
Renee Fish, Palm Harbor University High School, Palm Harbor, FL
Michael J. Kolen, University of Iowa
Thomas W. Tucker, Colgate University

Although the reviewers listed above have provided many constructive comments and suggestions, they were not asked to endorse the conclusions or recommendations of the panel reports, nor did they see the final drafts of the reports before their release. The review of these reports was overseen by Philip C. Curtis. Appointed by the NRC, he was responsible for making certain that an independent examination of these reports was carried out in accordance with institutional procedures and that all review comments were carefully considered. Responsibility for the final content of these reports rests entirely with the authoring panels and the institution.

As a final note, we would like to acknowledge that when copyright permissions were being sought from various sources, the IBO pointed out several inaccuracies in our listing of their programs. Since this report was already in the final stages of printing when these errors were noted, we correct them here for the entire report and extend our apologies to the IBO: The "program guides" to which we refer throughout the main report as well as the content panel reports should instead be labeled as "subject guides" in specific disciplines (e.g., Chemistry guide). The IB Diploma Programme is one of three academic programs. The IBO is now using the U.S. spelling of "Organization" as part of its official name rather than "Organisation" that is presented throughout this report. Finally, it also should be noted that permission to reprint AP materials does not constitute review or endorsement by the Educational Testing Service or the College Board of this publication as a whole or of any questions or testing information it may contain.

Contents

---

*Content Panel Reports are not printed in this volume but are available online. Go to http://www.nap.edu and search for *Learning and Understanding*.

LEARNING AND UNDERSTANDING

Executive Summary

This report presents results of a 2-year effort by a National Research Council (NRC) committee to examine programs for advanced study of mathematics and science in U.S. high schools. The committee focussed on the two most widely recognized programs in the United States, and the only two of national scope: Advanced Placement (AP) and International Baccalaureate (IB). The committee also identified alternatives to IB and AP and addressed specific questions about advanced study.[1] The committee's statement of task and study questions are found in Appendix C.

While international comparisons of the performance of advanced students served as a catalyst for the study, its primary motivator was the improved, research-based understanding of teaching and learning that has emerged recently, and its application to improving advanced study. In approaching its charge, the committee considered advances in the cognitive and learning sciences. The committee also examined research about the AP and IB programs using information provided by the College Board and the International Baccalaureate Organisation (IBO). Neither the AP or IB programs nor independent researchers, however, have yet gathered or published critical data that the committee sought. Therefore, the committee also relied on materials and expert testimony from AP and IB program officials and teachers for some of the data used in its analyses. More studies are needed to address the many issues that are raised by this report.

---

[1]The committee found that defining "advanced study" for secondary students is surprisingly difficult. Establishing a clear definition is problematic in part because these programs share a number of the objectives of other high school courses. Although many equate accelerated content (e.g., college-level material) with secondary-school advanced study, the committee concluded that acceleration alone does not define a quality program. Indeed, the inclusion of too much accelerated content can prevent students from achieving the primary goal of advanced study: deep conceptual understanding of the content and unifying concepts of a discipline.

The committee found that existing programs for advanced study are frequently inconsistent with the results of the research on cognition and learning. This report describes how program developers, schools, and educators can remedy this situation by considering all components of educational programs: curriculum, instruction, ongoing and end-of-course assessments, and teacher preparation and professional development.

Also examined in depth is the issue of equal access to advanced study. Advanced study is no longer only for an elite audience of exceptionally talented and privileged students; participation has become almost the norm for students seeking admission to selective colleges. Yet minorities, inner-city and rural students face serious limitations in accessing programs. These broader populations of students who could benefit from advanced study are currently limited by their prior educational opportunities, their schools' ability to provide effective learning environments, and the availability of qualified and effective teachers. Improvements in these areas could significantly expand the population that can be served effectively by advanced study.

Expertise on the committee included scientist-researchers, secondary teachers of AP and IB, science and mathematics educators working on teacher education and issues of access and equity, cognitive scientists, and educational administrators. Panels of experts in the disciplines (biology, chemistry, physics, and mathematics) also advised the committee. The four panel reports provided a critical basis for the committee's analysis and may be used independently of this volume. They are available online[2] and are summarized in Appendix A.

This report is intended for many audiences concerned with high school science and mathematics education in general and advanced study in particular, including program developers, high school and higher education faculty, university and high school administrators, policymakers, and parents.

CONTEXT OF ADVANCED STUDY

Advanced study has wide-ranging effects on curricula, teachers, and students, therefore, advanced courses must be considered within a broader context that includes the schools where the courses are offered, preceding grade levels, and higher education. Advanced study in science and mathematics makes special demands on facilities, financial resources, and personnel at both the middle- and high school levels.

---

[2]At http://www.nap.edu/catalog/10129.html.

Components

Teachers. Students learn best from teachers with strong content knowledge and pedagogical skills. Lack of access to high-quality teachers may preclude some students, especially minorities and those living in poverty, from pursuing advanced study. All 50 states require licensing of public school teachers; none requires special certification for those providing advanced study. High school teachers see themselves as subject area specialists. They teach up to 175 students per day, and have little opportunity to work with colleagues to improve curriculum or instruction. They frequently cite inadequate support, lack of student motivation, and student discipline problems as reasons for leaving teaching.

Coordination. Academic preparation for advanced study begins in middle school. Mathematics and science courses in these grades often lack focus, cover too many topics, repeat material, and are implemented inconsistently. In mathematics, states are moving toward offering algebra in eighth grade. Increasing numbers of middle schools are instituting integrated science curricula that de-emphasize disciplines. Middle and high school teachers rarely have opportunities to coordinate curricula or instruction for grades 7–12.

Curricular Differentiation. More than 80 percent of middle schools and many high schools direct or allow students to choose their classes in mathematics, science, and other subjects. Other schools offer core curricula that are narrowly focused on academic subjects and allow students few choices. Early differential placement steers some students away from rigorous academic programs. Research indicates that constrained curricula are more effective and equitable in helping students pursue advanced study.

Sequencing. The typical progression of courses in high school mathematics leading to calculus is Algebra I, geometry, Algebra II, trigonometry, and precalculus. Most state high school graduation requirements also include 2 years of science, although college-bound students traditionally take more, usually biology, chemistry, and then physics.

Standards. In science, standards developed by the American Association for the Advancement of Science and the National Research Council call for increased emphasis on inquiry and in-depth study of fewer topics. In mathematics, the standards from the National Council of Teachers of Mathematics emphasize learning of concepts and helping students understand mathematics more deeply. Forty-nine states have developed standards and curriculum frameworks in mathematics and science. All 50 states test their students and 27 states hold schools accountable for results. The AP and IB programs are not predicated on state or national standards in any subject area, but can complement standards-based reform efforts. Both provide nationally recognized external measures of student achievement, but schools can implement the programs in ways that conform to local or state standards.

Students. High school students face competing time pressures. Typical students work 15–20 hours per week, spend 20–25 hours socializing, 5 hours in extracurricular activities, and 15 hours watching television. Significant numbers of students—particularly those from low-income families—think so much about problems at home that they cannot concentrate in school.

Unequal Access

There is an enduring belief that advanced study confers advantages to students in college; thus, ever-increasing numbers enroll in AP courses and IB programs. However, access to advanced study is uneven. Some high schools offer multiple sections in many AP subjects; others provide none. These differences are associated with school size and location, and the availability of AP and IB in a school decreases as the percentage of minority or low-income students increases, especially in mathematics and science. Even where available, students from underrepresented and low-income groups take advanced courses less frequently than students from other groups. Effective strategies for improving student participation in advanced study include eliminating low-level courses with reduced academic expectations, enhancing professional development for teachers, hiring qualified teachers for rural and inner-city schools, providing information to parents about long-term benefits of participating in such programs, and increasing student access to skilled counselors and mentors.

High School–College Interface

To understand the role AP and IB play in college admission decisions, the committee surveyed deans of admission. The survey revealed that participation in these programs is of greatest importance for admission to the most selective colleges. Deans view such participation as an indication of students' willingness to accept academic challenges, but stated that the lack of such courses at an applicant's high school typically does not adversely influence admission if a student succeeded in the most challenging courses available at his or her school.

AP and IB examinations are administered each May, but scores are not available until July. Therefore, examination grades from the senior year do not influence college admission, but are used in credit and placement decisions. Students also use these credits to reduce course loads or to meet prerequisite or distribution requirements. As a result, some students may not have to take college courses in specific subject areas, such as mathematics or science. Some institutions minimize this practice by requiring that students enroll in courses at higher levels than those taken in high school. A survey of mathematics and biology departments revealed that the vast majority award credit and advanced placement for AP, and sometimes IB; the amount awarded usually depends on the student's score.

OVERVIEW OF THE PROGRAMS

Advanced Placement

Developed in 1955, AP is the predominant national program for advanced courses in U.S. high schools. Eleven separate courses are available in eight mathematics and science subjects. The College Board provides topic outlines for AP courses, generated largely by surveying colleges and universities. However, teachers are allowed considerable leeway in implementation. Elective, end-of-course examinations are designed to be comparable with "typical" introductory college-level courses in a subject area. Originally, the program served only top students from a few high schools. Today, approximately 62 percent of U.S. high schools offer AP. In May 2001, students took more than 450,000 AP examinations in mathematics and science.

International Baccalaureate

The IB program was developed in the late 1960s to provide an international standard of secondary education for children of diplomats and others stationed outside their countries. One goal was to prepare students for university work in their home countries. The IBO authorizes participating high schools; schools must offer a full IB Diploma Programme and cannot offer only a subset of IB courses. While some students take individual IB courses as they would an honors course, most are diploma candidates, taking a program of six or seven courses over two years.

Final examinations are part of the integrated IB Diploma Programme. Assessment consists of both external and internal components designed to measure content knowledge, depth of understanding, and use of specific higher-level cognitive skills for each subject. In May 2001, students from 272 U.S. public and private schools took 50,745 IB examinations, of which roughly 13,000 were in mathematics and science. Teachers also provide internal assessments of students' practical skills (for example, laboratory investigations in science, portfolios in mathematics), which are judged against established IBO assessment criteria.

Alternative Approaches

Other opportunities for advanced study in high school are available through local-, state-, and nationally sponsored programs. These include collaborative programs between high schools and postsecondary institutions, specialized schools for high-ability learners, distance learning programs, research internships, and academic competitions. Many programs award college credit to high school students, but less is known about transferability of credits earned in these alternate programs compared with qualifying scores on AP or IB examinations.

DESIGNING PROGRAMS BASED ON RESEARCH ON LEARNING AND PEDAGOGY

The goal of advanced study is to promote development of deep conceptual understanding and the ability to apply knowledge appropriately. Accordingly, the committee developed a framework to guide its analysis of advanced study and to evaluate the degree to which existing programs accomplish this goal. This model also can guide the development of new programs.

The concept of "learning with understanding" is concerned with knowledge and how it is organized. Effective instruction is focusesd on enabling learners to uncover and formulate the deep organizing patterns of a domain, and then to actively access and create meaning around these organizing principles. Learning with understanding also helps students develop the ability to evaluate the relevance of particular knowledge to novel problems and to explain and justify their thinking. As students learn and practice these skills of critical reflection, they become able to apply knowledge in multiple contexts, develop adaptive expertise, and serve as active members of learning communities.

Seven Principles of Human Learning

Seven research-based principles of learning can provide a framework for designing effective curriculum, instruction, and assessment—three facets of classroom activity that teachers can orchestrate to promote learning with understanding. These principles also underlie the design of effective preparation and professional development for teachers, which, along with curriculum, instruction, and assessment, helps create a system that focuses on student learning:

1. Learning with understanding is facilitated when knowledge is related to and structured around major concepts and principles of a discipline.
2. A learner's prior knowledge is the starting point for effective learning.
3. Metacognitive learning (self-monitoring) is important for acquiring proficiency.
4. Recognizing differences among learners is important for effective teaching and learning.
5. Learners' beliefs about their ability to learn affect learning success.
6. Practices and activities in which people engage during learning shape what is learned.
7. Socially supported interactions strengthen one's ability to learn with understanding.

Design Principles: Curriculum, Instruction, Assessment, and Professional Development

The committee's framework for appraising advanced study programs encompasses the intentional and systematic design of curriculum, instruction, assessment, and professional development within the context of advanced study. Consideration of these program elements is based on the principles of learning and on theory and research on instructional programs. Education systems frequently address each element separately, but all four must be aligned and work together synergistically to facilitate deep conceptual understanding. The following examples of design principles for curriculum, instruction, and assessment reflect what is known about human learning:

• Effective mathematics and science curricula are coherent, focus on important ideas within the discipline, and are sequenced to optimize learning. They provide ample opportunities for exploring ideas in depth and for developing familiary with the discourse and modes of inquiry of the discipline.
• Teaching for understanding begins with careful consideration of students' thinking. It employs multiple representations and tasks. Effective teachers create learning environments that foster development of students' understanding and skills. They orchestrate classroom discourse in which students conjecture, present solutions, and argue about the validity of claims.

- Assessment for understanding is aligned with instruction and with desired learning outcomes. It is multifaceted and continuous and includes both content and process dimensions of performance.

Successful implementation of advanced study that promotes learning with understanding also depends upon creating opportunities for teachers' continual learning, and requires sufficient resources to support professional development. Effective professional development for mathematics and science teachers emphasizes deep understanding of content and discipline-based methods of inquiry, provides multiple perspectives on students as learners, and develops teachers' subject-specific pedagogical knowledge. It treats teachers as active learners, builds on their existing knowledge and beliefs, and occurs in professional communities where there are opportunities to discuss ideas and practices as colleagues.

ANALYSIS OF AP AND IB PROGRAMS BASED ON LEARNING RESEARCH

Although the AP and IB programs predate contemporary learning research, it is important to use the principles emerging from that research to assess and improve the programs. The committee's analysis of these programs, based on these principles of learning and supported by the reports of the four disciplinary panels, yielded the following findings:

- *Principled conceptual knowledge*—Although the AP and IB programs espouse an emphasis on concepts and key ideas, this intention is largely unrealized in the sciences. Excessive breadth of coverage (especially in 1-year science programs) and insufficient emphasis on key concepts in final assessments contribute significantly to the problem in all science fields. Although emphasis on learning concepts and key ideas is more evident in mathematics, further improvement is needed, particularly in the assessments, which frequently focus on procedural knowledge at the expense of conceptual understanding.
- *Prior knowledge*—Except for mathematics, these programs do not specify clearly what prior knowledge is needed for success or help teachers to build on what students already know or to recognize student misconceptions. In all subjects, efforts to prepare students properly in the years preceding advanced study are often inadequate. Too many students, especially in physics, take a 1-year advanced course as their first course in the discipline—an inappropriate situation.
- *Metacognition*—Advanced study can increase students' metacognitive skills, but many programs and courses do not help students develop these skills.

- *Differences among learners*—AP and IB teachers who employ a variety of pedagogical approaches are likely to reach a broader range of learners. Using several sources of evidence of student progress also can provide a more accurate picture of what students know compared with any single measure, such as an examination. The single end-of year examinations and summary scores, as found in AP, do not adequately capture student learning.

- *Motivation*—Students have varied motives for enrolling in advanced study. Designing programs that are consistent with the findings of learning research can increase students' motivation to succeed in advanced study, encourage them to believe in their own potential, and increase the proportion of students who take and succeed in the course and final examinations.

- *Learning communities*—Teamwork and collaborative investigation are especially important in advanced study. The breadth of course content and the generally short duration of laboratory periods in many schools may be inadequate for such activities. Better use of the Internet and technologies for collaborative learning is needed.

- *Situated learning*—Students need opportunities to learn concepts in a variety of contexts. The AP and IB programs currently do not emphasize interdisciplinary connections sufficiently or assess students' ability to apply their knowledge in new situations or contexts. Additionally, advanced study courses might make better use of laboratory experiences by requiring students to plan experiments, decide what information is important, select experimental methods, and review results critically. These courses might also draw upon local resources (e.g., science-related industries) to give students experience with varied practices in mathematics and science.

Although AP and IB programs currently are not well aligned with learning principles, they can be revised with this research in mind. The resulting transformations are likely to make the programs more successful in enhancing deep conceptual learning and make them more accessible to additional students.

ANALYSIS OF AP AND IB PROGRAMS WITH REGARD TO CURRICULUM, INSTRUCTION, ASSESSMENT, AND PROFESSIONAL DEVELOPMENT

Curriculum

Students can study topics in depth and develop conceptual understanding only if curricula do not present excessive numbers of topics. Currently, AP and IB programs are inconsistent with this precept. In their written materials the College Board and the IBO acknowledge the importance of depth and focus, but the breadth of topics covered in their curriculum guides and assessments conveys a different message. Additionally, the College Board models AP course outlines on *typical* college introductory courses, rather than on the best college courses or educational practices based on research on learning and pedagogy. Since college-level courses vary substantially in content and pedagogy, this approach limits the potential quality of AP courses.

Instruction

Individual teachers have substantial leeway in implementing AP or IB courses. Therefore, the nature and quality of instruction vary considerably from classroom to classroom. AP and IB programs depart from the model of instruction outlined above by not providing adequate guidance concerning excellent teaching practices in advanced study.

Assessment

The central principle for designing assessments that foster deep conceptual understanding is that they must be aligned with learning goals and with curriculum and instruction derived from those goals. Because AP and IB assessments exert a powerful influence on curriculum and instruction, it is especially important to ensure that they are designed to foster deep conceptual understanding.

A striking inadequacy of the AP and IB programs is the lack of detailed research about what their examinations actually measure, including the kinds of thinking that the examinations elicit. This concern touches on the tests' validity and the appropriateness of the inferences drawn from test scores. For both the AP and IB programs, certain kinds of validity research are lacking, including attention to the broader social consequences (or consequential validity) of their assessments.

Because high-stakes assessments strongly influence instruction, it is imperative to understand the connections between assessment and instruction in both programs. If instruction is to enhance understanding, assessments should not be predictable from year to year, nor should their content or form be capricious. Assessments in some AP and IB courses are relatively predictable.

Professional Development

At present, neither the College Board nor the IBO supports systematic and continuing professional development for teachers. Professional development opportunities vary in quality and focus and do not consistently reflect the notions of learning, instruction, curriculum, and assessment presented in this report. The College Board does not adequately monitor professional development programs that support AP; teachers' participation in such programs is voluntary. The College Board and the IBO have made progress in providing Web-based resources, workshops, and mentorships, but many teachers still lack access to such resources and opportunities.

Accepting greater responsibility for teacher professional development is a daunting challenge for the College Board and the IBO, whose missions historically have been much more limited in focus. Without improved professional development, however, other efforts to improve advanced study are likely to founder.

USES, MISUSES, AND UNINTENDED CONSEQUENCES OF AP AND IB

Some misuses of AP and IB test scores may have unfortunate consequences, though these have not been studied in detail. For example, in an attempt to quantify the extent to which high schools challenge students, top public high schools have recently been ranked based on the number of AP and IB tests taken. AP and IB assessment data also have been used inappropriately to evaluate teachers or to compare schools. Because of this, the committee is concerned that teachers may emphasize to their students the mechanics of preparing for a test, rather than learning and understanding of important principles. Coverage of content may be superficial and opportunities for inquiry-based experiences insufficient. The committee also has learned that some teachers discourage students from taking AP or IB courses (or the final examinations) when poor performance is anticipated. This form of limiting access occurs in many educational settings, including the most competitive high schools.

Data from AP and IB test scores by themselves cannot support inferences about teacher quality and effectiveness. Students come to advanced courses with different levels of skill and mastery of content that make it difficult to determine the effects of a teacher's work on student achievement in any particular year. Nor should such data be used to measure school quality. Some schools offer other options that are equally rigorous but more suited to their students.

Unlike the IBO, the College Board has no clear standards as to what constitutes an AP course. With the growth of AP as a perceived standard of excellence and school quality, the incentive to use the AP name inappropriately also has increased. Some schools may label non-AP courses as AP, while others may sponsor AP courses without providing proper facilities and personnel resources.

Students can be affected adversely when preparatory courses are compressed or when students are allowed to skip prerequisite courses without first demonstrating mastery before taking an AP course. However, efforts to prepare students for advanced study often stimulate improvements in prerequisite courses; and this is to be strongly encouraged.

Advances in technology make it possible to create online AP courses and to provide other online support, such as professional development for AP and IB teachers. The potential for growth in this area is virtually unlimited, but so is the potential for problems if suitable quality controls are not established. For example, students who take an AP science course online and earn a qualifying score on the examination may earn college credit or placement without having had any advanced laboratory experience.

Decisions about awarding college credit or advanced placement for qualifying scores on AP and IB examinations are best made on an individual basis, using multiple sources of information. Decisions based on sampling average student performance in courses at typical colleges is not strong enough to infer that all, or even most, AP or IB students who earn a particular examination score are qualified for either credit or placement.

RECOMMENDATIONS

Recommendation 1:
The Primary Goal of Advanced Study

The primary goal of advanced study in any discipline should be for students to achieve a deep conceptual understanding of the discipline's content and unifying concepts. Well-designed programs help students develop skills of inquiry, analysis, and problem solving so that they become superior learners. Accelerating students' exposure to college-level material, while appropriate as a component of some advanced study programs, is not by itself a sufficient goal.

Recommendation 2: Access and Equity

Schools and school districts must find ways to integrate advanced study with the rest of their program by means of a coherent plan extending from middle school through the last years of secondary school. Course options in grades 6–10 for which there are reduced academic expectations (i.e., those that leave students unprepared for further study in a discipline) should be eliminated from the curriculum. An exception might be made for courses designed to meet the needs of special education students.

Recommendation 3: Learning Principles

Programs of advanced study in science and mathematics must be made consistent with findings from recent research on how people learn. These findings include the role of students' prior knowledge and misconceptions in building a conceptual structure, the importance of student motivation and self-monitoring of learning (metacognition), and the substantial differences among learners.

Recommendation 4: Curriculum

Curricula for advanced study should emphasize depth of understanding over exhaustive coverage of content. They should focus on central organizing concepts and principles and the empirical information on which those concepts and principles are based. Because science and technology progress rapidly, frequent review of course content is essential.

Recommendation 5: Instruction

Instruction in advanced courses should engage students in inquiry by providing opportunities to experiment, analyze information critically, make conjectures and argue about their validity, and solve problems both individually and in groups. Instruction should recognize and take advantage of differences among learners by employing multiple representations of ideas and posing a variety of tasks.

Recommendation 6: Assessment

Teachers of advanced study courses should employ frequent formative assessment of student learning to guide instruction and monitor learning. External, end-of-course examinations have a different purpose: they certify mastery. Both types of assessment should include content and process dimensions of performance and evaluate depth of understanding, the primary goal of advanced study (see Recommendation 1).

Recommendation 7: Qualified Teachers and Professional Development

Schools and districts offering advanced study must provide frequent opportunities for continuing professional development so teachers can improve their knowledge of both content and pedagogy. National programs for advanced study should clearly specify and monitor the qualifications expected of teachers. Professional development activities must be adequately funded and available to all teachers throughout their teaching careers.

Recommendation 8: Alternative Programs

Approaches to advanced study other than AP and IB should be developed and evaluated. Such alternatives can help increase access to advanced study for those not presently served and result in the emergence of novel and effective strategies.

Recommendation 9: The Secondary–College Interface

9(a): When awarding credit and advanced placement for courses beyond the introductory college level, institutions should base their decisions on an assessment of each student's understanding and capabilities, using multiple sources of information. National examination scores alone are generally insufficient for these purposes.

9(b): College and university scientists and mathematicians should modify their introductory courses along lines similar to those proposed in this report for high school advanced study. Departments should carefully advise undergraduates about the benefits and costs of bypassing introductory courses.

Recommendation 10: Changes in the AP and IB Programs

The following substantial changes in the AP and IB programs are recommended:

10(a): The College Board should abandon its practice of designing AP courses in most disciplines primarily to replicate typical introductory college courses.

10(b): The College Board and the IBO should evaluate their assessments to ensure that they measure the conceptual understanding and complex reasoning that should be the primary goal of advanced study. Programs of validity research should be an integral part of assessment design.

10(c): Both the College Board and the IBO should take more responsibility for ensuring the use of appropriate instructional approaches. Specifying the knowledge and skills that are important for beginning teachers and providing models for teacher development are likely to advance teacher effectiveness.

10(d): The College Board should exercise greater quality control over the AP trademark by articulating standards for what can be labeled an AP course, desirable student preparation for each course, strategies for ensuring equity and access, and expectations for universal participation in the AP examinations by course participants. When necessary, the College Board should commission experts to assist with these tasks.[3] These standards should apply whether AP is offered in schools or electronically.

10(e): The College Board and the IBO should provide assistance to schools in their efforts to offer high-quality advanced courses. To this end, the College Board should provide more detailed curriculum, information about best practices for instruction and classroom assessment, and strategies for enhancing professional development opportunities.

10(f): The College Board and the IBO should offer more guidance to educators, policymakers, and the general public concerning proper uses of their examination scores for admission, placement, and teacher evaluation. They should also actively discourage misuse of these scores.

10(g): The College Board and the IBO should develop programs of research on the implementation and effectiveness of their programs.

---

[3]The committee notes that the College Board has used this strategy in the past. For example, in 1997 the National Task Force on Minority High Achievement was convened to assist the College Board in outlining recommendations for substantially increasing the number of African American, Latino, and Native American undergraduates who achieve high levels of academic success.

1

Introduction

Excellence in science and mathematics education is a critical need and goal for the United States. Programs for advanced study, particularly the Advanced Placement (AP) and International Baccalaureate (IB) programs, are major contributors to science and mathematics education at the high school level. Large numbers of high school students seek access to these courses, and many colleges use them in their admission decisions. High school curricula are strongly affected by these programs, since schools often structure their courses in the middle-school and early high school years to facilitate participation in advanced study.

This report presents the results of a 2-year effort by a committee of the National Research Council (NRC) to examine programs for advanced study of U.S. high school mathematics and science (calculus, biology, chemistry, and physics). As part of the scope of the study, the NRC asked the committee to ". . . explore the current status of high school mathematics and science education by means of an in-depth look at programs designed for advanced students, such as the AP and IB programs." The study focuses on AP and IB because these are the only advanced secondary science and mathematics programs of national scope. However, the availability of and participation in these programs are highly variable, with large differences among schools and their student populations.

The primary purpose of this report is to use the results of recent research on learning, curriculum, instruction, assessment, and professional development as lenses to examine educational programs for advanced secondary science and mathematics in the United States. We are now in a position to ask whether the AP, IB, and other programs of advanced study as currently implemented are as effective as possible, and how they might be improved.

BACKGROUND

The National Science Foundation and the U.S. Department of Education commissioned this study following the publication of a disappointing assessment of the performance of U.S. students in advanced mathematics and physics, which was part of the Third International Mathematics and Science Study (National Center for Education Statistics [NCES], 1998). This international comparison appeared to show that U.S. students of advanced mathematics and physics lagged behind their counterparts in other countries. However, a more recent study indicates that this pessimistic assessment may have been unwarranted because the original sampling included many students that should not have been classified as being in "advanced" courses. Indeed, a second administration of the test to U.S. students enrolled in AP calculus and AP physics showed that, in this sample, the AP calculus students performed better than those in all other countries, and the performance of the AP physics students was substantially above the mean of the other countries (Gonzalez, O'Connor, and Miles, 2001). One important lesson from these comparisons is that the percentage of U.S. students taking bona fide advanced courses is too small compared with other countries.

Although international comparisons served as a catalyst for this study, the need to undertake the study was clear for other reasons as well. Perhaps most important, a greatly improved understanding of the conditions for successful teaching and learning has emerged in recent years. These advances have been summarized in several NRC reports, including *How People Learn: Brain, Mind, Experience, and School* (Expanded Edition) (NRC, 2000b). The present analysis demonstrates that programs for advanced study are frequently inconsistent with the findings of this body of research on cognition and learning. We show how program developers can remedy this situation by considering all the components of educational programs when developing their courses: curriculum, instructional methods, ongoing (curriculum-embedded) and end-of-course (summative) assessments, and opportunities for teacher preparation and professional development.

Another factor contributing to the urgency of this study is the rapid growth of the AP and IB programs. In 2000, there were 433,430 AP exams taken in math and science, compared with only 164,333 in 1990 (College Entrance Examination Board [CEEB], 2000c),[1] and the number is expected to continue to grow rapidly in the future. The IB program had about 19,000 degree candidates in 2000, and roughly 13,000 IB exams were taken in the

---

[1]The College Board, which oversees the AP program, does not keep track of who or how many students enroll in AP courses, but estimates that about 30–40 percent of students enrolled in a course do not take the exam. If that holds true for all courses, then 433,000 AP exams in science and mathematics translate to about 580,000 enrollments.

sciences and mathematics in the United States that year.[2] Clearly, these are no longer programs only for an elite audience; participation in some form of advanced study has become almost the norm for students seeking admission to the most selective colleges. Advanced study programs can affect students' future opportunities, and the quality and availability of these programs have become central concerns.

As the United States becomes more diverse, racial and socioeconomic gaps persist in high school students' access to and success in advanced study. While minority participation in advanced mathematics and science courses has increased substantially during the past 20 years (National Science Foundation [NSF], 1999), inner-city and rural schools, especially those with high percentages of minority and poor students, are still less likely to offer these courses (Ma and Willms, 1999). Many schools in low-income communities remain ill equipped to provide advanced study, in part because they are less likely than schools with greater resources to have highly qualified teachers or sufficient laboratories, equipment, and other curriculum materials (Darling-Hammond, 2000; Ferguson, 1991, 1998; Greenwald, Hedges, and Laine, 1996; Murnane, 1996; Wright, Horn, and Sanders, 1997). In addition to these gaps, there are parallel disparities in access within racially and ethnically diverse schools. In these schools, African American, Hispanic, and Native American students and those of low socioeconomic status are much less likely than white or Asian American students to enroll in upper-level mathematics and science courses even when such courses are available (Atanda, 1999; Horn, Nunez, and Bobbitt, 2000; Ma and Willms, 1999). Those who do enroll are much less likely to fare as well as white or Asian American students on national examinations. These facts represent a major challenge for advanced study programs.

A number of additional trends and concerns make this an appropriate time to analyze programs for advanced study of science and mathematics:

- *Changes in science and mathematics*—Rapid advances (e.g., the tremendous progress in molecular biology) mean that traditional course content may be inadequate for the future.
- *Demands for accountability*—There is increasing pressure from policymakers and the public for school accountability, and participation in advanced study is often used as a measure of school quality.
- *Connections to earlier years and higher education*—Since learning of science and mathematics tends to be hierarchical, advanced programs in

---

[2]These numbers are estimates based on IB Worldwide Statistics.

these subjects have major implications for the earlier years of schooling and vice versa. Similarly, as introductory college courses evolve and their emphases change (see, for example, NRC, 1999d), it is important to review the secondary courses that precede them.

  • *Teacher shortages*—A teacher shortage of immense proportions is projected to emerge in the next few years in many districts. These shortages are likely to be particularly acute for science and mathematics (National Commission on Mathematics and Science Teaching for the 21st Century, 2000; NCES, 2000b). Teaching in advanced programs requires extensive knowledge of both subject matter content and pedagogical methods. Thus it is unclear how the staffing needed to implement and maintain the quality of these programs will be provided in the future. This problem is especially severe in schools with large populations of minority and poor students, where shortages of qualified science and mathematics teachers are already daunting (National Commission on Mathematics and Science Teaching in the 21st Century, 2000).

  • *Economic forces*—The increasing demands of a knowledge-based economy add to the importance of providing advanced courses in mathematics and science for as many students as are motivated and prepared to enroll in them.

  • *Information technology*—Advances in information technology are transforming work, teaching, and learning, creating new opportunities for instructional delivery. For example, distance learning is now being used to deliver advanced study programs to schools that have few resources, small student populations, or insufficient numbers of teachers to offer a program within the school.

  • *Assessment*—Better understanding of the uses and impact of assessment with regard to classroom dynamics and student learning creates opportunities for fundamentally changing and improving programs of advanced study (see, for example, NRC, 2001a).

BRIEF OVERVIEW OF THE PROGRAMS

The AP program was launched in 1955 by the College Entrance Examination Board, commonly referred to as the College Board,[3] to provide college-level courses for advanced high school students. The program currently consists of 35 courses in 19 subjects, including 11 courses in 7 science and mathematics subjects.[4] An individual school can choose to offer any number

---

[3]The College Board is an independent, not-for-profit membership organization. Membership includes colleges, universities, and secondary schools.

[4]See http://apcentral.collegeboard.com/courses/overviews/ (February 11, 2002).

and combination of these courses. The AP program is built around elective, end-of-course examinations that are graded on a five-point scale. The College Board produces content outlines for its courses, largely by surveying colleges and universities about the content of their introductory courses. The national AP examinations are used by many colleges and universities as a basis for granting credit or advanced placement to incoming students. Additional information about the AP program is provided in Chapter 3.

The IB program was developed in the late 1960s to provide an international standard of secondary education for a mobile population—primarily the children of diplomats and others stationed outside their home countries for extended periods. One goal was to prepare these students to qualify for university admission in their home countries after schooling abroad. As with the AP program, a final examination developed by the International Baccalaureate Organisation[5] (IBO) is a major component of an assessment process that helps determine eligibility for university admission. The examination is supplemented by teacher-devised classroom assessments, such as a portfolio of laboratory reports. Schools cannot choose to offer individual IB courses; they must provide a program of interrelated courses that students seeking the IB diploma take during their junior and senior years. While some students take individual IB courses much as they would an honors course, approximately two-thirds are diploma candidates, taking a full program of six or seven courses over the 2-year period. A detailed course outline and specific goals are provided for the courses. Additional information about the IB program is provided in Chapter 4.

As a consequence of the growing belief that all students should have access to quality educational programs, many states and the federal government have advocated an expansion of programs such as AP. Former U.S. Department of Education Secretary Richard Riley called for at least one AP course in every school by 2002 and an additional course incorporated into a school's AP offerings each year for the remainder of the decade.[6] While Governor of Texas, George W. Bush said, "Making Advanced Placement available to students across Texas is one of the best ways to challenge students academically" (Callahan, 2000, [from AP Program 1999, p. 16]). Many states have advisory councils and other structures in place specifically to promote and improve AP offerings.

The U.S. education system has changed dramatically since these programs were first established, and the programs and their assessments are now being used in ways that initially were neither anticipated nor intended. The leaders of these programs are aware of the need for reform. For ex-

---

[5]The IBO is a not-for-profit educational foundation based in Geneva, Switzerland.
[6]See www.ed.gov/Speeches/02-2000/20000211.html (February 11, 2002).

ample, in 2000 the College Board convened a Commission on the Future of the Advanced Placement Program, asking it to focus on ways of maintaining the integrity and quality of the program while improving equity of access to accommodate greater student diversity.[7]

WHAT IS ADVANCED STUDY?

The committee found that defining "advanced study" for secondary students is surprisingly difficult. Establishing a clear definition of advanced study is problematic in part because these programs share many of the objectives of other high school courses. For example, all courses in mathematics and science, whether "advanced" or not, should encourage students to think about concepts in addition to factual information. Similarly, all courses should engage students in scientific or mathematical reasoning.

A number of overlapping definitions are often used to characterize advanced study for high school students in the United States. Some have tended to equate advanced study with accelerated or college-level learning. However, the committee finds this definition insufficient because as discussed in detail later in this report, the inclusion of too much accelerated content can prevent students from realizing the important goal of attaining deep conceptual understanding.[8]

Furthermore, introductory courses at colleges and universities often do not take advantage of the greatly improved understanding of the conditions for successful teaching and learning mentioned earlier. As a result, they are not necessarily good models for emulation at the high school level. It is possible to enrich students' learning beyond what is typically found in secondary curricula in other ways—for example, by adding depth or rigorous analysis, applications to new domains, or opportunities for investigation. Thinking of advanced study entirely in the context of obtaining college credit and placement is unnecessarily limiting.

For purposes of this report, therefore, the committee adopted a focus on helping students achieve deep conceptual understanding as the primary goal of advanced study. At the same time, committee recognizes that accelerated exposure to college-level content has an appropriate place in some pro-

---

[7]The sponsors of these programs have acknowledged and appreciate the importance of increased access for underserved students. However, it is probable that offering courses alone, without providing support systems for both students and teachers and appropriate prerequisite education in the earlier years, would prove unsuccessful. These issues are discussed at length in Chapter 2, this volume.

[8]Conceptual understanding involves the creation of rich integrated knowledge structures around an underlying concept. Understanding is not a static point in learning, but rather a continually developing mental activity.

grams, provided it is well integrated with the primary goal of nurturing conceptual understanding.

THE STUDENT CLIENTELE
FOR ADVANCED STUDY

For whom are programs of advanced study appropriate? Again the answer is not straightforward. This study did not examine programs intended only for the most exceptional learners, who might constitute at most a few percent of the student population. Exceptional learners sometimes require opportunities that differ significantly from what is needed or effective for other able and well-motivated students; they may need earlier access to advanced material and a faster pace (see Annex 6-1).

While it is important to provide challenging opportunities for the most talented students, the primary concern of this study is with programs available to a broader group of highly motivated students with solid academic preparation. This population is limited at least in part by the adequacy of students' prior educational opportunities, the ability of their schools to provide effective learning environments, and the availability of qualified and effective teachers. It is the committee's consensus that improvements in these areas could enlarge significantly the group of students for whom advanced study programs such as AP and IB are a realistic choice. *Therefore, instead of asking, "For whom is advanced study appropriate?" we think it much more useful to ask, "How can high school science and mathematics education at both the introductory and advanced levels be improved so that a larger number of students will have access to advanced study and a realistic chance of succeeding once enrolled?"* Achieving this goal will require fundamental changes in curriculum, approaches to teaching and learning, assessment tools, and teacher preparation and professional development. Both school systems and institutions of higher education will have to change in significant ways.

The pathways leading to advanced study begin early. If a student has not developed a sound conceptual understanding of algebra, geometry, and functions, for example, he or she may be lost even in a well-taught calculus class. The committee envisions a future in which the conceptual understanding and habits of mind essential to advanced study are successfully nurtured among a greater number of students than at present. In this hoped-for future, early tracking of some students into academically weak courses is avoided so that each child has a suitable opportunity to develop and demonstrate his or her individual academic abilities and talents.

It should be noted that the early high school years are important as well for students who do not go on to advanced study. The programs reviewed in this report have a profound influence on the course structure and course-taking patterns of all students throughout the high school years. Moreover, AP and IB teachers—who are often among the best in their schools—are a critical resource for the entire high school system.

STUDY CHARGE AND APPROACH

The charge to the committee was as follows:

> . . . to consider the effectiveness of, and potential improvements to, programs for advanced study of mathematics and science in U.S. high schools. In response to the charge, the committee will consider the two most widely recognized programs for advanced study: the Advanced Placement (AP) and the International Baccalaureate (IB) programs. In addition, the committee will identify and examine other appropriate curricular and instructional alternatives to IB and AP. Emphasis will be placed on the mathematics, physics, chemistry, and biology programs of study.

The committee was charged with answering the following questions:[9]

1. What does research tell us about the ways in which high school students learn science and mathematics?
2. To what extent do the AP and IB programs in mathematics and science incorporate current knowledge about cognition and learning in their curricula, instruction, and assessments?
3. To what extent do AP and IB programs encourage teaching approaches that are consistent with current research on effective instructional practices?
4. How do final assessments generally, and AP and IB assessments in particular, influence instructional practice?
5. What does research tell us about how teachers learn to teach, and about effective professional development opportunities?
6. What is the impact of student assessment on the learning process, and how could student assessment be used to improve student learning in advanced courses?
7. To what extent do the IB and AP programs reflect the best in current thinking about content and curriculum for teaching mathematics and science?
8. How can the goal of equitable and broad access to programs for advanced study best be pursued?

---

[9]The full text of the committee's statement of task can be found in Appendix C; only a subset of the questions to be addressed is presented here.

9. How does the interface with higher education affect programs for advanced study in secondary schools?

In approaching its charge, the committee considered research about how people learn and gain expertise in a discipline. The committee found surprisingly sparse empirical data about either the AP or IB programs. For example, systematic information is lacking about how the AP and IB programs are actually implemented in U.S. high schools. Systematic data about the AP and IB examinations are also scarce, as is information about the long-term effects of AP and IB participation on student learning and achievement. Because neither independent researchers nor the AP or IB programs have gathered and published much of the data the committee sought for this study, it was necessary to use instead available program materials and expert testimony from program officials and experienced AP and IB teachers. As this report notes throughout, more studies are sorely needed to address the many issues and questions raised herein.

The committee was composed of scientist-researchers, secondary teachers having considerable experience with both the AP and IB programs, scientists and educators with expertise in the preparation of teachers and in issues of access and equity, experts in the cognitive sciences, and educational leaders. (Biographical sketches of the committee members are provided in Appendix B.) The committee held seven 2- to 3-day meetings over a period of 2 years, convened several small-group meetings, and interacted extensively between meetings. Representatives of the AP and IB programs and experts on science learning met with the committee. Deans of admission and chairs of science and mathematics departments in a diverse group of colleges and universities were surveyed about their uses of AP scores. These surveys and their results are described in Chapters 2 and 10, this volume.

Given the differences among the four disciplines under the committee's charge, panels of experts in each of the disciplines were convened to advise the committee. Each panel included at least one representative from each of the following categories: an expert on pedagogy in the discipline, an accomplished university teacher-scholar, a secondary teacher involved in advanced programs, and an educational researcher with a strong base in the discipline. The panels met for two 2-day sessions during the summer of 2000. The charge to the panels, the set of questions they were asked to consider, and a summary of their findings are included in Appendix A. Each of the panel reports was submitted to a group of independent reviewers for analysis and improvement, using procedures identical to the review process for all NRC reports. The panels' analyses and recommendations were an important source for the information on which the analyses, conclusions, and recommendations of this report are based. The names and institutional affiliations of the panel members are provided in the front matter of the report. To keep the size of this volume reasonable, only summaries of the panels' findings and recommendations are included in Appendix A; the full text of their reports is available online for reading or downloading.[10]

AUDIENCES FOR THE REPORT

This report is intended to be useful to a variety of audiences concerned with high school science and mathematics curricula in general and advanced study in particular. Those who determine the shape of advanced study programs should find many opportunities to improve their programs along the lines suggested in this report. High school teachers should be interested in the analysis, which they can use both to develop useful teaching ideas and to press for changes in their schools that will enhance advanced study opportunities and make the programs effective for more of their students. It is hoped that university faculty members will see the importance of interacting with their secondary school colleagues and of encouraging deep conceptual understanding among their students, especially those who might become teachers. It is also hoped that university administrators will better appreciate the influence of their policies regarding admission and credit or placement for advanced study on both high schools and their students. Middle school and elementary school teachers should attain a better understanding of what they can do to prepare their students for advanced study at a later time and, in so doing, to enhance academic opportunities for all students. The report should be of value as well to policymakers and administrators at both the K–12 and university levels, who have a vital role to play in promoting the practices that research has shown to be effective and in providing the resources their teachers need to make advanced study successful for larger numbers of students. Finally, this report is intended to assist parents in being informed advocates for educational quality in science and mathematics.

OVERVIEW AND STRUCTURE OF THE REPORT

Chapter 2 provides essential background for this report, including the policy context of advanced study, the roles of middle schools and high schools in preparing students for these programs, and problems related to the supply of qualified teachers. It also addresses issues of equity and access to advanced study programs, factors that affect the success of students who enroll in advanced study, and the interface of secondary advanced study

---

[10]At www.nap.edu/catalog/10129.html/.

with colleges and universities. Chapters 3 and 4 introduce the AP and IB programs in some detail, while Chapter 5 provides a brief overview of some alternative advanced study programs. Chapter 6 summarizes the results of research on human learning that are critical for the present analysis. Chapter 7 extends these findings to the design of curriculum, instruction, assessment, and professional development as they relate to advanced study.

The report next turns to a detailed analysis of programs for advanced study, an analysis that is influenced strongly by the panel reports in the four individual disciplines. Chapter 8 presents an analysis of the programs from the perspective of research on learning, while Chapter 9 considers them from the perspective of curriculum, instruction, assessment, and professional development of teachers. Chapter 10 examines appropriate and inappropriate uses of these programs and their assessments of students. Finally, Chapter 11 presents the committee's recommendations for change.

2

Context of Advanced Study

There are approximately 36,000[1] public and private high schools in the United States (National Center for Education Statistics [NCES], 2001a). As a result of the U.S. tradition of local control of education, these schools vary widely along many dimensions, such as size, availability of facilities and resources, student and teacher characteristics, staffing levels, teacher preparation and qualifications, and stated goals and missions. Public, private, and parochial schools set their own educational standards[2] and are accountable to different oversight agencies. They implement widely varying curricula and administer different assessments, which are selected by their districts' or states' boards of education or boards of trustees. Local school boards organize their schools and implement policies related to ability grouping, course offerings, and staffing patterns in ways that reflect their differing missions, educational goals, and local political concerns and priorities. Thus, "high school" in the United States must be understood as a diverse array of institutions in which students, even those attending the same school, may have vastly differing opportunities and experiences, depending on their course of study.

Students' school experiences and academic achievement are most affected by the overall culture and atmosphere of their school, the organization and content of their school curriculum, and the training and qualifications of the teaching force they encounter during the course of their educational career (NCES, 2000b). It has been consistently demonstrated that disparities among schools along these dimensions have a profound effect on students' abilities to prepare for and fully participate in advanced study opportunities.

---

[1]This figure excludes special education, alternative, and other schools not classified by grade span.

[2]Public school standards are usually established by local boards of education, which follow polices established by state boards of education.

Advanced study does not exist in isolation. As advanced study programs are currently structured in the United States, they have wide-ranging effects on the curricula, teachers, and students in the schools where they are offered. In turn, they are affected by political, educational, and social contexts that shape their implementation in schools. This chapter reviews the policy context of advanced study (including its financing), its educational context (including student preparation for advanced study in both middle and high school and teacher preparation), disparities in opportunities for different groups of students to pursue and succeed in advanced study, and the connections between advanced study and higher education.

POLICY CONTEXT

Immediately following the release of *A Nation at Risk* by the National Commission on Excellence in Education (1983), intense public interest was generated in improving the achievement of U.S. secondary school students by reforming and restructuring U.S. high schools. Although most states and school districts have adopted the commission's recommendations for strengthening state and local high school graduation requirements,[3] U.S. high schools still face intense criticism from those involved in higher education, policymakers, education reformers, and the public for continuing to graduate significant numbers of students who are neither well prepared for college nor able to enter the workplace with the technological and problem-solving skills demanded by the new economy (American Federation of Teachers [AFT], 1999; Kaufman, Bradby, and Teitelbaum, 2000; National Association of Secondary School Principals [NASSP], 1996; National Commission on the High School Senior Year [NCHSSY], 2001a, 2001b; Powell, Farrar, and Cohen, 1985; Sizer, 1992).

High schools may not be failing to the degree that some of these reports indicate (see for example, Berliner and Biddle, 1996). However, the Mathematics and Science Report Cards of the National Assessment of Educational Progress (NAEP)[4] and data gathered from state education testing and the SAT I and II suggest that the schools are doing a less than stellar job in challenging all students to achieve at the same high levels.

In 1999 Richard Riley, then U.S. Secretary of Education, declared it was time to change U.S. high schools so they would be better aligned with the

---

[3]The Five New Basics recommended by the commission included 4 years of English; 3 years of mathematics; 3 years of science; 3 years of social studies; one-half year of computer science; and, for the college-bound, 2 years of foreign language.

[4]Available at http://www.nces.ed.gov/nationsreportcard/ (February 10, 2002).

demands and needs of modern times.[5] The needed changes, according to Riley, must include high expectations for all students, rigorous curricula, support for students who need help in meeting higher standards, an educational structure that is flexible in meeting students' needs, and well-prepared teachers who have adequate opportunities for professional development and the time to work together in achieving student and school goals. In light of all of the recent criticism leveled at high schools, many policymakers and educators have turned to AP[6] and IB to improve their academic programs (see for example, The National Education Goals Panel, Promising Practices, Goal 3,[7] and legislation in Virginia[8] and California[9]). Rod Paige, current U.S. Secretary of Education, has continued the Department of Education's support for AP in 2001–2002 by providing $6.5 million in grants to 18 states, the District of Columbia, and Guam so that thousands of students from low-income backgrounds can prepare for and take AP examinations.[10] Several states also have adopted policies to support IB that are similar to those for AP.

In the view of many educators and policymakers, AP and IB complement the nation's decentralized system of educational governance and the different approaches that states and districts have adopted with regard to academic standards, curriculum, and instruction. That is, AP and IB are national programs that are controlled locally. Both programs provide a basic structure, quality standards, and nationally recognized external measures of student achievement, but states and individual schools can decide which students are able to take the courses, who is qualified to teach them, and how the courses will be taught.

At least 26 states provide legislative support to AP programs in their schools by subsidizing examination fees or costs for teacher education, pro-

---

[5]Riley, 1999, available at www.ed.gov/Speeches/09-1999/990915.html (February 11, 2002).

[6]Secretary Riley called on all schools to add one AP course to their curricular offerings for each of the next 10 years (ending in 2010) so that every student in every high school in the United States could have access to at least ten AP courses. The Federal AP Incentive Act (1999) provided funds to help low-income students pay the fees for AP examinations.

[7]The National Education Goals Panel uses an increase in the number of AP examinations receiving a grade of 3 or higher per 1,000 students in grades 11 and 12 to recognize schools with promising practices (http://www.negp.gov [February 11, 2002]).

[8]Virginia's Board of Education established an accountability system that requires every school division in the Commonwealth to offer at least two AP courses (www.pen.k12.va.us [February 11, 2002]).

[9]Spending $20.5 million to make at least one AP class available for every high school student by the fall of 2000, although at first this might mean the students' going to a different location or watching the class on closed-circuit television (http://www.cisco.com/warp/public/779/govtaffs/people/issues/educational_reform.html [November 26, 2001]).

[10]Additional information about this support is available at http://www.ed.gov/PressReleases/10-2001/10012001b.html (October 26, 2001).

viding funds for materials and supplies for AP courses, offering incentives for initiating AP courses or hosting training sessions, encouraging or mandating publicly funded colleges and universities to accept AP credit, and/or supporting professional development opportunities. State policies related to IB are less well established.[11]

For many years, policymakers have focused on making advanced-level courses available to all students who are interested in participating. That goal has not yet been accomplished, but educators and policymakers have increased their efforts to provide many more students with equitable opportunities to learn and succeed in these courses. As discussed later in this chapter, the success of these efforts will depend on whether educational leaders assign top priority to increasing the number of underrepresented minority students who both are enrolled in advanced study and achieve at high levels.

The Role and Influence of Standards and Accountability

Reform is an ongoing and recurring theme in American education. The latest wave of educational reform, highlighted by calls for standards and accountability, began a little more than a decade ago. These efforts, which have garnered the broad-based support of education policymakers, business leaders, many educators, and the public, rest on three basic tenets: (1) all students should be held to the same high standards for learning; (2) high standards should serve as a basis for systems of assessment that can be used for the purpose of accountability; and (3) consequences should be imposed on schools, teachers, and sometimes students when students do not meet the established standards (Linn, 2000).

In the early 1990s, attempts at developing national standards for several subject areas met with varying degrees of success. The American Association for the Advancement of Science (AAAS) published *Benchmarks for Science Literacy* (1993), which contains science content standards based on a previous publication, *Science for All Americans* (AAAS, 1989). These publications outlined what the citizens of the United States should know about science. In 1996, the National Research Council (NRC) published the *National Science Education Standards* (NSES), a consensus document based on input from hundreds of scientists, science educators, and professional societies. The NSES relate to science content, teaching, teacher development, assessment, and the infrastructure required to support effective science education.

---

[11]The committee noted that Florida has instituted a state scholarship program that allows Florida students who graduate with an IB diploma to attend any state university for free. California recently enacted legislation that grants sophomore standing in college to students who earn an IB diploma in high school.

Both documents call for fundamentally different approaches to teaching and learning science for students in grades K–12, with emphasis on inquiry and in-depth study of fewer topics than was characteristic of most science education programs at the time.

In mathematics, the National Council of Teachers of Mathematics (NCTM) has taken the lead in developing content standards for grades K–12 (NCTM, 1989, 2000). Like their counterparts in science, the national mathematics standards emphasize teaching and learning concepts and helping students understand mathematics much more deeply. Both the national science and mathematics standards leave decisions about specific curriculum to the discretion of the teacher, school, or district.

Based in part on these efforts, during the past decade 49 states and the District of Columbia have established statewide academic standards for what students should know and be able to do in at least some subjects; many states also have developed curriculum frameworks to support their standards. All 50 states currently test how well their students are learning, and 27 states hold schools accountable for results (*Education Week*, 2001).

This expectation for academic standards and measuring of student achievement has again assumed national prominence with the passage in January 2002 of the *No Child Left Behind* Act, which requires all states to test children in reading and mathematics every year while they are in grades 3–8. National expectations for assessing science achievement will begin in the 2007–2008 school year. Schools will be held accountable for the results.

The question now, after a decade of standards-based reform, is whether this approach achieves the results envisioned by policymakers and educators. Some contend that the assessments being used to measure achievement are narrowing the curriculum and discouraging high-quality instructional practices. These critics contend that greater gains in learning would occur if policymakers and educational decision makers focused more on equity in educational funding, teacher quality, and professional development, and less on testing. Supporters of standards-based reform point out that test scores are on the rise in a number of districts, including those that have shown low achievement in the past, and that a focus on accountability has forced teachers and schools to attend to the learning and achievement of all students, not just those at the top.

The AP and IB programs complement standards-based reform efforts at the advanced level. Both programs provide content-rich curricula and nationally recognized external measures of student achievement, but can be implemented by states and individual schools in ways that conform to local standards and link with other curricular offerings.

Financing Advanced Study Programs at the Local Level

Implementing, expanding, and supporting high-quality advanced study programs in science and mathematics requires resources that some school districts have difficulty providing. Such is the case particularly in rural areas and urban school districts that are supported by a limited property tax base and serve a large number of high-poverty or minority students. There is substantial variation in available fiscal resources across states, as well as among districts within states. For example, Rubenstein (1998) found that within some districts, schools with higher levels of student poverty sometimes receive lower allocations of both money and other educational resources than more affluent schools within the same district.[12]

Establishing and supporting high-quality advanced study programs also means that school districts must allocate sufficient resources for teacher professional development, instructional resources, and adequate student preparation at the middle school level. Indeed, disparities in school funding can exacerbate the already low level of access to advanced study courses for students who reside in high-poverty localities. Some states, such as Indiana, South Carolina, California, and Texas, have implemented state funding initiatives to ensure that advanced study opportunities will be equitably distributed across all of the states' schools and school districts.

Teacher Qualifications, Certification, and Challenges

In the quest for greater student achievement, state governments have undertaken reforms that have as their goal better teaching and learning for all students (Council of Chief State School Officers [CCSSO], 1998). Despite these reforms and the hard work of school and school district personnel, gaps still exist between desired and actual student achievement. These gaps can be attributed largely to disparities in the qualifications and distribution of the teacher workforce (Darling-Hammond, 2000).

Teaching quality matters. Numerous studies of the effects of teachers on student achievement have revealed that the availability and effectiveness of qualified teachers are strong contributors to observed variances in student learning (Jordan, Mendro, and Weerasinghe, 1997; Sanders and Rivers, 1996; Wright, Horn, and Sanders, 1997). There is broad consensus that students learn more from teachers with strong academic skills than from those with

---

[12]Two reports by the NRC's Committee on Education Finance (NRC, 1999a, 1999c) examine the link between school finance and student achievement and educational attainment. Readers interested in issues of school finance as they relate to student achievement are encouraged to review these reports.

weaker academic skills (see for example, Ballou, 1996; Ferguson and Ladd, 1996; Hanushek, 1996). Further, the effects of teachers on student learning appear to be additive and cumulative, and affected students may not be able to compensate for being taught by an unqualified teacher (NCES, 2000b). Results of a recent survey of secondary school teachers, students, school administrators, and parents also indicate that students who experience top-quality teaching are more likely than those who experience poor teaching to have high expectations for their futures (Markow, Fauth, and Gravitch, 2001).

Data drawn from the Fast Response Survey System (as cited in NCES, 2000b) show that the highest-poverty schools and those with the greatest concentrations of minority students have nearly twice the proportion of in-experienced teachers as schools with the lowest poverty levels and concentrations of minority students (20 versus 11 percent). Also troubling are studies showing evidence of strong bias in the assignment of students to teachers of different levels of effectiveness (Jordan et al., 1997). For example, African American students are nearly twice as likely to be assigned to the most ineffective teachers and half as likely to be assigned to the most effective teachers as white or Asian students (Sanders and Rivers, 1996). It also should be noted that new teachers, who increasingly are expected to have credentials in specific subject areas, leave high-poverty schools at a rate far greater than teachers in affluent suburban schools (NCES, 2000b).

High turnover rates and inexperienced teachers not only have an effect on student learning, but also deprive new teachers of mentors. A high proportion of experienced colleagues in a school can provide strong resources for advice and guidance to new teachers, as well as offer opportunities for experienced teachers to discuss their practices and learn from the experiences of others.

Darling-Hammond, Wise, and Klein (1999) discuss what is required of teachers if the gap in student achievement is to be closed and the goals of reform are to be met:

> The new mission for education requires substantially more knowledge and radically different skills for teachers . . . . In order to create bridges between common, challenging curriculum goals and individual learners' experiences and needs, teachers must understand cognition and the many different pathways to learning. They must understand child development and pedagogy as well as the structure of subject areas and a variety of alternatives for assessing learning . . . teachers must be prepared to address the substantial diversity in the experience children bring with them to school—the wide range of languages, cultures, exceptionalities, learning styles, talents and intelligences that in turn [require] an equally rich and varied repertoire of teaching strategies. (p. 2)

Teacher Certification

All 50 states and the District of Columbia require public school teachers to be licensed. Requirements for regular licenses vary by state. However, all states require a bachelor's degree with a minimum grade point average, completion of an approved teacher-training program with a prescribed number of subject and education credits, and supervised practice teaching. One-third of the states currently require training in the use of information technology as part of the teacher certification process. Other states require teachers to obtain a master's degree in education, which involves at least a year of additional coursework after earning a bachelor's degree with a major in a subject other than education.

Many states offer alternative teacher licensure programs for those who have a bachelor's degree in the subject they will teach, but lack the education courses required for a regular license. Such programs were originally designed to ease teacher shortages in certain subjects, such as mathematics and science. Under other programs, states may issue emergency licenses to individuals who do not meet requirements for a regular license when schools cannot attract enough qualified teachers to fill positions. No states require special licensing for advanced study teachers. Further, the committee did not identify any colleges or universities that currently offer teacher preparation programs specifically designed for prospective teachers of advanced study.[13]

Teacher Shortages

Impending teacher shortages and the concomitant need to educate and retain more qualified teachers to staff the nation's schools have been predominant legislative and policy themes. Recently, some education policy experts have stated that the problem is more the distribution of qualified teachers than a teacher shortage. For example, these experts say that while there is a teacher shortage in secondary and middle schools, there is no such shortage in elementary schools; while there is a strong need for more single-subject teachers, especially in mathematics, physical science, special education, and bilingual education, there is no shortage of multisubject teachers or teachers of English or social studies; and while fast-growing cities in the South and dense urban areas will have a need for more teachers, suburban and more affluent schools will experience few shortages (Bureau of Labor Statistics, 1999; Eubanks, 1996; Ingersoll, 1999).

---

[13]According to *Education Week* (2001), the College Board is experimenting with developing a three-credit course colleges can offer to prospective AP teachers.

TABLE 2-1   Trends in Teacher Salaries Compared with Average Annual Salaries of Selected White-Collar Occupations, 1999

Teacher	Accountant III	Buyer/ Contract Specialist III	Attorney III	Computer Systems Analyst III	Engineer IV	Full Prof. Public Doctoral	Assistant Prof. Public Comprehensive
$40,574	$49,257	$57,392	$69,104	$66,782	$68,294	$78,830	$41,940

SOURCE: Adapted from http://www.aft.org/research/survey99/tables/tableII-5.html (January 29, 2002).

The committee takes the position that qualified teachers are the backbone of both high-quality advanced study programs and the gateway courses leading to advanced study. Consequently, teacher shortages in mathematics and science and the dearth of teachers willing to teach in high-poverty and rural areas have implications for both access to and the quantity and the quality of advanced study programs available to students across the country. Education policy experts agree with this appraisal and suggest that government agencies, colleges and universities, and school districts initiate and support efforts to attract and retain qualified teachers in specific subjects and for particular geographic regions (National Commission on Mathematics and Science Teaching for the 21st Century, 2000; National Commission on Teaching and America's Future [NCTAF], 1996; NRC, 2000a).

Attracting the number of new teachers needed to the profession and retaining current teachers is a major challenge for the nation. In addition, given the challenges teachers face in the classroom (as discussed later in this chapter), the United States has not been willing to compensate teachers at levels comparable to those of people in other professions with similar levels of education, training, and expertise. The AFT reports that beginning teachers with a bachelor's degree earned an average of $25,700 in the 1997–1998 school year; those with a master's degree earned slightly more. The estimated average salary of all public elementary and secondary school teachers during the 1998–1999 school year was $40,574 (AFT, 2001). This salary is considerably less than that earned by other white-collar professionals (see Table 2-1).

EDUCATIONAL CONTEXT

Preparing for Advanced Study: Middle Schools

Academic preparation for advanced study begins in middle school. However, middle schools face a number of factors that compromise their ability to impart to as many students as possible the desire and preparation necessary to aspire to advanced study.

Educators, policymakers, and researchers have recently begun to focus considerable attention on middle-level education because of several widely held concerns. Specific concerns include a lack of focus on core academic courses; teachers without the appropriate training to teach young adolescents, especially those with special needs who are placed in general classrooms; appropriate approaches to teaching challenging academic material to students in this age group; and a much greater emphasis than in primary schools on ability grouping, which restricts high-poverty and minority students' access to challenging curricula and high-quality instruction and effectively precludes many of these students from participating in advanced study in high school (NCES, 2000a).

Middle School Mathematics and Science

The mathematics and science curricula for middle school students vary widely both within and among states (CCSSO, 1999). In mathematics, two-thirds of the states report that fewer than half of their students are in the traditional grade 8 mathematics curriculum by the time they reach that grade; the majority are enrolled in algebra-based mathematics (CCSSO, 1999). States are moving toward providing eighth-grade students with greater exposure to algebra topics, whether in full-fledged Algebra I or in pre-algebra courses. However, McKnight et al. (1987), Porter, Kirst, Osthoff, Smithson, and Schneider (1993), and Shaughnessy (1998) all found that the course titles provide only a rough indication of the content students actually receive.

In science, most seventh-grade students are studying life sciences or a biology-based curriculum, while most eighth-grade students are focusing on a mix of earth science and physical science (Schmidt, McKnight, Cogan, Jakewerth, and Hourang, 1999). CCSSO reports that a growing proportion of middle schools are instituting integrated or coordinated science programs. Integrated science programs, which intentionally blur the disciplinary lines among biology, chemistry, earth science, and physics, treat science as an integrated whole, based on the position that science learning during the middle school years should not be separated by discipline. Coordinated science curricula treat the disciplines of biology, chemistry, physics, and earth science individually, for perhaps 9 weeks each, and focus on the overarching ideas in science that can be studied in terms of each discipline rather than focusing on facts and details, as is more typical of traditional courses in these subjects. Finding qualified instructors for integrated and coordinated middle school science courses is often difficult because many science teachers at this level have not been prepared adequately in even one area of science.

Schmidt, Finch, and Faulkner (1992) analyzed a random sample of eighth-grade state curriculum guides in mathematics and science and concluded that the curricula lacked focus, covered too many topics, were repetitious from grade to grade, and were implemented inconsistently across schools and classrooms, resulting in highly uneven exposure to a range of important curricular topics. This lack of rigor and coherence can have enduring long-term consequences for students, whether or not they decide to pursue advanced study later in high school.

If middle school is one of the gateways to advanced study (the other being introductory high school courses), it stands to reason that middle school and high school mathematics and science teachers should have structured opportunities to plan together and make decisions about the content and focus of the science and mathematics curricula for grades 7–12. However, a majority of high school teachers never interact with their peers from elementary and middle schools on the crucial issue of curricular alignment.[14] Fewer than 30 percent of middle school teachers report having had any contact with high school teachers in their discipline with regard to curriculum structure, content, or design (NCHSSY, 2001a, p.16).

Even where school districts encourage and facilitate such vertical integration, however, their efforts can be compromised by the fact that today's students are far more mobile than ever before. The transience of the U.S. population will continue to confound efforts to provide well-defined academic pathways through the various grade levels that would enable more students to take advantage of advanced studies in high school.

Challenges of Middle School Teaching

A great deal of research conducted over the past 15 years has led to the conclusion that "in-field" teachers (those holding certification in the subject area to which they are assigned) not only know more content than their "out-of-field" colleagues, but also are better able to communicate that knowledge to students in their classrooms (Darling-Hammond, 2000). However, mathematics and science teachers in middle schools are far more likely to be teaching mathematics or science classes without certification in the subject area as compared with high school teachers (NCES, 2000b). This lack of certification in specific subjects can have profound effects on preparing middle school students for higher-level or advanced work in high school.

---

[14]Through its Vertical Teams Initiative, the College Board provides a vehicle for cross-grade contact (see Chapter 3, this volume). In the Vertical Teams approach, teachers from the middle school level up through AP work with one another to ensure that students are prepared to participate successfully at the advanced level by aligning curricula and developing content-specific teaching strategies.

Ability Grouping in Mathematics

Schmidt et al. (1999) note that 82 percent of 13-year-olds in the United States are in schools offering two or more differently titled mathematics classes for students at the same grade level, each with different expectations for student learning. These students from different middle-grade courses sometimes funnel into the same high school courses, leading to a lack of continuity in their mathematics education. Of even greater concern is that this early mathematics placement contributes to sorting students into different "pipelines," some of which lead away from rigorous academic courses and programs. As noted below in the discussion of disparities in opportunities to pursue and succeed in advanced study, this problem is compounded for minority students and those of low socioeconomic status.

Early ability grouping at the middle school level has the most pronounced effect in mathematics because of the cumulative and sequential nature of the curriculum. Once students are placed in a mathematics sequence, it is very difficult for them to move to a more advanced sequence without doubling up (taking two mathematics courses during the same year) or attending summer school for an intensive and fast-paced version of a typical yearlong course. Summer school courses, because they are compressed, often do not provide a solid foundation of understanding for further study (see the report of the mathematics panel).

Several recent reports indicate that the process of determining which students will take advanced courses in high school begins with their placement in the first algebra course (Gamoran, 1987; Horn, Nunez, and Bobbitt, 2000; NCHSSY, 2001a).[15] Once considered a ninth-grade course, algebra is becoming an eighth-grade option in increasing numbers of school districts,[16] and some districts offer it to a small number of seventh graders.[17]

Placement in algebra is based most often on the results of standardized tests, teacher recommendations, and parental requests. It is not uncommon, however, for parental requests to take precedence over test scores. Studies have shown that, although counselors and school administrators use test scores or current mathematics placement to bar low-income students from high-level courses, they permit middle-class students with similar qualifications to enroll when parents intervene on their children's behalf (Orfield and

---

[15]Some research indicates that ability grouping begins much earlier than middle school, perhaps even as early as elementary school.

[16]In 1998, 18 percent of U.S. eighth-graders were enrolled in Algebra 1.

[17]This shift is beginning to place great strain on middle schools, as well as many of the teachers in those schools who may not have received appropriate preparation or professional development for teaching this subject well to younger students (NRC, 1998, 2000a).

Paul, 1995; Paul, 1995; Romo and Falbo, 1996), even though parents sometimes push for class options for which their children may not be prepared or ready.

While mathematics is often the subject in which students initially are separated by perceived ability, this division occurs throughout the curriculum. Because this system of matching students to courses begins even before high school, many low-income and minority students (as well as other students who have been inappropriately accelerated) enter high school unprepared for demanding science and mathematics courses.

During the last two decades, attempts have been made to dismantle formal "tracking" systems for students. Few principals today would admit to tracking in their schools. However, the differentiation of students by ability that tracking was intended to address persists in the form of nonacademic courses and varying levels of specific academic courses (such as Algebra 1, Honors Algebra 1, Algebra 1: Parts 1 and 2, Basic Algebra, Introduction to Algebra, Business Algebra [Lucas, 1999; Powell et al., 1985]), coupled with allowing students to choose which course or series of courses to take.

Preparing for Advanced Study: High School

Curriculum

The curriculum of most high schools is organized around subject areas: English, mathematics, science, social studies, and fine and performing arts. Typically, academic courses are offered at multiple levels of difficulty, and students are grouped for instruction on the basis of earlier performance, perceived ability, student persistence, or parental request. In most comprehensive high schools, there are fairly distinct curricula for those who are college bound and those who are not. Even among those headed for college, decisions are made continually about whether a particular student should take the more rigorous AP and honors courses or the traditional academic versions of those courses. These different "college preparatory" classes are often characterized by different grading scales[18] and degrees of depth. Many

---

[18]In some schools, the four-point grade-point average (GPA) system has been replaced by a weighted system. In a weighted system, final letter grades earned in honors or advanced courses are assigned a higher number of points to be used in the calculation of GPAs. For instance, using a four-point system, A = 4, B = 3, C = 2, and D = 1, whereas in one type of weighted system, A = 4.5, B = 3.5, C = 2.5, and D = 1.5. Thus, grades earned in honors or advanced courses help increase students' GPAs. Weighted grades were first devised to entice students to take more-rigorous classes without fear of hurting their class rank or GPA. Some colleges and universities readjust these weighted GPAs to their own systems when making decisions about which students to admit. There are many variations on this formula. Schools often devise a system that reflects their unique beliefs and goals.

students describe these alternative pathways as differing in tone and purpose, with the higher-level classes drawing more serious students who are more likely to stay on task (NCHSSY, 2001a; Office of Educational Research and Improvement [OERI], 1999).

Most comprehensive U.S. high schools offer a vast array of courses, and students are allowed to choose freely among them. This diversification and differentiation of curriculum is intended to address the differing abilities, interests, and preparation of the student body. However, diversification and freedom of choice also allow many students to choose poorly and consequently to leave school underprepared for either college or work (AFT, 2001; Frome, 2001; NCHSSY, 2001a).[19] More-rigorous state high school graduation requirements have helped address these concerns, but the continuing availability of many low-level academic courses and their effects on students' course-taking patterns and achievement remain a significant problem for students, schools, higher education, and prospective employers.

While most high schools organize their curriculum as described above, others take a different approach, offering a core curriculum. Such a set of course offerings is quite narrowly focused and composed mainly of academic courses, and the students have very few choices among them. Electives are typically academically oriented courses. A student is more likely to take academic courses if he or she is assigned to them, if enrolling in such courses is considered the norm among students at a school, or if there are few (or no) undemanding courses available. This core curriculum approach is one way schools might try to address disparities in course-taking patterns among students; research on other promising practices is greatly needed.

Lee and colleagues have evaluated the relative efficacy of the above alternative curriculum structures, defined as "differentiated" and "constrained," respectively, in both public and Catholic schools (Lee, 2001; Lee, Burkam, Chow-Hoy, Smerdon, and Geverdt, 1998; Lee, Croninger, and Smith, 1997).[20] Using two different nationally representative longitudinal datasets and multilevel analysis methods, they evaluated the effects of curriculum structure and other student- and school-related variables on two outcomes: (1) learning in mathematics during the high school years and (2) distribution of learning in a school according to students' social class. The studies demonstrated that

---

[19]Although almost 70 percent of high school graduates now go on to college, only about 28 percent of them complete a bachelor's degree, and only 8 percent complete an associate's degree by the time they reach age 28 (NCES, 2001a). Of the high school graduates who go to college, approximately 30 percent need to take a remedial course in basic subjects such as English and algebra before they can begin college coursework (Kirst, 2000).

[20]The constrained curriculum model is more common in Catholic than in public schools in the United States (Bryk, Lee, and Holland, 1993; Lee, 2001; Lee and Bryk, 1989).

the constrained curriculum was both more effective (i.e., it induced higher levels of learning among all students in the school) and more equitable (i.e., socioeconomic status was less strongly correlated with learning in schools with a constrained curriculum). Indeed, holding all students to the same high standards and eliminating low-level academic courses is recommended by many organizations, including the NASSP (1996), the Southern Regional Education Board (Bottoms, 1998; Kaufman et al., 2000), the AFT (2000), the NCHSSY (2001a, 2001b), and the American Youth Policy Forum (2000).

A constrained curriculum does not imply an absence of differentiation among students. Rather, differentiation in constrained curricula is related to the pace at which students progress through the curriculum, not the content of the courses. As a result, some students may graduate from high school having completed calculus, while others may take longer to master algebra or geometry and graduate having completed only Algebra II. It is important to reiterate that both the path and the content of the courses along the path are the same, or nearly so, for all students, regardless of their future educational plans or perceived abilities (an exception might be made for classes designed to meet the needs of special education students). What differs is the time and support students need to move along the path and how far they progress. To be successful, some students will require additional academic support, such as "double dosing" (taking the same course over more than one class period). Such students may have to skip some other activity in their school day to do so, but after-school and Saturday academic classes, tutoring, and summer "bridge" classes can help them develop academic competencies (e.g., analytic reading and writing) or give them a head start on the curriculum they will be expected to learn should they pursue advanced coursework. The idea is that remediation is reduced as students demonstrate greater learning and achievement. Additionally, some school districts, understanding that students differ in the amount of time they may need to complete high school graduation requirements when expectations are high, have opted to allow their students to complete high school in 3, 4, or 5 years in accordance with individual achievement and educational needs (see, e.g., Johnston, 2000). This flexibility is consistent with recommendations made by the American Youth Policy Forum (2000).

High School Mathematics and Science

Many states have set 3 years of high school mathematics as a requirement for high school graduation, following the recommendation of the National Commission on Excellence in Education (1983) (*Education Week*, 2000). Research on patterns of student achievement in mathematics and science demonstrates that the amount of time spent in instruction and the number

TABLE 2-2 Percentage of All High School Students Taking Higher-Level Mathematics Courses by Graduation, 1998 and Change 1990 to 1998

Geometry or Integrated Mathematics 2		Algebra 2 or Integrated Mathematics 3		Trigonometry or Precalculus		Calculus or AP Calculus	
1998	% Change 1990 to 1998	1998	% Change 1990 to 1998	1998	% Change 1990 to 1998	1998	% Change 1990 to 1998
72%	+11%	63%	+14%	39%	+10%	12%	+3%

SOURCE: Adapted from CCSSO (1999).

and level of courses taken are strongly related to achievement (Adelman, 1999; Jones, Davenport, Bryson, Bekhuis, and Zwick, 1986; Jones, Mullis, Raizen, Weiss, and Weston, 1992).

The typical progression of courses in high school mathematics leading to calculus begins with Algebra I and is followed (although not always in this order) by geometry, Algebra II, trigonometry, analysis or precalculus, and calculus.[21] Table 2-2 indicates the number of students taking higher-level mathematics classes in 1998 and the changes in the percentage of students doing so between 1990 and 1998.

National consensus standards for mathematics and science have been available for the past decade (American Association for the Advancement of Science [AAAS], 1993; NCTM, 1989, 2000; NRC, 1996) and frequently have served to guide individual states in developing their own standards, curriculum frameworks, and assessments to improve learning in these subjects. In many states, however, standards in mathematics and science have been developed in the context of local political considerations and needs rather than with an eye to regional or national cooperation and consensus, or remain enmeshed in debates about the appropriate ways in which students should learn these subjects. Thus, expectations for what students should know and be able to do vary greatly among states (Gandal, 1997).

It should be noted that instructional time and course taking in mathematics and science vary widely among U.S. schools. Such variation relates to ability (Benbow and Stanley, 1982; Benbow and Minor, 1986), but also is correlated with students' socioeconomic status (Goodlad, 1984; Horn, Hafner, and Owings, 1992; Lee, Bryk, and Smith, 1993; McKnight et al., 1987; Oakes, 1990). While the data reported in Table 2-2 for mathematics and in Table 2-3 for science do not reveal differences in course taking among students of different racial and ethnic groups, such is the case primarily because many

---

[21]There are numerous remedial and basic mathematics courses below Algebra I, and some 10 percent of public high school graduates in 1998 never progressed beyond them (NCES, 1998).

TABLE 2-3   Percentage of All High School Students Taking Higher-Level Science Courses by Graduation, 1998 and Change 1990 to 1998

Biology		Chemistry		Physics	
1998	% Change 1990 to 1998	1998	% Change 1990 to 1998	1998	% Change 1990 to 1998
92%	-3	54%	+9%	24%	+4%

SOURCE: Adapted from CCSSO (1999).

states do not report data in this fashion. Of the 13 states that do report mathematics enrollment by race/ethnicity, enrollment of African American and Hispanic students in higher-level mathematics courses lagged behind that of whites and Asians in the same courses in all cases.

Most state high school graduation requirements include the completion of at least 2 years of science (*Education Week*, 2000), although college-bound students traditionally take more. These students usually take science in the sequence of biology, chemistry, and physics, with some taking earth science before biology. Physics is the least frequently selected science, often because most students have completed their graduation requirements in science by the junior year.

Table 2-3 indicates the number of high school students who had taken a specific science course by the time they graduated in 1998 and the changes in the percentages of students in those courses between 1990 and 1998. Although the increases in enrollment in upper-level science courses are not as dramatic as those for higher-level courses in mathematics, Table 2-3 indicates that more students now enroll in chemistry and physics. Recently, there has been an effort to change the order in which science courses are taught, with physics serving as the introduction to the science course sequence (Roy, 2001). Should this effort gain momentum, the numbers of students who graduate with a credit in physics could rise dramatically during the next decade.

Several states have recently implemented integrated or coordinated science programs for ninth- or ninth- and tenth-grade students. Students leaving an integrated or coordinated science program often go on to more specialized or advanced science courses during their last 2 years of high school (CCSSO, 1999). This move toward integrating science during the first 2 years also may account for the small decrease in the number of students who have taken biology, since that course is typically offered to ninth or tenth graders.

Challenges of High School Teaching

There are approximately 1.4 million teachers of grades 9–12. These secondary school teachers see themselves primarily as subject area specialists.

In general, high school teachers are members of subject-based departments that operate quasi-independently within a high school. Most academic departments are directed by department chairs, who make decisions about curriculum, instructional materials, textbooks, and teaching assignments.

Secondary school teachers typically are responsible for five periods of instruction per day.[22] Teaching responsibilities for high school teachers generally exceed 100 students and in some districts reach nearly 175 students. With such high enrollments, it is difficult for many high school teachers to know their students well or to adjust pedagogy to meet individual students' needs, particularly when there are special needs. Within the average school day, most high school teachers have 13 minutes of instructional planning time for every assigned teaching hour, and consequently have little opportunity to work with colleagues on curricular or instructional planning (Darling-Hammond, 1999b; NCTAF, 1996).

In a study of teachers' work, Louis (1992, p. 150) reports that what matters most to secondary school teachers is time. To be effective, teachers need time to remain abreast of changes in their subject areas and in the pedagogy related to their disciplines. They need time to plan effectively and collaboratively, to receive and analyze feedback about their teaching, and to reflect on their own teaching practice. However, many high school teachers report that they have little time during the school day to interact with other teachers (Choy et al., 1993, p. 128).

The National Institute on Student Achievement, Curriculum, and Assessment (OERI, 1999) describes two different teacher approaches to dealing with the lack of time for activities besides teaching. Some teachers indicate that they do what they can during school hours; what is not finished during the school day remains uncompleted. Others extend their working hours far beyond contract time to allow for collaboration and planning with other teachers, for grading, or for preparing for their own classes. In urban schools, teachers may not be able to remain in their buildings after hours because of safety concerns, making it even more difficult for any collaborative planning or collegial interactions to take place.

Secondary school teachers are more likely than teachers at other levels to report feeling isolated and unsupported (Bureau of Labor Statistics, 1999; NCES, 2000b; OERI, 1999). They also report that there are many competing demands on their own and their students' time that interfere with instruction. High school teachers who leave the profession frequently cite as their major reasons for doing so concerns about inadequate support from their school's administration; nonacademic demands, such as cafeteria duty; poor student motivation to learn; and student discipline problems (National Sci-

---

[22]This varies in schools that use alternative scheduling options.

ence Teachers Association [NSTA], 2000). Isolation is an especially frequent complaint of advanced study teachers, who are often the only members of their departments assigned to teach particular classes, such as AP physics or IB chemistry. Efforts to combat this isolation have led both the College Board and the International Baccalaureate Organisation (IBO) to establish online teacher education and support networks.

Students

The U.S. Department of Education (NCES, 2001a) estimates that there will be more than 15 million students in grades 9–12 in public and private high schools in the United States in the fall of 2002 and an additional 235,000 home-schooled students in these grade equivalents (Parent Survey of the National Household Education Surveys Program, as cited in Basham, 2001). The majority of secondary school students say that seeing friends is the most important reason for going to school; only a quarter of secondary school students cite academics as the most important reason (Hart Research Associates, 1999).

The popular media have reported on the stress many high school students feel because of the competing demands placed on their time—demands that both detract from and enrich their academic endeavors (see for example, Hart Research Associates, 1999; Schneider, 1999; Springer and Peyser, 1998; Noonan, Seider, and Peraino, 2001; Hong, 2001; Gratz, 2000). For example, in the United States approximately 60 percent of high school sophomores and 75 percent of seniors are employed (Bachman and Schulenberg, 1993; Steinberg and Dornbusch, 1991). It is now commonplace for students, particularly those bound for college, to work 15–20 hours per week during the academic year to earn spending money. In addition, as compared with their counterparts in other countries, U.S. teenagers spend a disproportionate amount of their free time each week in activities that not only fail to support learning, but may actually undermine it. On average, U.S. teens spend 20–25 hours socializing, 5 hours participating in extracurricular activities, and 15 hours watching television during each week of the school year (NCHSSY, 2001a).

Students in advanced study programs are more frequently caught between competing demands on their time as compared with other U.S. high school students. They are involved in field trips that take them out of their academic classes. They are also tapped regularly for academic competitions, honor society committees, student government planning and activities, and fundraising for clubs, all of which remove them from the classroom or impinge on needed study time after school. These students often also play in school orchestras or march in school bands, and they frequently assume leadership positions with school clubs or serve as editors for school publications.[23] Many of these students consistently carry the maximum number of academic subjects allowed by their schools' schedules, often starting on their homework as late as 10:00 pm. Added to all of this activity is a rushed school schedule that includes a 25–30 minute lunch period in a crowded cafeteria as the only break in the day. Problems at home and with friends and concerns about school safety and personal well-being distract many secondary school students from their academic pursuits. Fully 25 percent of secondary school students report that it is difficult for them to concentrate in class because they are worried about problems at home. This finding is most prevalent among low-income students: 55 percent of these students versus 17 percent of students whose families have few economic worries report that they think so much about home that they cannot concentrate in school (Hart Research Associates, 1999).

Moreover, 40 percent of students say that students who interrupt classes with bad behavior are a major problem that interferes with learning. Indeed, many parents and students view advanced study courses as temporary havens from such disruptions. Almost a quarter of the students surveyed said that teachers not knowing or caring about them as individuals is a big problem as well.

DISPARITIES IN OPPORTUNITIES TO PURSUE AND SUCCEED IN ADVANCED STUDY

Students' educational opportunities and achievement are strongly tied to the beliefs and values of those who educate them (Rosenthal, 1987; Rosenthal, Baratz, and Hall, 1974; Rosenthal and Rubin, 1978; Rutter, McNaughan, Mortimore, and Ouston, 1979). Offering advanced courses in most if not all academic subjects is one way to give students the message that teachers and administrators view participation in higher education as expected and attainable, and that they value the efforts and persistence required to prepare for college.

Most students perform poorly when their teachers do not believe in their abilities, in large part because such beliefs translate into fewer learning opportunities (Lee, 2001; Lee and Smith, 1996; Raudenbush, 1984; Rosenthal and Jacobson, 1968). Many teachers set different learning objectives for students according to perceptions of their abilities. For example, mathematics and science classes taught by teachers who report that their students are of "high" ability focus on developing reasoning and inquiry skills, whereas

---

[23]While these activities are voluntary, and many more students than those in advanced study participate, advanced study students are disproportionately represented among participants. Some attribute this situation to the public's perception of college admission practices.

classes in which teachers report that their students are of "low" ability emphasize instead the importance of mathematics and science in daily life (Gamoran, Nystrand, Berends, and LePore, 1995; Oakes, 1990; Raudenbush, Rowan, and Cheong, 1993; Weiss, 1994). All too often, students who are seen as being of low ability are disproportionately poor or of color (Ingersoll, 1999; Oakes, 1990). Differentiation of coursework and content by the perceived ability of students is characteristic of both formal and informal tracking in most U.S. secondary schools.

Disparities in Participation

High school students can take an advanced class in science and mathematics only if (1) their school offers such classes, (2) the school provides them access to the courses, and (3) they are prepared for such courses. A recent study in California revealed that AP offerings in that state's 1,100 high schools vary greatly (Oakes et al., 2000): 13 percent offer multiple sections of more than 15 different AP courses; 30 percent provide only single sections of 2 or 3 different AP courses; and 16 percent offer no AP classes at all (Carnevule, 1999; Hebel, 1999). Although these differences in AP offerings are associated with several factors, such as school size and location, there also is a clear correspondence between the availability and breadth of a high school's AP course offerings and its racial composition. Regardless of the size of the school, the availability of AP courses decreases as the percentage of African Americans, Hispanics, or students of low socioeconomic status in the school population increases, as compared with comprehensive public high schools that serve predominantly white and middle-class students (see Table 2-4). This differential access to AP classes is most stark and most consequential in mathematics and science. The problem also is compounded by the fact that even when schools do offer high-quality advanced mathematics and science courses, students of color and those of low socioeconomic status are much less likely to enroll in them (Atanda, 1999; Horn et al., 2000; Ma and Willms, 1999; Oakes, 1990).

As noted earlier, parental involvement can play a strong role in students' course selections. Students are more likely to take higher-level mathematics and science courses if their parents are highly educated and knowledgeable about the college admission process and help guide their children's course selection (Ekstrom, Goertz, and Rock, 1988; Horn et al., 2000; Lee and Ekstrom, 1987; Useem, 1992). When asked to explain the disproportionate enrollment of whites and Asians in advanced classes as compared with other racial or ethnic groups, however, educators attributed this disparity to students' ability or wise choice of courses without considering the influence of parents on these decisions (Oakes and Guiton, 1995). Some faculty members dismissed

TABLE 2-4 School Racial/Ethnic Disparities in Mathematics and Science Offerings in California, 1998-1999

Proportion African American and Hispanic	Number of AP Math/Science Offerings
Greater than 70 percent	3.8
Less than 30 percent	5.3

SOURCE: Adapted from Oakes et al. (2000).

the disproportionate representation of Hispanics in lower-level courses, even those whose test scores were comparable to the scores of higher-placed white and Asian students, attributing the disparities to differences in students' motivation and choices or to cultural differences in educational values or family support. And studies of schools under court-ordered desegregation have found them to have course placement practices that result in consistently skewed enrollments in favor of white or Asian students over and above what can be explained by measured achievement (Welner, 2001).

Disparities in Outcomes

Even when minority students participate in high-level courses such as AP, end-of-course test results reveal significant differences in outcomes for students from different racial and ethnic groups (see Table 2-5). The disparity in scores on AP assessments between African American, Hispanic, and Native American students on the one hand and white and Asian students on the other are large (as they are for most standardized tests). Additionally, the proportion of minority students who earn scores of 4 and 5 on AP assessments is small (AP examinations are scored on a scale of 1–5, with 5 being the highest score).

It is unclear whether these disparities result from assessments that are biased or reflect others factors, such as the multiple inequities that affect minorities long before they are able to take AP courses or assessments. In any case, education policymakers, school officials, and college leaders must evaluate and implement educational reforms that will improve the academic achievement of economically and educationally disadvantaged students. As a means of improving outcomes, the College Board and many school districts are focusing on improving teaching and learning in the courses that lead to advanced study. As described earlier, this means school districts must redesign the organization and structure of their schools and the allocation of resources to meet the educational needs of *all* students.

TABLE 2-5   Mean Scores[a] and Standard Deviations[b] on Selected Advanced Placement Examinations, Categorized by Subject and Racial/Ethnic Group

Subject	American Indian/ Alaskan	Black/ African- American	Chicano, Puerto Rican, and Other Hispanic[c]	Asian/ Asian American	White	Other and Not Stated[d]	National Average
AP biology	2.68 [1.23]	2.12 [1.17]	2.32 [1.29]	3.28 [1.31]	3.15 [1.26]	3.18 [1.32]	3.08 [1.30]
AP chemistry	2.17 [1.21]	2.00 [1.14]	2.08 [1.24]	3.07 [1.36]	2.86 [1.33]	2.94 [1.36]	2.84 [1.35]
AP Physics B	2.44* [1.23]	1.77 [1.05]	1.98 [1.20]	2.75** [1.32]	2.82 [1.28]	2.77** [1.31]	2.73 [1.30]
AP Physics C: Mechanics	3.05** [1.54]	2.33 [1.32]	2.62 [1.41]	3.26** [1.38]	3.32 [1.34]	3.21** [1.37]	3.25 [1.37]
AP Physics C: E&M	3.11** [1.63]	2.52 [1.26]	2.74 [1.39]	3.30** [1.43]	3.35 [1.39]	3.13* [1.37]	3.29 [1.40]
AP Calculus AB	2.54 [1.33]	2.12 [1.23]	2.41 [1.33]	3.09 [1.34]	3.11 [1.30]	3.09 [1.33]	3.03 [1.33]
AP Calculus BC	3.20* [1.55]	2.77 [1.42]	3.10 [1.48]	3.66 [1.38]	3.63 [1.36]	3.65** [1.38]	3.60 [1.38]

SOURCE: Adapted from College Entrance Examination Board (2000c).
[a]The differences between any given group mean and the national mean are significant at .01 except where indicated: *difference between group mean and national mean is significant at .05; **difference between group mean and national mean is not significant.
[b]Given in brackets.
[c]This column shows the weighted mean and standard deviation as calculated from three groups reported by the College Board—Chicano/Mexican American, Puerto Rican, and Other Hispanic.
[d]This column shows the weighted mean and standard deviation as calculated from two groups reported by the College Board—Not Stated and Other and Not Stated.

Some of the most effective strategies for improving student success in advanced study go far beyond merely adding more advanced study classes in high schools with underserved student populations (although access to these classes is important). Strategies that have proven effective include reducing class size (Grissmer, 1999); eliminating low-level academic courses that do not prepare students academically (Frome, 2001; NASSP, 1996); enhancing professional development to help teachers incorporate research-based instructional, curricular, and assessment strategies in their classrooms (see Chapter 7, this volume); hiring and retaining qualified teachers to teach in rural and inner-city schools; providing information to parents about the long-term benefits of students' participation in rigorous academic programs

(Dornbusch, 1994; Eccles and Harold, 1996);[24] implementing and supporting supplementary educational opportunities; and increasing student access to skilled counselors and mentors who can help them plan and implement strategies for educational attainment and achievement.

CONNECTIONS BETWEEN ADVANCED STUDY AND HIGHER EDUCATION

High School–College Interface Coordination and Articulation

Most people agree that an important goal of high school is to prepare students for further education and future work. However, a high school diploma currently does not guarantee success in either domain. This situation derives partly from a decentralized and disconnected system of K–12 education in which students encounter differing sets of requirements and expectations as they move from elementary school to the middle grades and on to high school. The disjuncture is exacerbated further by the lack of articulation and coordination between secondary and higher education in terms of what students need to succeed academically in college (Kirst, 1998).

In 1999 almost 66 percent of high school graduates nationwide had completed some college by the time they reached age 28. This number represents an enormous increase as compared with the proportion of 28-year-olds who had completed some college in 1971 (43 percent). Yet despite this increase in matriculation, the proportion of high school graduates who have completed a baccalaureate degree by the time they reach age 28 has risen by only 10 percentage points (NCES, 2000a).

Many policymakers and higher education faculty view students' inadequate preparation for the rigorous demands of college as a failure on the part of high schools. Others contend that the situation represents not a failure on the part of high schools, but a misunderstanding of what it means to be prepared. The diverse nature of colleges and the corresponding diversity of their academic offerings and expectations contribute markedly to this lack of understanding. Given this diversity, teachers and guidance counselors can be unclear about what students should know and be able to do before they begin college work.

A cursory review of the placement examinations administered to incoming freshmen at many institutions is all that is required to reveal just how varied these expectations are. Even in the same state, each public institution

---

[24]See also The National Coalition for Parent Involvement in Education at http://www.ncpie.org/Resources/Subject_HigherEducation.html (February 11, 2002).

of higher education often has a different set of expectations for placement of students in its system, making it doubly difficult for high schools to know just what preparing their students for college means (Kirst, 1998). This lack of understanding may leave some students with limited college options many years before they are ready to make such a choice.

What is clear, however, is a pervasive and enduring belief that AP or IB courses offer an advantage to students in the college admission process. This belief has led to ever-increasing numbers of students enrolling in multiple AP courses or seeking IB Diplomas (see Chapters 3 and 4, this volume). The popular media, college guidebooks, and even the colleges themselves promote the potential positive edge in admission gained from participation in these programs.

Advanced Study as a Link Between High School and College

Advanced study programs such as AP span the boundaries of secondary and higher education. The content and structure of advanced study programs and the learning experiences they offer to high school students can provide one of the foundations for academic success in higher education. Students and their parents look to these programs to facilitate students' admission to college, to help them succeed in college-level work once admitted, and to yield college credit and the possibility of proceeding directly to more advanced courses when the students matriculate in college. High school teachers expect these programs to provide motivated and well-prepared students with opportunities to gain the prerequisite content knowledge and habits of mind that will make them successful in college.

In turn, colleges and universities want to enroll highly qualified students who have the background and motivation to succeed in college courses. They want students who are well prepared and well educated. Colleges and universities look to and rely on advanced study to prepare students for the rigors of higher education. High school advanced study courses in science and mathematics are particularly important in establishing a foundation on which to build further study in these disciplines. Students, parents, high school guidance counselors, and even some college faculty may view these introductory courses in science and mathematics as "gatekeepers." Science and mathematics are among the most hierarchical subjects in higher education and typically require sequential courses of study extending over many years. If the advanced study programs that serve as introductions to these disciplines are not well constructed, subsequent learning is likely to be adversely affected.

The availability of both government and private funds has begun to catalyze fundamental changes in the ways science and mathematics are taught at the undergraduate level, especially in introductory courses (see, for example, NRC, 1999d; Rothman and Narum, 1999). Cutting-edge concepts and skills from the disciplines are being integrated into introductory classes and laboratories. Information technologies increasingly are being woven into the fabric of teaching and learning for large numbers of undergraduates. However, this teaching and learning revolution has yet to reach many campuses, and advanced high school courses in the sciences continue to be modeled on traditional approaches. This tendency is reinforced in AP science courses by the College Board's practice of basing its course outlines on surveys of institutions that accept large numbers of AP students. This practice can reinforce the status quo for AP courses instead of encouraging change to reflect emerging best practices in the disciplines involved.[25]

The Role of Advanced Study in College Admission Decisions

How Admission Decisions Are Made. Although much is known about how colleges make admission decisions, there is clearly a limit to what can be known about actual practices across institutions. The committee recognizes that many different individuals ultimately make these decisions, and that the decisions they make are based on particular circumstances and available information of varying quality. Thus, the discussion below can explore only in part the full range of processes and practices involved.

The primary role of admission officers at all colleges and universities is to assemble a class from among the qualified applicants. In some states, legislative mandates determine who must be admitted to public colleges and universities. For example, the Top 10 Percent Law (officially House Bill 588) guarantees that Texas high school graduates who rank in the top 10 percent of their senior class will be admitted to any state institution of higher learning. At other postsecondary institutions, both public and private, admission decisions are made primarily on the basis of numerical formulas that include a student's high school grade-point average (GPA), class rank, completion of specified numbers of courses, and performance on the ACT (American College Testing Program) or SAT I and sometimes one or more SAT II subject tests. Some of these institutions also consider information on applicants'

---

[25]An exception to this trend is in AP calculus, which is based on emerging research about teaching and learning in that subject. This difference between calculus and the science subjects that were investigated by the committee is considered in greater detail in Chapter 10 and in the panel reports prepared for this study (a summary of these reports is provided in Appendix A; the full reports can be found at http://www.nap.edu/catalog/10129.html).

experiences, extracurricular activities, talents, and backgrounds. Students who meet established standards are typically admitted as long as space is available. This approach to admissions allows institutions to identify qualified applicants efficiently from a very large pool. With this approach, AP and IB play a role only when grades earned in those classes are given extra weight in computing GPAs or establishing class rank. Students who do not have access to AP or IB courses are at a disadvantage in this type of admission process unless provisions are in place to give equal weight to other kinds of advanced courses available to them. Thus, colleges and universities that use a formula to make admission decisions often give special consideration to grades earned in honors or college preparatory courses as well as to AP and IB grades.

In contrast with both of the systems described above, some institutions, particularly those interested in shaping their incoming classes in accordance with institutional goals and priorities, use a very different approach. Admission officers at these colleges individually read applications (sometimes more than once), consider information about students that is more subjective in nature, and examine how each student might contribute to the values and goals of the institution. Evaluations of students in these situations usually take into account both what an individual applicant has accomplished and the context of the high school from which he or she will graduate. For example, students who take no honors or AP classes at schools that offer such programs are viewed differently from those who take no such classes at schools where they are unavailable. Similarly, those who attend schools where participation in extracurricular activities is limited by school policy are not evaluated with the same expectations for participation as those who attend high schools that encourage participation in a wide variety of activities. School profiles,[26] reports of admission officers who visit many high schools, and the academic reputations of particular schools are used to pro-

---

[26]A profile is a concise overview of the high school and its offerings. Profiles vary in quality, but a good one will indicate the highest-level courses offered in each academic area, describe the levels available (for example, honors, gifted and talented, college preparatory, remedial) for each grade, and make clear the degree of challenge. This profile allows an admission reader to compare the applicant's transcript against the offerings of the school. In addition to course-level information, a profile also includes demographic information about both the school and the community; economic information, including percentage of school population on free or reduced lunch; the diversity of the student body; the percentage of graduates attending 4-year colleges; educational options in the community (mentorships or access to college courses taught on local college campuses, for example); college acceptance lists (where previous graduates were accepted or matriculated); SAT/ACT ranges; GPA distribution; and AP or IB score distributions by subject that serve as important indicators of how well the high school classes are aligned with the AP or IB program syllabi.

vide admission officers with needed information about the high schools attended by applicants.

The Roles of AP and IB in the Admission Process. To better understand the role played by AP and IB courses and examination results in college admission decisions, the committee conducted an informal survey of deans of admission from 264 U.S. colleges and universities.[27] Approximately half responded. The survey was designed to shed light on three broad issues related to the college admission process: (1) how AP and IB courses on an applicant's transcript are used in admission decisions, (2) the extent to which applicants' chances for admission are affected if they do not take IB or AP courses because the courses are not offered at their high schools, and (3) the role played in admission decisions by AP and IB examination grades or by a lack of reported results.

The survey revealed that, regardless of their specific goals, the most important priority for admission officers at selective schools is to admit students who can take advantage of the academic strengths of the institution as well as contribute to the education of their peers. Because past performance is deemed a strong predictor of future performance, admission officers carefully review applicants' transcripts to determine how well and to what extent the applicants have taken advantage of the school- and community-based opportunities available to them in high school.[28] Admission personnel generally view the presence of AP or IB courses on a transcript as an indicator of the applicant's willingness to confront academic challenges.[29]

The presence of AP and IB courses on a student's transcript (if such courses are available at the applicant's high school) is of greatest importance for admission to highly selective schools seeking students who have taken

---

[27]Using the 1994 Carnegie classifications for ranking undergraduate institutions, schools were placed into four broad categories: national universities, national liberal arts colleges, regional universities, and regional liberal arts colleges. Institutions from these four categories were then sorted by their selectivity in the admission process, as defined by the percentage of applicants admitted. Surveys were sent to the 50 most selective national liberal arts colleges and the 50 most selective national universities, as well as every seventh school on the remaining lists (a total of 264 institutions). Reminders were sent to deans who had not returned their survey forms by the deadline. This process resulted in a return of surveys from 133 institutions. Admission selectivity among the sample of surveys that were completed ranged in percentage of applicants accepted from a low of 11 percent to a high of 100 percent.

[28]Admission officers use two primary sources of information for determining what was available to students at different high schools: first-hand information gathered by admission staff during recruiting trips, and the high school profile, discussed above.

[29]AP and IB courses may also serve as indicators of the quality of the academic program offered by the applicant's high school and hence assist in comparing students from different schools.

maximum advantage of the academic opportunities available to them. AP and IB courses are somewhat less important factors for admission at colleges where a larger percentage of applicants are admitted. Nonetheless, many of these colleges use the presence of AP and IB courses as an indicator of the strength of the applicant's academic preparation. AP and IB play little to no role in admission decisions at colleges where the vast majority of applicants are accepted.

There are generally two types of high schools that do not offer AP or IB courses. First are both public and private schools that, for institutional reasons, elect not to offer AP and IB and instead provide their own rigorous curricula. Many of these high schools have national reputations for excellence, and admission officers know the levels of challenge the students in these schools experience. Second are schools typically located in areas where sufficient resources or qualified personnel are not available to mount such a program or where the demand for such courses is deemed to be low. The committee was concerned primarily with the outcome for students from this second group.

When asked what the effect on admission decisions is if AP or IB classes are not available at an applicant's high school, deans from virtually every college or university replied that a lack of AP or IB courses at an applicant's high school would not have an adverse effect on a student's gaining admission to their institution if the student had taken the most challenging courses that were available and done well in them. Some admission officers indicated that they might look for evidence that students lacking access to rigorous opportunities in school tried instead to participate in similar kinds of academic opportunities outside of school. A very small number of deans indicated that there might be indirect consequences for students from schools with limited advanced course offerings. For example, a small number of deans reported that they are more likely to "dip deeper" into a class (i.e., accept students with a lower class rank) in high schools with solid academic programs than in schools with less solid programs. Thus, the number of AP and IB courses is sometimes used as an indicator of a school's academic commitment. Of course, while offices of admission consciously avoid penalizing students who do not have access to advanced study courses or programs in their high schools, the lack of access to such courses also could result in students' from these schools being less prepared and less successful if they are admitted to selective institutions.

The survey also addressed the issue of students who have access to AP and IB courses at their high schools but choose not to enroll in them. Deans from the most selective schools responded consistently that this decision would likely place an applicant at a disadvantage. When evaluating a student's program against a high school's course offerings, the most selective schools effectively require, in the absence of some compelling reason, that successful applicants take the most demanding curriculum available to them. For some students, this may mean they are expected to take four to six AP courses during their high school years or three higher-level IB courses during their senior year. It also implies that students who attend schools where AP and IB courses are offered as junior year options are expected to have taken such courses in their junior year as well.

AP and IB Examination Grades and the Admission Process

AP and IB examinations are administered each May, and scores are not usually available until July. Therefore, final examination grades for AP and IB courses taken during the senior year of high school are not a factor in admission decisions, although they are a factor in credit and placement decisions. Many educators contend that this makes it easy for seniors to reduce their level of commitment to academics once admission letters have been mailed, sometimes as early as December of the senior year for those students who have applied for early decision or rolling admission.

If an applicant has taken AP or IB classes in tenth or eleventh grade but has not submitted scores, deans at most of the more selective colleges and universities included in the committee's survey indicated that they interpret the student's decision cautiously. Many observed that AP examinations are expensive and that applicants may not have taken them for financial reasons. Others noted that teaching is uneven from school to school and that it would be unfair to make assumptions about an applicant on the basis of information not provided. If, however, a student fails to submit scores, he or she has, in the words of one respondent, "missed a chance to strengthen the application." A few of the most selective schools actively search for AP or IB scores on an applicant's transcript; deans from these schools mentioned that the lack of an examination score would be addressed in a student interview if the opportunity arose.

Given the increase in the number of examinations being administered to sophomores and juniors, it is anticipated that examination scores may play a greater role in the admission process in the future. Deans from colleges and universities familiar with the IB program noted to the committee that the practice of some high schools of providing predicted scores[30] was helpful in the evaluation of an applicant.

---

[30]IB teachers are required to submit "predicted grades" for each student before the year's end. Predicted grades are used for a variety of purposes, including teacher evaluation and determination of grade distributions. The decision whether to release predicted grades to students, and presumable to colleges, is left to the individual high schools (IBO, 2000d). See additional details in Chapter 4, this volume.

College Credit and Placement Based on Advanced Study

The College Board and the IBO do not award credit or mandate specific placements, although both provide some guidance about appropriate practice. Thus individual colleges and universities (or departments within them) decide whether to award credit for AP and IB examination scores they regard as sufficiently high.

More than 2,900 colleges and universities accept AP test scores, and approximately 750 postsecondary institutions recognize IB scores. IB students traditionally have more difficulty than their AP counterparts obtaining college credit or placement for their scores. This situation is changing somewhat as colleges become more familiar with IB course content and requirements and gain more experience with IB students. However, because of the lingering reluctance of some schools to grant credit or placement for IB, some IB students also take AP assessments. This is a challenging undertaking for IB students because both sets of examinations are administered in May, and the dates may overlap.

Reducing Time to Degree

One of the factors contributing to the rapid increase in AP and IB enrollments is the perceived potential benefit of earning inexpensive college credits that can reduce time to degree and consequently decrease overall tuition costs.[31] The extent to which students actually take advantage of this opportunity for acceleration in college and the resulting savings in tuition, is not well documented, however. Some students spend the same amount of time as other undergraduates, using these credits instead to reduce overall course loads, to pursue coursework that their schedules would not otherwise allow, or to take additional courses in a subject area.

Using AP and IB for Placement or Exemption from Required Courses

As noted above, in addition to being able to graduate early, students can use their AP and IB credits to reduce overall course loads or to meet college prerequisite or distribution requirements, freeing time in their schedules to

---

[31]Approximately 1,400 institutions offer sophomore standing to students with sufficient AP credit (College Board, http://www.collegeboard.org/ap/students/benefits/soph_standing.html [November 27, 2001]). Increasing numbers of colleges (for example, state universities in California, Florida, and Washington) are awarding credit and sophomore standing to IB students with IB diplomas.

take courses they find more interesting or challenging.[32] Indeed, for many high-achieving students, the opportunity to place out of introductory courses and move directly into upper-level classes is a greater motivator than early graduation. Some colleges explicitly support this use of AP and IB scores by offering upper-level course placement to students who earn qualifying scores even if the institution does not award credit. Many high school counselors and teachers encourage their students to use their AP and IB credits in this manner when they enter college, especially when the introductory courses they would otherwise be required to take are large lecture classes or are perceived not to be sufficiently challenging.

At the same time, using credits from these examinations to fulfill distribution requirements means that students can potentially graduate from college without ever having taken courses in certain subject areas. For example, a student with AP biology credits may never have to take another course in science. Some institutions have attempted to minimize this practice, requiring that students address the school's distribution requirements by enrolling in courses that are at higher levels than those taken in high school.

In contrast, some students decide not to use their AP or IB credits to place out of introductory courses because they believe they will benefit from taking the subjects again in college. The biology, physics, and chemistry panels that provided information for this study agreed that most students would benefit from retaking these courses in college. The mathematics panel did not agree, suggesting that there is typically little benefit for qualified AP or IB students in retaking introductory calculus in college unless their institutions require them to do so.

Students also may forego upper-level placement because they want to avoid the risk of doing poorly in upper-level courses during their first year in college or because they believe retaking a course in college would result in their receiving a higher grade than if they enrolled in a more advanced course. Deans from a very small number of institutions participating in the committee's survey indicated that they offer transitional courses to students who place out of introductory-level courses but do not advance to the next course because of either the student's own decision or that of the institution.

It may also be noted that students who take AP and IB courses and then repeat those same courses in college present a particular challenge to college faculty. It can be difficult to teach these students in the same class with those who may have only a basic understanding of the subject.

---

[32]Some colleges do not allow students to use AP or IB credits to fulfill distribution or major requirements; others grant AP or IB credit for first-year courses only after students have successfully completed a second-level course in the same subject.

Institutional Decisions

In general, colleges and universities make decisions about granting AP and IB credit and placement in the same way they decide about accepting credits from other colleges. That is, university or department officials consider the content of the course, its perceived difficulty, associated laboratory activities (in the case of science courses), and the student's level of achievement. They compare the course with similar offerings at their own institutions. Placement (rather than credit) decisions also may take into account the capabilities of the particular student and may be aided by the use of a department's own placement test. This process is consistent with recommendations made by the College Board to its member institutions. In some publicly funded institutions,[33] the granting of credit for a given AP or IB score may be legislatively mandated or set by institutional policy.

The IBO does not provide guidelines for colleges to use in making decisions about credit or placement. IB is an international program, and consequently IB students attend colleges in many countries, each with its own standards and examination policies. However, the IBO offers to assist administrators and department heads at U.S. colleges or universities who are unfamiliar with the IB program in making appropriate decisions with regard to the acceptance of IB examination scores for credit or placement.

In science, decision making at the department level may involve interviewing the student and reviewing his or her high school course syllabus and laboratory notebooks. In other departments, examination scores alone may suffice. In mathematics, most departments accept an AP examination score in calculus without question. This practice is the result of faculty experience with what AP students know and are able to do, and the similarity between AP and college calculus courses.

Denial of Credit or Placement

Although the College Board encourages colleges to award academic credit for an AP score of 3 or higher, and the American Council for Education endorses this stance (College Entrance Examination Board, 2000a), nearly half of the colleges in the United States that accept AP credits do not abide by the College Board's standards (Lichten, 2000). Lichten found that while most 4-year colleges accept 4's and 5's for credit, only 55 percent accept 3's. Overall, only 49 percent of AP test takers receive college credit, even though

---

[33]This point applies only to publicly funded institutions.

two-thirds of them are qualified for college credit according to the College Board.[34]

There are various reasons for the reluctance of some colleges to award college credit as generously as entering students have come to expect and as frequently as the College Board recommends. For example, university faculty and administrators may not believe that students taking AP courses have undertaken work that is equivalent to the courses at their institution or that students have engaged the concepts of the discipline as deeply as they would in college.

Variability of Credit and Placement Decisions

Survey of Mathematics and Biology Departments. To gain a better understanding of the ways in which postsecondary institutions make credit and placement decisions about AP and IB, the committee sent an informal questionnaire about these issues to the departments of biology and mathematics at 131 colleges and universities.[35] The respondents represented national universities and liberal arts colleges, as well as regional colleges and universities located in the Midwest, North, South, and West. The institutions that responded included research universities, colleges, highly selective institutions, and institutions with open-admission policies.

It is important to note that a precise interpretation of the survey data was difficult. Response rates were less than ideal. The survey questions unfortunately did not probe sufficiently for detail or allow respondents to qualify their answers. Nevertheless, the data do provide useful information about how placement decisions are actually made.

The majority of the biology departments that responded to the survey offer two different introductory biology courses—one designed for potential majors and the other for everyone else. Other survey findings include the following:

---

[34]The College Board is currently studying the validity of a grade of 3 on AP examinations.

[35]Departments of biology and mathematics to which survey forms were sent were selected from a list of schools gathered from the Gourman Report: *A Rating of Undergraduate Programs in American Universities* (Gourman, 1999). Also selected were departments in every third school from the alphabetical list of the Oberlin Conference schools and every seventh school from the Carnegie Foundation's listings of institutions of higher education by institutional type (Bachelors I and II, Masters I and II, and Doctoral I and II institutions—available at http://www.carnegiefoundation.org). This process resulted in the selection of 131 schools. The chairs of the biology and mathematics departments from these institutions were sent the questionnaire by electronic mail. Responses were received from 43 chairs (33 percent) from departments of biology and 59 chairs (45 percent) from departments of mathematics.

- The vast majority of these departments award college credit for AP, and sometimes for IB.[36]
- The amount of credit awarded almost always depends on the score earned. For example, a student with an AP score of 5 or an IB score of 7 might earn up to eight credits (the equivalent of two semester courses with laboratory), while a student with a score of 3 or 4 might earn only earn four credits.
- Some departments are willing to accept an AP score of 3 or an IB score of 5, but the majority look for 4's or 5's on AP tests and 6's or 7's on IB tests. Two institutions grant credit or placement only for an AP 5 or an IB 7.
- Credit and placement policies at most institutions do not vary significantly between majors and nonmajors.
- A small proportion of the schools reported using indicators other than the test scores in making placement or credit decisions. In order of descending frequency, these additional factors are student interviews, placement tests, the high school's reputation, and the student's laboratory manual.
- Only two of the schools that responded have developed a special course as a transition to higher-level science for students with AP or IB credits.

Approximately half of the mathematics department chairs that responded to the survey indicated that their departments offer only one sequence of calculus. The others offer different sequences—one for mathematics, engineering, and physical science majors and the other for life science and other majors. A variation on this last organizational structure is a third sequence for business majors. Additional survey findings are as follows:

- A large majority of the mathematics departments offer *credit* to students with qualifying AP scores without considering any additional factors. However, almost a third require a departmental test and/or an interview with the student before determining *placement* in courses beyond the introductory level.
- Mathematics departments routinely offer credit for scores of 4 and 5 on AP Calculus AB or BC examinations. Among the schools that accept IB, most consider a score of 5 or higher on the Higher Level examination to be acceptable.[37]

---

[36]Many of the biology departments were unfamiliar with the IB program and had never been asked to consider an IB score for credit or placement. These institutions restricted their responses to AP.

[37]Many respondents did not know of a policy for accepting IB credits, and some of the departments reported that they do not award IB credit.

- Very few departments indicated that they would accept any scores from the IB Standard Level course in Mathematics Methods.
- Special sections of mathematics (both higher-level calculus and other areas of mathematics) are sometimes offered to students who score 4 or higher on an AP calculus examination. This practice is most common among schools that emphasize mathematics and engineering.

EPILOGUE

From the perspective of higher education, advanced study in mathematics and science has both advantages and disadvantages. In theory, both the AP and IB programs should lead to learning of science and mathematics content at a more advanced and deeper level than would occur if students had taken only introductory high school courses in these subjects. Furthermore, by creating de facto standards for the kinds of knowledge and skills students are expected to learn in a subject area, these programs allow colleges and universities to gauge more easily the academic experiences that applicants and entering students have had during their high school years as compared with students who did not enroll in these courses or programs.

As detailed in Chapters 3 and 4, however, the academic experiences of the students in these programs can be highly variable. Additionally, some college bound students may not have access to such opportunities even where they do exist. Therefore, it remains a challenge to provide appropriate college courses for this broad array of first-year students. This is a concern in particular for smaller institutions that cannot offer a large number of options for incoming students in each discipline.

3

The Advanced Placement Program

The Advanced Placement (AP) and International Baccalaureate (IB) programs are the two most widely known and nationally recognized models for advanced study. Students in AP and IB courses are provided opportunities for both acceleration and advanced study in high school mathematics and science. Both AP and IB are examination-based programs, designed for well-prepared and highly motivated students in their last 2 years of high school. Both certify a student's level of knowledge with a score on an end-of-course assessment that is recognized and valued nationally and internationally. And both programs are being challenged by a rapid expansion in the number of participating schools and students and by uses of test scores that probably were unforeseen when the programs were first established nearly 50 years ago.

Despite their ostensible similarities, the two programs are actually quite different with respect to their goals, their organization, and the ways in which they assess student learning. This chapter presents a detailed review of the AP program; a similar review of the IB program is provided in Chapter 4, this volume. The first section gives an overview of the AP program; the sections that follow address in turn AP curriculum, instruction, assessment, and professional development.

OVERVIEW

The AP program is the predominant national model for advanced courses in high school. It was established in 1955 to challenge able and well-prepared secondary students with college-level work. Supported by the Educational Testing Service (ETS), the College Board develops AP course descriptions and yearly end-of-course examinations that represent an attempt to mirror the coverage typical of college-level introductory courses. On the basis of demonstrated achievement on the examinations, students may be awarded college credit or advanced placement in higher-level college courses (see Chapter 2, this volume). A high school can elect to offer one or more AP courses simply by scheduling the courses and assigning a teacher. Individual students can elect to take any number of AP courses, as their high school allows, and there is no requirement from the College Board that students who take AP courses and receive the AP designation on their high school transcript take the examination.[1]

The College Board has developed an AP Diploma that is being offered in the academic year 2000–2001 in 20 school districts across the United States. To earn the diploma, students must complete five AP courses and receive a qualifying score (3) on each of the five examinations. The five courses must include at least one in each of the core areas of mathematics, science, language arts, and history, along with one AP elective course. The College Board plans to offer the AP Diploma in all schools in the 2001–2002 school year.

During the past 45 years, the AP program has grown from a small program that served only the top students from largely suburban public and private high schools to one that now is available in a much more diverse group of approximately 62 percent of the nation's high schools. The program experienced a decade of rapid growth during the 1990s as the number of students taking AP examinations increased from 206,000 to more than 760,000 a year. The number of examinations administered in a year rose from 277,000 in May 1990 to 1,277,000 in May 2000 (College Entrance Examination Board [CEEB], 2000c).

In its report *Access to Excellence*, the Commission on the Future of the Advanced Placement Program (CFAPP) (CFAPP, 2001) describes significant challenges to the program that have accompanied this rapid growth. Since approximately 34 percent of students enrolled in AP courses do not take the AP examinations, the first challenge noted is how the program can maintain the quality of courses and examinations and the validity of the AP credential. Second, students from urban, rural, and poor districts are underrepresented among those who take the AP examinations, and minority students are less likely than other students to take AP courses when they are offered and to achieve success on the examinations. Therefore, the commission notes the critical importance of finding ways to increase the equity of access to AP courses. The report sets forth goals and recommendations that would broaden the aim of the program by positioning it to enable many more students to experience college-level courses and earn college credit while in high school.

---

[1]Some states and school districts require that students who receive an AP credit on their transcript take the corresponding AP examination. This requirement is most common in districts where students receive financial support for taking the examinations.

At the same time, the commission emphasizes that the AP program needs to adhere to the following set of expectations to maintain program quality and oversight:

- While continuing to reflect college-level expectations and cooperation between schools and colleges, AP courses and examinations also should reflect changes in the disciplines and in pedagogy and provide models of effective instruction.
- The reliability of the AP examinations in measuring student achievement at the introductory college level must be ensured.
- Standards for AP programs in schools and school systems, for AP teachers, and for teachers' professional development should be formulated and implemented.
- The program should focus on expanding access for underserved schools and populations by strengthening the preparation of students in courses that precede AP courses.

AP CURRICULUM

Consistent with the purpose of the program, AP courses are designed to be equivalent to general introductory college courses with respect to the range and depth of topics covered, the kinds of textbooks used, the kinds of laboratory work done by students, and the time and effort required of students (CEEB, 2001a). A course description for each AP course briefly outlines the topics that may be included on the end-of-course examination, describes the examination format, and provides sample questions. The course description and teacher's guide for each AP subject area are available for a fee to teachers, who can use them as the basis for developing the curriculum for their own courses (course descriptions can now be downloaded from the College Board's Web site for free). Individual teachers are given great leeway in structuring AP courses for their classrooms. Thus, the curriculum for AP courses varies from classroom to classroom in both design and implementation, including which topics are emphasized, how the topics are related, how the content is sequenced, and how much time is spent on laboratory activities.

Development of AP Courses

College faculty members in each discipline, along with experienced AP teachers, are recruited by the College Board to serve on a development committee for each AP course. The traditional strategy for determining the content and skills to be covered in an AP course and on the AP examination has been to survey the department faculty from colleges and universities receiving the most AP score reports in a discipline. The faculty who serve on the subject-specific development committees synthesize the information from these surveys and construct a course description they believe best represents the consensus view of the college-level introductory course (CFAPP, 2001, p. 22). The development committee for a course develops both the topic outline and, with help from ETS experts, the course examinations. The committee prepares the course description for each subject and compiles a list of the textbooks used most frequently in the corresponding college course. Development committees for AP science courses may also recommend laboratory activities that are representative of work done by college students in the corresponding introductory course. This entire process is repeated every 5 to 6 years.

One result of this process is that until curricular changes have become common in introductory college courses, those changes are not reflected in the AP course descriptions and examinations. Thus, some disciplinary leaders have contended that, with the growth in AP participation and the program's influence on high school curricula, the AP course development process has the potential to slow the implementation of desirable curricular reforms.

In contrast, the development of AP calculus during the 1990s provides a model for implementing rather than impeding curricular change. The AP Calculus Development Committee used a broader, more forward-looking strategy for revising the description and the examination specifications for this course by collaborating with experts in mathematics content, curriculum, and pedagogy. The committee became an active participant in the calculus reform movement at the college level and the National Council for Teachers of Mathematics–driven standards movement at the precollege level.[2] According to CFAPP, "We believe that such strategies must be replicated whenever AP course descriptions are reviewed and revised. Leaders in the disciplines, pedagogy, and research must all play a role in order to create the highest quality curriculum possible" (CFAPP, 2001, p. 12). This committee concurs with that recommendation.

Content of AP Courses

Each AP course description, or acorn book to use the popular term, includes a topic outline. The major topics on the outline for biology, chemistry, and physics are accompanied by percentages. However, the percent-

---

[2]More information about the AP calculus development process is available at *AP Calculus for a New Century* by Dan Kennedy, http://www.collegeboard.org/ap/calculus/new_century/index.html (November 26, 2001).

ages may have different meanings for different subjects. For example, in the course description for AP biology, the percentages for each major topic and subtopic to be covered in a course are indicated (CEEB, 2001a, pp 5–6). In the course description for AP physics, the "percentage goals for the examination" are given (CEEB, 2001d, pp.16–20). In AP chemistry, the percentages indicate "the approximate proportion of questions on the multiple-choice portion of the examination that pertain to that topic" (CEEB, 2001c, pp. 6–8).

A listing of subtopics is provided for each major topic. The portion of the AP chemistry topic outline related to chemical bonding illustrates the level of detail provided by the topic outlines for each subject (CEEB, 2001c, p. 6):

B. Chemical Bonding
  1. Binding forces
     a. Types: ionic, covalent, metallic, hydrogen bonding, van der Waals (including London dispersion forces)
     b. Relationships to states, structure, and properties of matter
     c. Polarity of bonds, electronegativities
  2. Molecular models
     a. Lewis structures
     b. Valence bond: hybridization of orbitals, resonance, sigma and pi bonds
     c. VSEPR [valence shell electron pair repulsion]
  3. Geometry of molecules and ions, structural isomerism of simple organic molecules and coordination complexes; dipole moments of molecules; relation of properties to structure

The topic outline is intended to indicate the scope of the course, but not necessarily the order or depth in which topics are taught. Teachers are told that although the examination is based on the outline, they may wish to add further topics (CEEB, 2001b, p. 12).

Laboratory Requirement for AP Science Courses

Because each AP course is developed independently, information on laboratory work provided to teachers of AP science courses varies among disciplines. There is a common recommendation that at least one double period per week in AP chemistry and AP physics and two double periods per week in AP biology be spent in laboratory work. The AP physics course description does not recommend specific laboratory exercises, but rather presents survey results on laboratory emphases in typical introductory college physics courses and describes the diversity of approaches used. The May 2002–May 2003 course description for AP chemistry includes *A Guide for the Recommended Laboratory Program for Advanced Placement Chemistry* (CEEB, 2001c, pp. 36–51). The guide recommends 22 laboratory activities,[3] with the qualification that it is unlikely that every student will complete all 22 activities while enrolled in an AP chemistry course (CEEB, 2001c, pp. 45–49). Students who have completed a first-year chemistry course will likely have been exposed to many of these activities prior to the AP course. For AP biology teachers, an AP biology student laboratory guide and accompanying teacher's guide are available. Like the recommended chemistry activities, many of the biology laboratories will likely have been part of a first-year biology program. Biology teachers are encouraged to substitute alternative investigations as appropriate if they will enable students to meet the objectives stated in the guide.

While the importance of including laboratory work in the curriculum is emphasized to teachers, the interrelationships among curriculum, assessment, and instruction are also highlighted. The AP physics course description suggests that laboratory experiences should help students understand the topics being considered in the course and may improve test performance overall (CEEB, 2001d, p. 8). The description for AP chemistry states, "Data show that student scores on the AP Chemistry Exam improve with increased time spent in laboratory. This correlation is expected to be even stronger now that a question concerned with laboratory experiences is included on the examination each year" (CEEB, 2001c, pp. 43–44). Recent guidelines given to the AP science course development committees include a charge to assess knowledge about laboratory skills and experimentation.

Additional Guidance Provided to Teachers About Curriculum Development

The College Board asks AP biology teachers to stress understanding of concepts rather than memorization of terms and technical details. The rationale provided is that students who understand the topics on a conceptual level will do better on the national examination. Teachers are told that the AP biology examination will assign increasingly less weight to specific facts, and that students should be encouraged to focus on understanding important relationships, processes, mechanisms, and potential extensions and applications of concepts. According to the College Board, questions on future

---

[3]The recommended activities include some processes and procedures that can often be combined and incorporated into a single laboratory investigation.

examinations can be expected to test students' ability to explain, analyze, and interpret biological processes and phenomena more than their ability to recall specific facts (CEEB, 1999a). With regard to the issue of depth vs. breadth, the AP physics course description states, "concentration on basic principles of physics and their applications through careful and selective treatment of well-chosen areas is more important than superficial and ency-clopedic coverage of many detailed topics" (CEEB, 2001d, p. 4).

Although the stated goals for AP courses emphasize the importance of depth of understanding of fundamental concepts, the materials provided to teachers give little specific and detailed advice for designing a coherent curriculum. The AP biology course description goes the furthest in articulat-ing the principal concepts underlying the discipline and in organizing knowl-edge around them: "Emphasizing concepts over facts makes the content of a biology course less overwhelming and more meaningful. A biology course has more structure and meaning when the key concepts for each topic are placed in the broader context of unifying themes" (CEEB, 2001a, p. 4). To this end, the course description identifies three main subject areas that are crosscut by eight biological themes. The College Board presents a brief, open-ended framework for conceptual knowledge and encourages teachers to continue the articulation and organization of knowledge themselves (see Table 3-1).

TABLE 3-1   Some Applications of the Energy Transfer Theme to the Three Main Subject Areas

Theme	I. Molecules and Cells	II. Heredity and Evolution	III. Organisms and Populations
	Plants transform light energy into chemical energy.	A cell must spend energy to transcribe and translate a gene because entropy decreases as monomers are organized into complex macromolecules.	Energy flows from producers to consumers in an ecosystem.
III. Energy Transfer	A proton gradient across membranes powers the synthesis of ATP in mitochondria, chloroplasts, and prokaryotes.	Energy released by the hydrolysis of ATP is used by cells in DNA synthesis, transcription, and translation.	Ion pumps in membranes reestablish a transmembrane resting potential after a neuron fires an impulse or a muscle fiber contracts.

SOURCE: Adapted from CEEB (2001a, p. 17).
NOTES: ATP = Adenosine Tri-Phosphate. The College Board encourages teachers to continue identifying ways in which the eight major themes can be applied to the three major subject areas.

The teacher's guide for AP biology (Schofield, 2000) encourages teachers to develop a curriculum for conceptual or thematic understanding. The guide illustrates a shift in emphasis of AP biology examination questions away from factual listings of information, as illustrated by the 1989 free-response question about cell energetics, and toward conceptual understanding, as illustrated by the 1995 question. The following examples are taken from that guide (Schofield, 2000, pp. 24–25).

Factual free-response question about cellular energetics from the 1989 AP biology examination:

Explain what occurs during the Krebs (citric acid) cycle and electron transport by describing the following:
  a. The location of the Krebs cycle and electron transport chain in the mitochondria
  b. The cyclic nature of the reactions in the Krebs cycle
  c. The production of ATP and reduced coenzymes during the cycle
  d. The chemiosmotic production of ATP during electron transport

Conceptual-thematic free-response question about cellular energetics from the 1995 AP biology examination:

Energy transfer occurs in all cellular activities. For three of the following five processes involving energy transfer, explain how each functions in the cell and give an example. Explain how ATP is involved in each example you choose:

  • Cellular movement
  • Active transport
  • Synthesis of molecules
  • Chemiosmosis
  • Fermentation

AP INSTRUCTION

Little is known, other than anecdotally, about what actually happens in AP classrooms as teachers engage with students in the teaching–learning process. Teachers make decisions every day and in every class period about what to teach and how. Many factors influence these decisions, including teaching philosophies; experience with various teaching strategies; the teacher's own educational background, experience, and familiarity with various topics in the discipline; and student outcomes. In typical honors courses, teachers generally feel freer to follow their own interests and pursue topics within the broad course outline in which their content knowledge is most secure. In AP courses in which teachers focus on preparing their students for success on an AP examination, there is internal accountability if students take the external examination (Herr, 1993), although little can be said about accountability if large numbers of students in the course do not take the test. Differences among schools also influence how a course is implemented. Scheduling and length of class periods, available facilities and resources, and existing state standards and assessments for courses preceding the AP course all help shape a course differently in each locality.

AP Course Descriptions and Teacher's Guides

AP program materials address instruction only in a very general way. For example, a letter to teachers from Gasper Caperton, President of the College Board, is included as a preface to the May 2002–May 2003 course descriptions for AP biology, calculus, chemistry, and physics. He states, "This AP Course Description provides an outline of content and description of course goals, while still allowing teachers the flexibility to develop their own lesson plans and syllabi, and to bring their individual creativity to the AP classroom." Consistent with this message, for example, the May 2002–May 2003 AP physics course description features a message from the development committee encouraging the following broad instructional goals (CEEB, 2001d):

- Basic knowledge of the discipline of physics, including phenomenology, theories and techniques, and generalizing principles.
- Ability to ask physical questions and to obtain solutions to physical questions by use of qualitative and quantitative reasoning and by experimental investigation.
- Fostering of important student attributes including appreciation of the physical world and the discipline of physics, curiosity, creativity and reasoned skepticism.
- Understanding connections of physics to other disciplines and to societal issues. (p. 3)

The course descriptions in the other subjects also provide statements of goals and emphases that suggest a focus for instruction, such as the value of active learning, but do not address strategies or specific models for instruction in any detail.

Instructional strategies that might be employed effectively in achieving the instructional goals specified for AP courses may be among the teaching strategies and techniques included with the sample course outlines presented in the AP teacher's guides. However, the following two examples of strategies provided by teachers in the teacher's guide for AP biology (Schofield, 2000) are indicative of the degree of variability in instruction that might be found in AP biology classrooms:

"The primary goal of the class is to ensure that students leave having experienced an intense course of college-level biology. I do this mainly through lectures and discussions, during which time students are able to ask plenty of questions." (p. 45)

"I try to provide my students with a variety of teaching techniques that encourage both independent and group activities." The strategies described by this teacher include student discussion of journal and newspaper articles, student presentations of course topics, use of computer simulation software and a yearlong independent experimental research project. (pp. 58–59)

The section of the May 2002–May 2003 course description for AP chemistry entitled *A Guide for the Recommended Laboratory Program for Advanced Placement Chemistry* (CEEB, 2001c, pp. 36–51) clearly states goals for the laboratory program that include inquiry and student experimentation:

The program of laboratory investigations should be seen as a cyclic continuum of inquiry rather than a linear sequence of steps with a beginning and an end . . . the ideal program should not only allow students to gain experience with traditional laboratory exercises, . . . but also provide opportunities for students to carry out novel investigations. (CEEB, 2001c, pp. 39–40).

The stated goals for laboratory work (CEEB, 2001c) encourage students to:

- Think analytically and to reduce problems to identifiable, answerable questions.
- Design and carry out experiments that answer questions.
- Draw conclusions and evaluate their validity.
- Propose questions for further study.
- Communicate accurately and meaningfully.

The teacher's guide for AP chemistry (Mullins, 1994) describes a variety of laboratory programs, but does not address the context in which they might be effective in meeting the stated goals. Most of the programs described in the guide are based on typical published manuals for college-level introductory chemistry laboratory programs that prescribe both a purpose and a step-by-step procedure for students and allow few opportunities for inquiry or student-designed investigations. Some course descriptions include laboratory components that may be more effective in providing these opportunities, including "small-scale inquiry labs" (Mullins, 1994, p. 74) and preparation of a botanically based universal indicator (p. 86).

Similarly, the stated goal for the 12 biology laboratory investigations is to encourage higher-level thinking and provide opportunities for students to learn concepts, acquire skills, and engage in problem solving. The manuals, however, while providing important information to teachers about materials and procedures that are essential features of a biology laboratory program, specify the questions to be investigated, as well as step-by-step procedures. They provide no guidance to teachers about establishing a laboratory program that would enable student inquiry and no support for the goal stated in the AP Biology course description that students gain personal experience in scientific inquiry.

The report from the CFAPP is also relatively silent about instruction. It recommends only that the College Board set high standards for AP course delivery and provide demonstrations via video and other media of "best practice" teaching approaches (CFAPP, 2001, p. 10).

Messages About Instruction Conveyed by AP Examinations

Recent guidelines given to the development committees for AP science courses include a charge to assess knowledge about laboratories and experimentation. One of the free-response questions on each AP science examination will be a laboratory question. The format of the second section of the chemistry examination was changed in 1999 with the introduction of a required laboratory-based question. The 1999 question referred to a traditional experiment designed to determine the molar mass of an unknown gas. Commentary on the question in the 1999 released exam for AP chemistry states that the goal of the question is to determine whether students understand how an experiment works, as well as the chemistry behind it. Students having performed the experiment (or a similar one involving the determination of moles of a gas collected over water) in the laboratory may have had an advantage, as the question asked them to explain the purpose of steps in the experiment and list measurements that must be made. However, the question also could have been answered on the basis of knowledge of variables needed in the calculation, without a student's having actually completed the laboratory. And although one of the stated goals for the AP chemistry laboratory program is for students to design and carry out experiments, students have not yet been asked to design an experiment on an AP chemistry examination. Thus the program materials may be sending conflicting messages, since the examination questions indicate that experience with designing experiments is not necessary for success.

AP ASSESSMENT

The AP examinations, administered nationally in May of each year, provide the foundation for curriculum and instruction in AP courses. They are timed examinations, with about 50 percent of the total time devoted to multiple-choice questions and the rest to free-response, essay, or problem-solving questions.[4] Students can elect to have their examination scores reported to their choice of colleges, where the scores may be considered in decisions about placement in a college course, awarding of credit for the introductory course in the subject, or both (see Chapter 2, this volume).

AP courses are intended to represent general introductory-level college courses. The AP examinations are designed to allow students to demonstrate mastery of the concepts and skills learned in the course, enabling some students to undertake, as freshmen, second-year work in the sequence at their institution or to register for courses in other fields for which the general course is a prerequisite.[5] Consequently, AP examinations must be valid and reliable measures of student achievement at the college level. "Continued acceptance by colleges and universities of the validity of the content of AP courses, the validity and reliability of the AP Examinations, and the integrity of the scoring process is critical to AP's success" (CFAPP, 2001, p. 6).

How AP Examinations Are Developed

Content specifications for AP examinations are determined during the development of AP courses. The development committee for each AP course is responsible for deciding the general content of the examination and the ability level to be tested. The examination is constructed using the topic percentages from the AP course descriptions as a guideline for the distribution of questions. The development committee helps write and review test questions, as well as materials (including the AP course descriptions) that

---

[4]These percentages do not necessarily reflect the weighting of scores as a final examination grade is determined.

[5]The policies of colleges and universities vary widely with respect to the score they will accept to award credit or placement and how that score translates into college credit or placement. Indeed, individual departments within an institution of higher education often have very different policies and expectations. This issue is considered in greater detail in Chapter 2 this volume.

are distributed to schools. The committees also help create and give final approval for each examination.[6]

The committees, representing both secondary- and college/university-level teachers, work closely with ETS content specialists and psychometricians to ensure that the examination scores will mean the same thing to from year to year and from student to student. AP validity studies are designed to validate the use of AP for college credit by measuring the comparability of student knowledge of content and processes with that of students in introductory-level college courses (see Chapter 10, this volume, for a discussion of these studies). Most of the multiple-choice questions are written by committee members and pretested in college classes to obtain some estimate of the degree of difficulty and comparability with college courses. For optimal measurement, the AP development committee endeavors to design a multiple-choice section such that the average raw score is between 40 and 60 percent of the maximum possible raw score. Questions at varying levels of difficulty are included. Using many questions of medium difficulty ensures that clear distinctions will be made between students earning grades of 2 and 3 on the one hand and 3 and 4 on the other (CEEB, 2000b, p. 1). Some previously administered questions are included to link the current form of the examination to previous forms, thus maintaining reliability from year to year and examination to examination. The committees write, select, review, and refine free-response questions. One important aspect of test development is determining which item type and format are best for assessing a given topic or skill area. AP development committee members work with AP content experts and ETS statisticians to make this determination. Free-response questions are designed so that students will have to use analytical and organizational skills to solve problems, predict the products of chemical reactions, and formulate answers to questions (CEEB, 2000b, p. 2). The College Board does not, however, employ systematic research to determine the validity of test items in measuring cognitive processes.[7]

As questions are being written and refined, the development committees propose preliminary scoring standards that are based on consistent criteria from year to year. The committees also develop a formula for assigning composite scores based on differential weights for the multiple-choice and free-response questions.

---

[6]see http://www.collegeboard.org/ap/techman/whois/apdevcom.htm (November 26, 2001).

[7]The committee has been informed that an effort is presently under way by the College Board to begin the collection of validity data.

TABLE 3-2   College Board Recommendations Regarding Students Qualifications for Receiving College Credit, Placement, or Both

AP Grade	Qualification
5	Extremely well qualified
4	Well qualified
3	Qualified
2	Possibly qualified
1	No recommendation

SOURCES: CEEB (2001a, 2001b, 2001c, 2001d).

How AP Examinations Are Scored

In scoring, the number of correct and incorrect answers in the multiple-choice section of an examination is determined, and a correction for guessing is applied. The procedures for scoring the free-response sections are similar to those used by other testing programs to score essays or constructed-response items. Faculty consultants score the free-response questions during AP readings, which are held at various sites (usually college campuses) throughout the United States each June.[8] Because it is essential that students' responses be scored consistently, "a great deal of attention is paid to the creation of detailed scoring guidelines, the thorough training of all faculty consultants, and various 'checks and balances' applied throughout the AP Reading."[9] Composite scores are created using formulas developed by each development committee.

AP uses a five-point scale for awarding final grades on the examinations. The qualification for college credit that is described for each AP grade is shown in Table 3-2. As indicated, those students who earn a score of 3, 4, or 5 are described by the College Board as qualified for credit and/or enrollment in advanced courses at colleges and universities.

Boundaries for awarding AP grades are reset annually at a grade-setting session for each examination. Participants in these sessions usually include the chief faculty consultant, the AP director or associate director from the ETS, the College Board director or associate director of the AP program, ETS content experts for the discipline, and an AP program statistician. Grade distribution charts for each examination are available on the subject pages of the AP Web site.[10]

---

[8]All of the examinations from a subject area are graded at the same site.
[9]See http://www.collegeboard.org/ap/techman/chap3/scorefc.htm (February 11, 2002).
[10]See http://apcentral.collegeboard.com/courses/overviews/ (February 11, 2002).

How Examination Results Are Reported

AP grade reports are sent in July to the college(s) designated by the student, to the student's secondary school, and to the student. The report includes the grade earned and an interpretation of that grade for each AP exam taken by the student in the current year. A report to AP teachers is sent for each examination taken by five or more students at participating schools. The report compares these students' performance with that of the national candidate group. Mean scores for the multiple-choice questions grouped by four or five major topics and for each free-response section are compared. The free-response booklets of a school's senior AP students are released to the schools after October 15 of the year in which the exam is taken if the booklets have not already been requested by a postsecondary institution.

The free-response questions on the AP examinations are released to students and teachers after the exam has been administered. They are also posted on the AP Web site, along with scoring guidelines and student samples with scoring commentary, after the examinations have been graded.

Entire released examinations, including both the multiple-choice and free-response sections, are published about every 5 years for each subject.[11] The publication provides the following:

- Multiple-choice questions and answer key, and the percentage of candidates who answered each question correctly.
- Free-response questions and scoring guidelines.
- Sample student responses with commentary (the actual scores these students received, with a brief explanation).
- Statistical information about students' performance on the examination.

How the College Board Determines Whether AP Examinations Accomplish Their Purpose

AP examinations must be valid and reliable measures of students' achievement at the college level. Colleges need to know that the AP grades they receive for their incoming students represent a level of achievement equivalent to that of students who take the corresponding introductory course in college. The College Board conducts college comparability studies to confirm that the AP grade scale is properly aligned with current college standards. Periodically, instructors from some of the 200 colleges receiving the largest number of AP grades for an examination administer the AP examina-

---

[11]Free-response questions are released annually.

tion or portions thereof to college students who are completing the corresponding college course. The performance of the college students on the examination is compared with that of the AP students. When AP grades are set, the composite score cut points are established so that the lowest composite score for a grade of 5 is roughly equal to the average composite score of college students earning a grade of A. The lowest composite score for a grade of 4 is roughly equal to the average composite score for students with a grade of B. The average composite score of students receiving a grade of C is used to set the lowest AP grade of 3. Similar logic is used in setting the lowest composite score for a grade of 2 (Morgan and Ramist, 1998).

AP PROFESSIONAL DEVELOPMENT

What Is Known About the Preparation and Credentials of AP Teachers

Very little is known about the teaching experiences and preparation of teachers who are teaching AP courses. The College Board is currently conducting a survey of AP teachers with the goal of describing their characteristics and identifying teacher attributes that affect the success of students.[12] Until the results of this study are available, information about the teachers involved with the AP program must be based on descriptions provided in program materials.

The College Board (CFAPP, 2001, p. 6) states, "AP is an enterprise that relies on a culture of dedication, volunteerism, and altruism among AP teachers." The College Board (CFAPP, 2001, p. 2) estimates that there were approximately 100,000 teachers teaching AP classes in the United States during the 1999–2000 school year. Assigning teachers to AP courses is usually a school-level decision; the College Board does not certify teachers and has relatively little to say about the matter of teacher qualifications. School administrators attending an AP workshop reported that arbitrary assignment of teachers to AP courses is used only when absolutely necessary and that in many cases, teachers apply specifically to take an AP assignment (Burton, Bruschi, Kindig, and Courtney, 2000).

Professional Development Experiences of AP Teachers

Although the College Board does not require participation in AP professional development activities, each of the AP teacher's guides encourages such participation. Stipends and travel support may come from local schools

---

[12]See http://www.collegeboard.org/ap/research/abstract24.html (February 11, 2002).

or school districts or from the states and the federal government, or a teacher may receive no support at all. Consequently, many of the teachers who participate in AP professional development activities do so on their own time and at their own expense.

The two principal types of professional development available to AP teachers nationally are 1- and 2-day AP workshops offered by the College Board's regional offices and AP summer institutes, usually 5 days long and offered by a variety of independent agencies. During the 1999–2000 academic year, more than 56,000 AP teachers (about 56 percent of the approximately 100,000 teachers teaching AP classes in the various disciplines) participated in professional development workshops and summer institutes (CFAPP, 2001, p. 2). Teachers who participate may have widely differing professional development experiences, depending on which workshop or summer institute they attend. Recognizing the variability in content and uneven quality of the workshops and summer institutes, the College Board recently developed and implemented quality standards for AP workshop consultants and AP summer institutes (College Board, 2000, 2001).

Generally, teachers, guidance counselors, and school administrators attend the 1- or 2-day workshops to learn the rudiments of teaching an AP course and to be apprised of the latest developments and expectations for each course. Major topics covered include the following:

- Advice on preparing students for the AP examinations.
- Practical information on starting or revising an AP course.
- Insights into the structure, content, and grading of the AP examinations.
- New technology applications.
- Updates from the College Board and the ETS.

AP teachers attending the summer institutes explore a variety of instructional strategies that can be employed both to help their students learn and understand the material and to prepare them for success on the national examination. The strategies discussed range from covering every topic to emphasizing concepts, principles, and a "scientific attitude," and from teacher-centered, content-based lecture delivery to a variety of student-centered pedagogies (Burton et al., 2000). AP science teachers attending summer institutes often perform and discuss laboratory activities with the guidance of experienced AP instructors. They follow actual laboratory procedures; learn to handle equipment and materials; and discuss time frames, pitfalls, possible shortcuts, reasonable laboratory results, good follow-up questions, and ways of integrating the laboratory experience most profitably into the classroom setting (Schofield, 2000, p. 13). Fifty summer institutes responded to a 1999 survey in which directors were asked to provide evaluation data about their workshops. Workshop participants from these 50 programs indicated that sharing ideas and experiences, networking, and having good discussions with other teachers were of the activities of most value to them. Many of the participating AP teachers reported feeling isolated and unsupported after they left the institutes and workshops, as most of them returned to schools where they were the only AP teacher in a discipline (Burton et al., 2000).

Experienced AP teachers often cite the experience of serving as a faculty consultant for the annual AP reading as a highly valued professional development experience. In June 2000, approximately 5,000 college faculty and high school teachers participated in the 1-week sessions. The College Board cites three of the most common reasons given by readers for applying to return after their first experience:[13]

- High school and college faculty exchange ideas on an equal playing field.
- Networks are established among participants.
- Practice gained in establishing and applying rubrics makes participants better teachers.

The CFAPP recommends that teacher professional development become the area of greatest emphasis for technological investment and development: "Technology can supplement face-to-face workshops and institutes, providing ongoing support to teachers throughout the year" (CFAPP, 2001, p. 11). Services currently provided to teachers by the College Board include an AP electronic mailing list for each discipline—*AP Central*; the College Board's online site for the AP program, with information about AP courses, publications, workshops, and summer institutes; and videoconferences with the teachers who develop the AP courses and examinations. The College Board presents no information about local professional development activities available for AP teachers, but AP teacher's guides for the individual disciplines refer teachers to their respective professional organizations, which often sponsor sessions on AP at state and national conventions.

The CFAPP report warns that the current models for AP professional development are and will continue to be insufficient. An estimated 100,000 new AP teachers will be needed between now and the end of the decade, and many of them will be teaching AP for the first time. The commission states: "The College Board, working in cooperation with schools, school systems, colleges and universities, governments and others, must make an unconditional commitment to teacher professional development. Without

---

[13]See http://www.collegeboard.org/ap/readers/index.html (November 26, 2001).

this commitment, access to AP will not improve and quality will decline" (CFAPP, 2001, p. 10). Specific recommendations include (1) developing and implementing a mentoring system using experienced and retired AP teachers as mentors, (2) identifying successful strategies for preparing teachers to teach AP, and (3) evaluating and incorporating new models of professional development that support instructional and curricular changes. The commission also recommends that the College Board expand the development and implementation of the AP Vertical Teams program. This program focuses on collaborative planning workshops at which teachers in grades 7–12 are involved in redesigning middle school and high school curricula to give students good preparation for AP and other advanced courses.

4

The International Baccalaureate Programme

Given the differences in their origins and goals, it is not surprising that the International Baccalaureate (IB) and Advanced Placement (AP) programs differ significantly. This chapter presents a detailed review of the IB program; a similar review of the AP program is provided in Chapter 3. The first section gives an overview of the IB program; the sections that follow address in turn IB curriculum, instruction, assessment, and professional development.

OVERVIEW

The International Baccalaureate Organisation (IBO), a nonprofit educational foundation headquartered in Geneva, Switzerland, was founded in the 1960s with the mission of fostering in member schools international understanding and responsible world citizenship, as well as intellectual rigor and high academic achievement (IBO, 1997a). The IB Diploma Programme consists of a comprehensive precollege curriculum for highly motivated students in the last 2 years of high school that allows students to fulfill the requirements of various educational systems and aims to incorporate the best elements of many different national models (IBO, 1997a). Each of the IB courses in mathematics and the experimental sciences incorporates a formative internal assessment component and culminates in an internationally administered external examination. Students who complete the program and receive qualifying scores on the examinations are awarded the IB Diploma.[1]

---

[1]Although the IBO does not represent its courses as replacements for college courses, some college and university policies allow for granting credit or placement. A database listing these institutions and describing their policies can be accessed at the IBO Web site at http://www.ibo.org/ibo/index.cfm/en/ibo/services/universities (November 28, 2001).

The requirements for the IB Diploma are designed to engage students in an integrated program of studies as they complete courses and examinations in one subject from each of six different subject groups.[2] Students study some subjects in depth by selecting at least three but no more than four courses at the Higher Level (HL) and explore others more broadly at the Standard Level (SL). This approach represents a deliberate compromise between the early specialization preferred in some national systems and the breadth found in others (IBO, 1998b, p. 2, 2001a, 2001b, 2001c, p. 1). HL courses are 2-year courses. SL courses may be completed in 1 year if scheduling allows for the required number of hours, although many IB schools offer 2-year SL courses.[3]

In contrast to the AP program, which aims to provide discrete college-level courses for students in high school, the IB courses are part of an integrated program designed to prepare students for college. The IB mathematics program offers a selection of mathematics courses designed to meet the varying needs, interests, and abilities of college-bound high school students. The IB Mathematical Methods SL course is designed to provide a sound mathematical background for students who expect to study subjects at the university level that have a significant mathematical content. The IB Mathematics HL and Further Mathematics SL courses offer more rigorous preparation. Another fundamental difference between the AP and IB mathematics programs is that the IB mathematics courses are not calculus courses; rather, they focus on many advanced mathematics topics that may include calculus.[4] Similarly, students are offered both HL and SL courses in each of the experimental sciences; this accommodates students with a strong interest in science while also providing sound preparation in science for those who wish to focus on other subjects.

Three additional requirements are designed to give IB Diploma candidates the opportunity to pursue their own interests while at the same time developing a broad understanding of the bases of knowledge in both the humanities and the sciences. Theory of Knowledge is a 2-year course of study unique to IB and mandatory for every diploma candidate. "It challenges students and their teachers to reflect critically on diverse ways of knowing and areas of knowledge, and to consider the role which knowledge plays in a global society. It encourages students to become aware of

---

[2]Language (a student's first language and a study of world literature), a second modern language, the social sciences, the experimental sciences, mathematics, and the arts and electives.

[3]For IB courses, 240 hours of teaching is recommended for HL courses and 150 hours for SL courses.

[4]For a detailed discussion of the content of these courses, including their calculus component, and an analysis of how they fit into typical U.S. high school mathematics programs, see the report of the mathematics panel, available at http://www.nap.edu/catalog/10129.

themselves as thinkers . . ." (IBO, 2000b, p. 3). The curriculum for the course centers on a series of questions, including those designed to help students understand the nature of knowledge in mathematics and the sciences.[5]

IB Diploma candidates must also satisfy the Extended Essay requirement by undertaking original research and writing an essay of some 4000 words. This requirement offers students the opportunity to investigate a topic of special interest and acquaints them with the independent research and writing skills expected at the university level. It allows them to deepen their study by investigating a topic that was introduced in one of their higher-level courses or to add breadth to their program by studying a subject not included in their diploma courses. A third requirement—the Creativity, Action, and Service requirement (CAS)—encourages students to become involved in extracurricular activities.

A student who satisfies the Theory of Knowledge, Extended Essay, and CAS requirements and achieves a cumulative score of at least 24 points on the six examinations (each of which is graded on a scale from 1 to 7) is awarded the IB Diploma. An IB Certificate is awarded to students who take any number of individual IB courses and the subsequent examinations, but do not fulfill all of the requirements for the diploma.

During the past three decades, an increasing number of U.S. high schools have joined IB schools worldwide in offering the Diploma Programme. In May 2000, 18,511 students from 255 U.S. public and private schools took 50,745 IB examinations. Approximately two-thirds of those students were candidates for the IB Diploma,[6] and one-third were certificate candidates (May 2000 Summary). Although these students represent less than 2 percent of U.S. high schools, their increasing numbers indicate that the IB program is experiencing a period of rapid growth in this country. The number of IB examinations administered in the United States has increased by an average 16 percent annually every year since 1994. The number of schools applying to International Baccalaureate of North America (IBNA) has tripled over the

---

[5]The central questions examined include the following: How do I or how do we know that a given assertion is true, or a given judgment is well grounded? How is knowledge gained? What role does personal experience play? Do we construct reality, or do we recognize it? How is a mathematical proof different from, or similar to, justifications accepted in other areas of knowledge? Has technology, for example computers and electronic calculators, influenced the knowledge claims made in mathematics? Is the scientific method a product of western culture or is it universal? To what extent can science be understood through the study of just one discipline, for example physics? Are the models and theories created by scientists accurate descriptions of the natural world, or are they primarily useful interpretations for prediction, explanation, and control of the natural world? (IBO, 2000b, pp. 3–4)

[6]According to Paul Campbell, director for programs, International Baccalaureate of North America (IBNA) (personal communication), approximately 70 percent of diploma candidates earn the IB Diploma.

past several years and has been stable recently at 50 to 60 applications per year.[7]

A high school must offer all the components of the diploma program and be authorized by the IBO to use IB curriculum and assessment materials, register candidates for the IB examinations, and qualify them for the IB Diploma. U.S. schools that are interested in joining the IBO complete a self-study and submit a formal application to IBNA. Receipt of the application is followed by an on-site visit by representatives from IBNA that focuses on evaluating faculty commitment and qualifications; physical facilities, including the library and science laboratories; and commitment at the school level. The process of becoming an IB school can take 2 years or more as IBNA evaluates the ability of both the school and the school district to commit resources to providing the administrative structure, faculty, and facilities needed to support the offering of the IB Diploma Programme. IBNA maintains a relationship with member schools that includes monitoring test registration and administration.[8] Every 5 years, each IB school conducts a self-evaluation and submits a school review to IBNA.

IB CURRICULUM

IB mathematics and science courses are designed to be components of an integrated program, and this objective is reflected in the curriculum materials. The IB program guides for courses in each discipline, including mathematics and the experimental sciences, present common aims and objectives. A discussion of the program model, a description of the examination, and detailed information and guidance for teachers about meeting the internal assessment requirements are common to all of the subject guides for experimental science. The guides also provide a topic outline and a detailed syllabus for each course. Teachers use the guides as the basis for determining the structure of their curriculum. Thus like the curriculum for AP courses, the curriculum for IB courses, as it is designed and implemented, can vary from school to school in sequence and emphasis. However, the specificity of the IB syllabus and the requirements for the IB internal assessment lead to less variability in the content of the curriculum and the nature of the laboratory and other practical experiences provided to students than is the case in the corresponding AP courses. The extent to which the IBO specifies curriculum for IB courses is described in detail in the discussion that follows.

---

[7]Paul Campbell, director of programs, IBNA (personal communication).

[8]Schools are not able to maintain membership in the IBO without registering students in IB courses for the examinations and ensuring the security of the examinations.

Development of IB Courses

The IB course development process is guided by the IBO's vision of a rigorous, comprehensive, and balanced college preparatory curriculum. A curriculum review committee with international membership is responsible for articulating, implementing, and maintaining the vision in each subject area. The International Baccalaureate Curriculum and Assessment Centre (IBCA) in Cardiff, Wales, has primary responsibility for curriculum development. IBCA staff representatives, most of whom are former IB teachers, work with teachers representing IB schools from around the world on the curriculum review committees. The committees for all subjects in a discipline convene jointly at IBCA because changes in the mathematics or experimental sciences programs impact all of the subjects in that discipline. The role of the curriculum review committees encompasses identifying topics to be included, as well as reviewing the assessment structure and writing the assessment statements for each topic. The mathematics curriculum review committees are also responsible for specifying presumed knowledge and skills for each IB mathematics course.

An important distinguishing feature of IB curriculum review is the systematic involvement of classroom teachers in a "consultative process" (IBO, 1999d). The recent revision of the IB Experimental Sciences curriculum illustrates the process well. The process began with a review of responses to questionnaires sent to each IB biology, chemistry, and physics teacher. Teachers were asked about the instructional time spent on each topic in the syllabus and on laboratory work for each topic, as well as about the technology resources available to them. The biology, chemistry, and physics curriculum committees then made revisions to the diploma guides for each subject. Revised versions of the guides were posted on a password-protected Web site for further teacher review and comment before being published.

Content of IB Courses

The *IB Diploma Programme Guide* for each subject includes a detailed topic outline. It provides IB teachers with some guidance in identifying fundamental concepts by grouping "essential principles of the subject" in material designated as the core.[9] The core topics are common to both the SL and HL courses in a subject, with additional topics being specified for the latter.

---

[9]In the experimental sciences, 80 hours of instruction is recommended for core material in SL courses, with an additional 55 hours for HL courses. In mathematics courses, 105 hours is recommended for SL and 195 hours for HL courses.

The guides also provide outlines for optional topics.[10] Teachers of each IB experimental science subject at an IB school must collaboratively select two *options* to include in their curriculum. Options are generally selected on the basis of teachers' backgrounds and areas of expertise, as well as available local resources. The options for IB mathematics courses allow for studying a topic in more depth. Teachers select one option, and the selection made can determine the nature of the course, resulting in very different experiences for students. In the United States, for example, the Mathematics Methods SL option Further Calculus is often selected over the other two options—Statistical Methods and Further Geometry—to provide students with a course that is comparable to the AP Calculus AB course. The experimental science courses offer options that allow in-depth study of a topic, such as the physics options Astrophysics and Relativity. Many, like the physics option Biomedical Physics, focus on interdisciplinary topics. Schools are also allowed to submit an option of their own design for approval. That some schools have taken advantage of this opportunity is indicated by the addition of Medicine and Drugs, previously a local option, to the most recent revision of the IB program guide for chemistry.

The IB program guides provide considerable information about what students are expected to know by specifying *assessment statements*, expressed in terms of *learning outcomes*, for each topic in the experimental science courses. The guides also give estimated teaching hours for each topic, but do not recommend a sequence for the presentation of topics. To illustrate the considerably greater detail provided in the IB guides than in the AP course descriptions, the treatment of ionic bonds in IB chemistry can be contrasted with the AP topic outline for Chemical Bonding included in Chapter 3, this volume. The latter outline simply lists "ionic" as one of the binding forces that might appear on the AP chemistry examination. AP chemistry teachers must infer the desired depth of treatment of the topic by reviewing old examination questions. In contrast, the *Programme Guide for IB Chemistry* (IBO, 2001b, p. 51) gives the following six assessment statements for the same topic:

Topic 4: Bonding
4.1 Ionic Bond (2 hours)

 4.1.1 **Describe** the ionic bond as the result of electron transfer leading to attraction between oppositely charged ions.

 4.1.2 **Determine** which ions will be formed when metals in groups 1, 2, and 3 lose electrons.

---

[10]Mathematics courses include one 35-hour option. Experimental science courses include two options—15 hours each in SL courses and 22 hours each in HL courses.

4.1.3 **Determine** which ions will be formed when elements in groups 6 and 7 gain electrons.

4.1.4 **State** that transition metals can form more than one ion. Restrict examples to simple ions e.g., Fe^{2+} and Fe^{3+}.

4.1.5 **Predict** whether a compound of two elements would be mainly ionic or mainly covalent from the position of the elements in the periodic table, or from their electronegativity values.

4.1.6 **Deduce** the formula and **state** the name of an ionic compound formed from a group 1, 2, or 3 metal and a group 5, 6, or 7 non-metal.

The assessment statements for experimental science use 26 action verbs to indicate expectations for each topic. Some of these verbs are highlighted in bold in the preceding example ("describe," "determine," "state," "predict," and "deduce"). The guides define each verb and associate it consistently throughout the syllabus and on the IB examinations with one of three content objectives:

- Demonstrate an understanding.
- Apply and use.
- Construct, analyze, and evaluate.

Use of the action verbs conveys important information to teachers about the expectations for depth and breadth of content. Teachers and students are expected to be familiar with the definitions of these verbs. They must be aware that, for example, "predict" and "deduce" are associated with the third objective (construct, analyze, and evaluate) and require deeper understanding than "state," which is associated with the first objective (demonstrate an understanding) and requires only memorization.

Laboratory Requirement for IB Experimental Sciences Courses

The IB program has more to say about laboratory experimentation than does the AP program, as the score for a student's laboratory work (assessed internally by the teacher and moderated externally by the IBO) makes up 24 percent of a student's final examination score. The program guides do not recommend any specific laboratory exercises, but provide general guidance for the design of a laboratory program. The *Vade Mecum: Procedures Manual for IB Coordinators and Teachers* specifies that the laboratory activities in IB Experimental Sciences courses must include hands-on investigations in the

TABLE 4-1   Summary of Eight *Assessment Criteria* for IB Experimental Sciences and Two or Three *Aspects* of Each Criterion

Assessment Criteria	Aspects
Planning (a)	Defining the problem or research question; formulating a hypothesis or prediction; selecting variables.
Planning (b)	Selecting appropriate apparatus or materials; designing a method for the control of variables; designing a method for the collection of sufficient relevant data.
Data collection	Collecting and recording raw data; organizing and presenting raw data.
Data processing and presentation	Processing raw data; presenting processed data.
Conclusion and evaluation	Drawing conclusions; evaluating procedure(s) and results; improving the investigation.
Manipulative skills	Carrying out techniques safely; following a variety of instructions.
Personal skills (a)	Working within a team; recognizing the contributions of others; exchanging and integrating ideas.
Personal skills (b)	Approaching scientific investigations with self-motivation and perseverance; working in an ethical manner; paying attention to environmental impact.

SOURCES: Adapted from IBO (2001a, 2001b, 2001c).

laboratory or in the field, as well as problem-solving activities involving data analysis (IBO, 2000d, p. 4). At least 25 percent of the teaching program (not including time spent writing up the experiments) must be devoted to the Practical Scheme of Work (PSOW, described in greater detail below).[11] Teachers are provided extensive detail about the criteria for the internal assessment of laboratory work, as they must offer opportunities for their students that match the relevant assessment criteria. Specific criteria for the internal assessment guide science teachers in setting the stage for students to design and carry out their own experiments.

The IB internal assessment for the experimental sciences uses eight assessment criteria to evaluate the work of both HL and SL candidates (Table 4-1). These are described in the guide for each of the IB experimental sciences courses. For a particular criterion, a student's laboratory work is judged to see whether the requirements for different aspects of the criterion have been fulfilled completely, partially, or not at all. For example, forming a hypothesis is one of the three aspects of the planning (a) criterion. The following example (Table 4-2) is given in the guide for each of the IB experimental sciences courses.

---

[11]At least 60 hours for HL students and 40 hours for SL students (IBO, 2000d, p. 3), which includes 10–15 hours that candidates must spend on their Group 4 project (IBO, 2000c, p. 3).

TABLE 4-2   Example of Expectations of Students to Meet the Requirements of One Aspect of the Planning (a) Criterion

Formulating a Hypothesis or Prediction

Complete	Partial	Not at all
Relates the hypothesis or prediction directly to the research question and explains it, quantitatively where appropriate.	States the hypothesis or prediction but does not explain it.	Does not state a hypothesis or prediction.

SOURCES: Adapted from IBO (2001a, 2001b, 2001c).

The guides also provide a discussion of the criteria to guide teachers. "It is generally not appropriate to assess planning (a) for most experiments or investigations found in standard textbooks, unless the experiments are modified. It is essential that students be given an open-ended problem to investigate" (IBO, 2001a, 2001b, 2001c, p. 24). A separate publication, *Teacher Support Material: Experimental Sciences—Internal Assessment* (IBO, 1999e), provides teachers with exemplars of student laboratory reports that fulfill all aspects of the criteria completely, as well as examples of those that do not.

Teachers of the various experimental science subjects in an IB school must jointly submit to the IBO a PSOW, a summary of all the investigative activities their students carry out. Each PSOW must include at least a few complex investigations that make greater demands on the students than those posed by simple experiments. It must also include the date and a brief description of each investigation and an estimate of the time spent. The PSOW is accompanied by a copy of the instructions given to students for each activity. A script of any verbal instructions offered also must be included. These materials are used in moderating the internal assessment grades to ensure, for example, that if students are offered credit for planning, the teacher has not given them procedures. "The main criticism made by moderators was that the investigations were too directed with no real freedom for the candidates to develop the investigation for themselves" (IBO, 1998a). The PSOW also must include an interdisciplinary project involving all of the IB science students at a school in identifying and investigating an issue of local interest. The project requirements emphasize sharing of concepts and theories from across the disciplines, as well as the processes involved in scientific investigation, rather than products.

The PSOW is evaluated yearly, and teachers receive feedback and suggestions for improvement. More detail about the scoring and moderation of the internal assessment and about the feedback the IBO provides to schools on their laboratory programs is provided later in this chapter.

IB INSTRUCTION

There is variation from classroom to classroom in what is actually taught in an IB course, how much of the topic outline is covered, how much time is devoted to different topics, and what instructional strategies are used. However, the detail provided in the IB guides regarding expected student outcomes directs teachers toward the use of specific instructional strategies. Teachers are told that internal assessment tasks should be built into classroom teaching whenever possible. Internal assessments should form part of the learning experience of the students and should not be seen as an addition to the teaching schedule (IBO, 1999b).

IB Programme Guides and Teaching Notes

IB mathematics programme guides provide general guidance on instruction, but also offer specific suggestions about instructional strategies. The objectives for students given in the mathematics program guides include the following:

- Organize and present data in graphic, tabular, and/or diagrammatic form.
- Formulate a mathematical argument, and communicate it clearly.
- Recognize patterns and structures in a variety of situations.
- Use appropriate technological devices as mathematical tools.

Teaching notes for each topic in the syllabus for each mathematics course provide suggestions for teachers, while stating that "it is not mandatory that these suggestions be followed" (IBO, 1998b, p. 9). The following are examples of alternative strategies presented in the teaching notes for the Mathematical Methods SL guide: "an informal investigative/experimental approach to statistical inference is envisaged" (IBO, 1997b, p. 21), and "problems might be best solved with the aid of a Venn diagram or tree diagram, without the explicit use of these formulae" (IBO, 1997b, p. 18). The teaching notes also include suggestions for linking content to help students see connections, such as linking the study of the second derivative in the Further Calculus option to the study of exponents and logarithms in the core content (IBO, 1997b, p. 23).

The experimental sciences guides do not address instruction directly, other than to indicate consistently that there is no single best approach to teaching IB courses and that teachers should provide a variety of ways of acquiring information that can be accepted or rejected by each student, allowing different routes through the material (IBO, 2001a, 2001b, 2001c, p. 11). The IB program guide for chemistry tells chemistry teachers, for example, that the "chemistry course includes the essential principles of the subject but also, through selection of options, allows teachers some flexibility to tailor the course to meet the needs of their students" (IBO, 2001b, p. 35). References to instruction also appear in annual subject reports, such as the following example from the 1999 IB chemistry subject report (IBO, 2000a):

> The main areas of weakness involved applications of principles to specific situations. This process is always a challenge to students. Students need to be exposed repeatedly to the application of basic concepts to new situations. This can be done through examples used in the classroom, by homework assignments which provide a variety of appropriate situations requiring skills beyond recall of information, and by tests and examinations which use questions similar to those used in the IB examination. (p. 401)

As indicated in the discussion of curriculum, the use of action verbs in the experimental science assessment statements informs teachers about the depth of treatment required. Teachers then make decisions about the best way to prepare their students for the required outcomes. For example, "describe the ionic bond as the result of electron transfer leading to attraction between oppositely charged ions" (IBO, 2001b, p. 51) means students must be able to recall the definition of ionic bond. Teachers then make individual instructional decisions about the most effective ways to help their students learn this information. At a level requiring deeper understanding, the ability to "predict molecular polarity based on bond polarity and molecular shape" (IBO, 2001b, p. 52) is an outcome that cannot be achieved by memorizing a breadth of detail, but only by building the necessary understanding during a variety of practical experiences with molecular shapes, bond character, and electronegativities. Teachers must decide how best to accomplish this and are guided by the assessment statement to set up a variety of situations in which students can build understanding and experience.

Messages About Instruction Conveyed by IB Examinations

In specifying aspects of a subject to be assessed, the IB internal assessment criteria require that teachers structure the classroom and laboratory environment so that students have the opportunity to acquire and develop the skills to be evaluated.

IB mathematics teachers are encouraged to integrate the internal assessment assignments for the mathematics portfolio into their teaching. Related teaching and learning strategies discussed in the Mathematical Methods SL guide (IBO, 1997b, p. 51) include the following:

Candidates need to be provided with the opportunities to experiment, explore, make conjectures and ask questions. Ideally, the atmosphere in the classroom should be one of enquiry.

Small groups could work through some relatively simple assignments in order to learn skills associated with portfolio activities.

Students may be unaware of certain strategies associated with experimentation, or "playing," which are an important part of investigative work, particularly if they have only experienced more formal modes of working.

Similarly, IB experimental science teachers are given guidance in providing a variety of practical experiences for their students. Sample laboratory investigations are offered and analyzed in the IB *Teacher Support Material: Experimental Sciences—Internal Assessment* (IBO, 1999e). The program guides provide direction for preparing students for experimentation without specifying laboratory activities. For example, "the teacher might present the aim of an investigation generally in the form 'investigate the factors that affect X.' Students should be able to realize that certain factors will influence X and clearly . . . identify a focused research question" (IBO, 1999e, p. 4). The criteria for personal skills (a) require that a teacher assess a student's work within a team, defined as follows: "Teams, whose members collaborate, can be formed with a wide variety of people. The views of all team members are respected and actively sought" (IBO, 1998a). Teachers must therefore provide opportunities for students to learn how to work effectively in teams. Teachers are encouraged to use the online curriculum center to share ideas about possible investigations and add resources to the relevant sections of the online subject guides.

IB ASSESSMENT

Assessment in IB mathematics and science courses has two components—external and internal. The external assessment consists of a written examination that is administered internationally over a period of 2 days in May of each year (in November for split-session schools). The examination tests knowledge of both the core and optional topics. The internal assessment component comprises the teacher's formative assessment of students' practical work (laboratory investigations in science courses and portfolios in mathematics courses) judged against established assessment criteria. This component is conducted by teachers within the school environment and is moderated externally by the IBO. In the experimental sciences, the external and internal assessments make up 76 percent and 24 percent of the final examination mark, respectively. IB teachers submit internal assessment marks and a predicted final examination grade for each of their students. The latter is the teacher's prediction of the grade the candidate will achieve in the subject, based on all the evidence of a candidate's work and the teacher's knowledge of IB standards (IBO, 2000d, p. F14).

The IB assessments are designed to gauge the educational achievement of candidates against the range of objectives specified for each subject. The structure of each written external examination paper "allows candidates to demonstrate their achievement in terms of content knowledge, depth of understanding and use of specific higher level cognitive skills, as described by the subject objectives."[12]

The internal assessment component addresses skills that cannot be demonstrated satisfactorily within the context of a written examination. As stated in the guides, the purpose of the internal assessment for the IB mathematics portfolio is to "provide candidates with opportunities to be rewarded for mathematics carried out under ordinary conditions, that is, without the time limitations and stress associated with written examinations" (IBO, 1998b, p. 47). The requirements for the internal assessment in the experimental sciences are focused on the candidates' skills in laboratory investigation, including planning; data collection and processing; evaluation of procedures and results; manipulative skills; and personal skills, including working with a team (IBO, 2001a, 2001b, 2001c, pp. 20–22).

How IB Assessments Are Developed

Examinations for each IB course are written by chief examiners and deputies and are overseen and approved by the examination board at IBCA. Teams of experienced senior examiners prepare the examinations for each administration in a process that is coordinated and overseen by IBO academic staff. Separate examinations are developed for SL and HL courses in a subject area. Single senior examiners normally write individual examination questions, which are directly linked throughout the examination development process to the assessment statements and the objectives to be measured as outlined in the program guides for each subject. "The questions are not field tested, partly because it is difficult to find a suitable trial group of candidates without the possibility of compromising security. New questions are written for each examination session—they are not banked." Moreover, "for each session, the senior examining team aims to prepare a different form of the examination which is of the same standard of demand as in previous sessions. In practice it is very difficult to achieve a high level of precision."[13]

The IBO also does not calculate the internal reliability of the examina-

---

[12]George Pook, assessment director, IBCA (personal communication, May 31, 2001).
[13]George Pook, assessment director, IBCA (personal communication, May 31, 2001).

tions, as it is not one of the assumptions of IB assessment that all the items in each written examination paper will assess the same trait. Thus, high correlation of a candidate's performance on different parts of the assessment is not expected. Like the College Board, the IBO does not make use of systematic validity research regarding the cognitive characteristics of its examinations.

As part of the curriculum development and review process in each subject, the IB curriculum committees specify and describe the internal assessment criteria. The examiners in each subject meet to develop common understandings about how to assess each of the criteria. The IBO communicates the assessment details to classroom teachers and moderators in each subject through program materials and workshops.

The assessment structure for each subject is reviewed periodically as part of an overall curriculum review. Proposals for revisions to the assessments are developed by the curriculum review committees through a process similar to that described for curriculum review. The proposals are then reviewed by the Diploma Review Committee, which consists of chief examiners representing each subject group and senior academic staff from the IBO.

After each examination session, candidates' responses are scrutinized closely to determine whether they are in line with expectations for each question. Additionally, all IB teachers are asked to complete feedback forms following the examinations, answering questions about both the emphases of the examination and the content and form of individual questions. Much attention is paid to teachers' comments about the suitability of examination papers in achieving the intended objectives. Information gained in this manner is fed into the examination development process for future sessions.

How IB Assessments Are Scored

The IB grading system is criterion referenced. Each student's performance is measured against seven grade descriptors, given in the form of levels of performance that candidates should be able to demonstrate. The different levels of performance are closely related to the course objectives and are clearly specified for mathematics and the experimental sciences. The descriptors are equally applicable to both HL and SL examinations. As an example, grade descriptors 7, 4, and 1 for the experimental sciences follow (IBO, 1999c):

Grade 7   Excellent performance

Displays comprehensive knowledge of factual information in the syllabus and a thorough command of concepts and principles. Selects and applies relevant information in a wide variety of contexts. Analyzes and evaluates data thoroughly. Constructs detailed explanations of complex phenomena and makes appropriate predictions. Solves most quantitative and/or qualitative problems proficiently. Communicates logically and concisely using appropriate terminology and conventions. Shows insight or originality. Demonstrates personal skills, perseverance and responsibility in a wide variety of investigative activities in a very consistent manner. Works very well within a team, and approaches investigations in an ethical manner, paying full attention to environmental impact. Displays competence in a wide range of investigative techniques, paying considerable attention to safety, and is fully capable of working independently.

Grade 4   Satisfactory performance

Displays reasonable knowledge of factual information in the syllabus, though possibly with some gaps. Shows adequate comprehension of most concepts and principles but with limited ability to apply them. Demonstrates some analysis or evaluation of quantitative and qualitative data. Solves basic or routine problems but shows limited ability to deal with new or difficult situations. Communicates adequately but responses may lack clarity and include some repetitive or irrelevant material. Demonstrates personal skills, perseverance and responsibility in some investigative activities, although displays some inconsistency. Works within a team and generally approaches investigations in an ethical manner, with some attention to environmental impact. Displays competence in a range of investigative techniques, paying some attention to safety, although requiring some close supervision.

Grade 1   Very poor performance

Recalls fragments of factual information and shows very little understanding of any concepts or principles. Rarely demonstrates personal skills, perseverance or responsibility in investigative activities. Does not work within a team. Rarely approaches investigations in an ethical manner, or shows awareness of the environmental impact. Displays little competence in investigative techniques, generally pays no attention to safety, and requires constant supervision (IBO, 1999c).

The senior evaluating team uses these descriptors when determining the examination marks, which reflect the combined raw scores for the written examinations and the internal assessments. Examiners look to assign candidates the grade that matches their performance most comprehensively by determining the various grade boundaries for the raw scores the candidates achieve. Each time the examinations are administered and marked, the senior examiners meet to decide what marks equate to the same level of performance as in previous sessions.

The process begins by using the grade boundaries suggested by examiners on the basis of their reading of student responses on the written examination. Individual examiners mark students' responses on the examinations using a set of assessment criteria or mark schemes, which are accompanied by notes about the range of content that might be expected. Scripts with raw scores just below or above the proposed boundaries are reread carefully and evaluated with reference to the criteria described above. Inter-examiner reliability is ensured by a system of moderation in which each examiner sends a sample of his or her marking to a more senior examiner for checking. If the senior examiner's remarking of the sample indicates a slight disparity in standards, a statistical adjustment based on linear regression is made to all of the assistant examiner's marks. If there is substantial disagreement or inconsistency, all of the assistant examiner's work is remarked. Analysis of these moderation samples indicates that in the vast majority of cases, different examiners' marks are within 5 percent of each other, and that in very few cases is the difference more than 10 percent.[14]

Schools submit marks for internal assessment to IBCA by a given deadline in April of each year. A moderation process is also used to ensure reliability and an equivalent standard among schools for the internal assessment marks in both mathematics and the experimental sciences. Each school must submit for moderation five marked sets of candidates' work in each subject, selected to represent the full range of quality of work submitted by students in that subject. If the moderators' remarking of the students' work samples indicates a disparity in standards, a statistical adjustment is made to all the internal assessment marks of the teacher involved, and a moderator who is an experienced IB teacher remarks the work. In mathematics, for example, each moderator reviews about 50 portfolios. Each then sends a sample of five sets of student work to a senior moderator, who repeats the grading and sends samples of that work to a principal moderator in each subject. The senior moderator also sends a report to the IBO for inclusion in the chief examiner's report.

How Examination Results Are Reported

IBCA communicates examination results directly to the secondary schools. The schools, in turn, are responsible for ensuring that the results are communicated to candidates. IBNA communicates the results to colleges and universities. The results include scores on each examination taken, as well as marks for the Theory of Knowledge course and the Extended Essay and cumulative scores for diploma candidates. A profile of candidates' grades is available to schools for each examination session. The profile is only for candidates whose examinations are entered by that school and includes predicted grades; examination grades, including marks for each paper; and

---

[14]George Pook, assessment director, IBCA (personal communication, May 31, 2001).

internal assessment grades, indicating any adjustments made. All sections of the examination papers are made available to teachers for use in their classrooms 24 hours after the testing date.

The IBO publishes yearly detailed reports for each subject that include mark bands for each score, general comments on the application of mark schemes to free-response problems, and comments on the strengths and weaknesses of the candidates in the treatment of individual questions. The subject reports also describe areas of the program and examination that appeared to be difficult for candidates, as well as areas in which candidates appeared to be especially well prepared. Recommendations are offered for teachers regarding assistance and guidance that should be provided for future candidates. Examples from the May 2000 chemistry subject report include the following: "Overall, it appeared that the weaker candidates . . . did not fully understand the concept of intermolecular forces and typically described covalent bond strengths as affecting boiling points. This is something that teachers might place greater emphasis on in class" (IBO, 2000c, p. 5).

The subject report also includes a detailed discussion of the internal assessment and recommendations directed at improving the laboratory program. For example, the May 2000 report states: "Overall most schools presented a suitable Practical Scheme of Work, although some schools presented programs that were significantly deficient, either in the total experimental hours completed or in the degree of syllabus coverage . . . . The depth and breadth of the experiments was generally found to be good. New teachers are clearly considering the depth of the syllabus when designing experiments, at times with limited resources. These efforts are recognized and applauded" (IBO, 2000c, pp. 17–18). The biggest problem continues to be in providing students with opportunities to demonstrate the internal assessment planning (a) and planning (b) criteria: "These skills cannot be properly assessed if teachers provide students with the purpose, hypothesis and/or procedures for experiments. Some teachers consistently gave far too much direction in their instructions (purpose, method, data table, sample calculations etc.). Candidates have been deprived of the opportunity to design realistic methods for the control of variables. Teachers must use open-ended questions in order to facilitate the assessment of Planning (a) and Planning (b)" (IBO, 1999a, p. 414).

Yearly detailed narrative reports are made available to individual schools, for a fee, on the performance of their students as a group for each subject examined. The reports include comments on students' general examination techniques, along with suggestions for improvement, comments on overall performance in each section of the examination, analysis and evaluation of candidates' performance on individual questions, and recommendations and guidance for future candidates. Examiners write these reports at the time of marking and then add statistical data and a description of the mark schemes (IBO, 2000d, p. B1). The reports are substantial (7–10 pages) and include the following detailed information:

- Comments on the candidates' approach to answering the questions on each test paper, with suggestions for improvement.
- Quantitative information on the numbers of candidates answering particular questions.
- Comments on the overall performance of candidates in relation to all portions of each examination paper.
- An analysis and evaluation of candidates' performance on individual questions in relation to the marking scheme.
- Recommendations and guidance for future candidates.

Each school can also receive a *Moderation Report on the Internal Assessment* that provides information on the differences between the teachers' marks for their students and the marking by the moderator for the internally assessed samples of work. This information lets teachers know whether they are applying the standards correctly (i.e., the average mark awarded by the teacher is within 10 percent of the average mark awarded by the moderator) and consistently (i.e., the correlation between teacher and moderator marks is 0.85 or greater). Also provided are written comments from the moderators on feedback forms for each subject (International Baccalaureate Form 4/IAF, Internal Assessment Feedback Form: Group 4). These comments are provided in the form of responses to questions about clerical/procedural details, as well as the students' experimental work, including the following:

- Were the investigations/projects appropriate for the assessment of particular criteria?
- Was the practical program of the correct duration?
- Was the syllabus coverage (core, additional high level, and options) appropriate?
- Was the practical scheme of work of appropriate complexity?

IB PROFESSIONAL DEVELOPMENT

What Is Known About the Preparation and Credentials of IB Teachers

Because the credentials of prospective IB teachers are submitted as part of a school's application for membership in the IBO, initial staffing decisions and teaching assignments for IB courses are made as part of a comprehensive school plan. IB teaching assignments may be given to experienced or novice teachers. The IBO has established neither teacher qualifications nor standards for faculties, although the application process does ensure that, at least initially, prospective IB teachers attend an IB workshop (see the next subsection). The IBO also does not certify teachers and is not involved in monitoring staffing changes after a school has become an IB school. Consequently, there is not much more information available about the qualifications of IB teachers than exists for AP teachers.

Professional Development Experiences of IB Teachers

One prerequisite for a school's obtaining permission to offer the IB program is that every teacher who will teach IB courses must attend a 3- to 5-day workshop offered by IBNA. Teachers new to an already authorized school also must attend an IB workshop, preferably before they begin to teach IB courses. In addition, the IBNA regional office is responsible for conducting weeklong professional development workshops for IB teachers and administrators during the summer, as well as 3- to 5-day workshops during the school year. IBNA has also facilitated the establishment of regional organizations for IB schools. These organizations are supported by IBNA in holding conferences and workshops several times each year. Schools and/or school districts budget resources annually to support attendance by teachers and administrators at these sessions, which are held both nationally and regionally. Experienced IB teachers typically work with representatives from IBNA to prepare materials for and plan and conduct the sessions.

Both the conferences and workshops focus on providing guidance and resources for the implementation of IB programs and development of course curricula. Workshops focus on general topics unique to IB, including the following:

- Restructuring of the school schedule and course registration to accommodate IB course requirements.
- Internal assessment.
- Restructuring of the ninth- and tenth-grade curriculum to prepare students for IB courses.
- Characteristics of IB students.
- Use of international examples and illustrations in the curriculum.

Experimental science workshops focus on designing laboratory experiences that will enable students to meet specific internal assessment criteria. The most recent focus has been on the planning criteria, as the IB examiners have found that the practical work done in most classrooms does not afford students opportunities to practice the skills needed in planning their own experiments. In most mathematics workshops, time is spent on preparing teachers to teach an unfamiliar and expanded mathematics curriculum, including vectors and matrices; probability and statistics; and the optional topics—statistics, abstract algebra, and further geometry.

A dialogue exists between IB teachers and the IBO that is not a feature of the AP program. Every teacher completes feedback forms following each examination, answering questions about both the emphases of the examination and the content and form of individual test items. The results are summarized by IBCA and provided both to teachers and to the development committees, driving changes in curriculum and instruction the following year, as well as in the assessment instrument itself. After the examinations have been graded, each teacher receives a subject report (general comments about all of the student responses worldwide on the examination) and a school report (specific comments about their students' performance on the written examination and internal assessment, as well as comments and suggestions about the practical program in each discipline at the school). The comments provided to the schools and teachers serve as the impetus for corresponding changes in the instructional program aimed at improving students' test scores. Additionally, the IBO maintains an online curriculum site so IB teachers can receive the most current information about the curriculum.

5

Other Opportunities and Approaches to Advanced Study

Advanced Placement (AP) courses and International Baccalaureate (IB) programs are designed to meet the educational needs of high school students who are motivated and prepared for academic challenges beyond those that characterize most high school curricula. They are the only two nationally recognized, comprehensive, multisubject programs offered for this purpose in the United States. This chapter reviews other current opportunities for advanced study and some of the more common alternative models for providing college-level learning to high school students. It also describes some of the more widely recognized enrichment programs that provide opportunities for advanced study in settings other than classrooms, including internships and mentorships and academic and research competitions.[1] Many students, even those enrolled in AP, IB, or other formal programs, take advantage of some of these enrichment activities.

ALTERNATIVES FOR PROVIDING COLLEGE-LEVEL LEARNING IN HIGH SCHOOL

There are many opportunities for high school students to engage in college-level learning through local and state-sponsored programs. Some of these alternative programs follow the AP content outlines; others do not. Although many of the programs award college credit to high school students, less is documented about the transferability of credits earned by students in these alternative programs than is the case for credits earned through

---

[1] Some students who pursue independent study document their learning and eligibility for college credit by taking one of the subject tests offered as part of the College-Level Examination Program (CLEP). Traditionally, CLEP examinations have been taken by adults who have been out of school for a long time. However, the College Board is beginning to encourage high schools to offer both AP and CLEP opportunities to their students (http://www.collegeboard.org/clep/clephs/html/hs004.html [November 27, 2001]).

qualifying scores on AP or IB examinations. As a result, an increasing number of students who participate in alternative college-level learning programs or in courses taught in specialized schools that do not offer AP classes document their achievement for college credit and/or placement by taking AP examinations in the appropriate subject area.[2] (IB does not allow students to take subject examinations unless they have completed the corresponding course at a school authorized to offer the IB program.)

The committee did not have the information or resources needed for a careful evaluation of the effectiveness of any of these alternative opportunities, but does note that such evaluation is necessary because there is tremendous variability among these programs, even those ostensibly designed for the same purpose. Further, there are no standardized external assessments, such as those used in the AP and IB programs, to measure student learning or the quality of the programs themselves. The committee suggests that systematic evaluation of these models be conducted to provide objective data about their quality and their effects on students, teachers, high schools, colleges, and universities.

Collaborative Programs

With the exception of AP, the most prevalent option for college-level learning has evolved from collaborative efforts among universities, 2- or 4-year colleges, and high schools. In some cases, the colleges, universities, or high schools involved initiate these collaborations; others are mandated by state legislatures or other policymaking entities. Although these collaborations differ in terms of funding sources, site of instruction, faculty, class composition, and the use of technology (Russell, 1998), they frequently take one of the following forms:

- College courses taught in high schools.
- Dual-enrollment options.
- Concurrent enrollment options.
- Prematriculation enrichment programs designed for specific groups of students, including talented, minority, and able but underprepared or unmotivated students.

Rationales for promoting college-level learning for high school students include (1) strengthening the high school curriculum and raising expectations for high school students; (2) decreasing the total number of credits students need to complete college, thus reducing, at least potentially, both the time required for the baccalaureate and costs to parents, students, and

---

[2]Lee Jones, College Board director of AP programs (personal communication), 2001.

taxpayers; and (3) offering the potential to enrich students' undergraduate college experiences by reducing the need to take some introductory courses and allowing earlier entry into more-advanced courses, facilitating double majors, and permitting students to enroll in a more enriched array of electives (Greenberg, 1992; Johnstone, 1993). Others point to the positive social consequences of college and high school partnerships, asserting that such partnerships provide opportunities for students who attend schools where AP, honors, and gifted-and-talented courses are not readily available (Tafel and Eberhart, 1999).

College Courses Taught in High School

College courses taught in high school are typically the product of cooperative educational program agreements between high schools and colleges to offer college courses for credit in the high school. The postsecondary institutions are usually responsible for the curricular content and for standards, administrative support, and program monitoring. High school faculty, supervised by college faculty, frequently teach these courses.[3]

Both college and high school administrators and faculty have been raising concerns about the widespread implementation of these types of programs. Their concerns revolve around the following:

- Qualifications of the teachers who teach the courses.
- Policies for awarding college credit.
- Characteristics of a "qualified" student.
- Impact on the high schools' curricula.
- Difficulties associated with maintaining an atmosphere in high schools that is commensurate with the instructional/social setting and expectations of a college class.
- Impact on the workload of high school teachers selected to teach university-level courses.
- Instructional models that stress teacher-dominated class discussions to cover the scope of a college course.
- Costs.

Dual Enrollment

Dual-enrollment options usually involve high school students taking college courses that allow them to earn both college credit and credit to-

---

[3]Syracuse University's Project Advance is one of the oldest and most widely recognized programs of this type. Information about this program can be accessed at http://supa.syr.edu/ (November 27, 2001).

ward a high school diploma so that high school graduation is not delayed. These programs enable students to attend nearby colleges, sometimes at reduced tuition rates. State departments of education and/or local school boards certify the majority of dual-enrollment programs. In most cases, students attend the college as full-time students and use the college credits obtained to meet high school graduation requirements. At least 38 states have formal dual-enrollment agreements between public high schools and community colleges (Reisberg, 1998), and according to data gathered by the State Higher Education Executive Officers (Russell, 1998), the phenomenon shows no signs of abating. Tech Prep,[4] 2+2,[5] and middle-college high school[6] programs are usually built around dual-enrollment agreements. Yet a recent report published by the Association of American Colleges and Universities (Johnstone and Del Genio, 2001) finds fault with a number of these dual-enrollment arrangements, including those between 2-year colleges and high schools.

Concurrent Enrollment

Concurrent-enrollment programs allow high school students to take courses at local colleges or universities for credit while still in high school. One key difference between college courses taught in high school and concurrent enrollment is that students in the latter programs enroll in courses either taught by college faculty at the college's campus or delivered to the high school site by the college, whether through visits by faculty or electronically. In some cases, school districts cover a portion of the tuition costs, especially if they are unable to meet the educational needs of particular

---

[4]Tech Prep is a nationwide career development system that provides a high school student with a planned program of study that incorporates academic and career-related courses articulated between the secondary and postsecondary levels. The program leads to a diploma, degree, or 2-year apprenticeship certificate. All partners (secondary, postsecondary, and private sector) develop a Tech Prep program cooperatively. The program may also articulate from a community college to a 4-year baccalaureate degree. The program most typically provides technical preparation in a career field such as engineering; technology; applied science; a mechanical, industrial, or practical art or trade; agriculture; health occupations; business; or applied economics.

[5]2+2 programs allow students to complete 2 years of a vocational program in high school and the second 2 years at a community college.

[6]Students at middle-college high schools usually take high school and college courses on a community college campus. The programs began as a means to serve capable but unsuccessful students. Their purpose is to serve as a transition between high school and college for at-risk youth.

students. Students who participate in concurrent-enrollment programs typically earn college credit for their coursework,[7] but may or may not earn high school graduation credit. The decision to award high school graduation credit is almost always made by the local school district.

Frequently, students who take advantage of this type of arrangement have exceeded the offerings of their home high school in a particular discipline or want to take a course in a discipline not offered at the high school. Concurrent-enrollment opportunities are quite common in mathematics, particularly in geographic areas where there may not be enough students to offer courses such as AP calculus or those beyond AP calculus, such as Multivariate Calculus, Linear Algebra, or Differential Equations. In these cases, students may be allowed to enroll in a nearby college mathematics course with the district covering the college tuition or, in some cases, with the college offering reduced or free tuition as a community service. Students who participate in concurrent-enrollment programs usually attend high school full time and college part time.

Concurrent-enrollment options are quite prevalent in colleges. According to a 1997 State Higher Education Executive Officers' survey,[8] approximately 90 percent of postsecondary institutions admit qualified high school students to college courses prior to graduation through concurrent-enrollment agreements. As of 1997, 204,790 students had participated in dual-enrollment, college-in-high-school, or concurrent-enrollment programs during the previous school year. In addition, many colleges and universities offer programs that enable academically advanced and highly motivated students to pursue college-level course work on a part-time basis through early morning, late afternoon, and summer classes. They do so in the belief that concurrent-enrollment programs permit students to supplement high school work with more advanced material, to pursue interests, or to build on special talents. Some colleges also report that they gain from concurrent-enrollment programs an opportunity to recruit highly able students to their campuses for full-time study after graduation from high school.

The proliferation of dual-enrollment and concurrent-enrollment programs has sparked debate among professors about whether students are unwisely

---

[7]Colleges routinely accept the credits they have awarded to high school students in their concurrent-enrollment programs. However, transferability to other institutions is generally at the discretion of the receiving institution. In many cases, concurrent-enrollment credits are not deemed transferable if students also use such credits to meet high school graduation requirements.

[8]A complete version of the data gathered in the survey, including detailed summaries of the status of college-level learning policies and programming within all 50 states, is available through University Microfilms International, Publication No. 9833590, Volume/Issue 59-05A, 300 North Zeeb Rd., P.O. Box 1346, Ann Arbor, MI 48106-1346.

skipping entry-level classes at the colleges they ultimately attend and ending up in advanced courses for which they are under- or unprepared. A primary concern cited is the lack of standardized plans of instruction for the courses offered in these programs. Also noted is the lack of any general measure of the quality the curriculum or the instruction that could be used in determining whether to award credit or advanced standing to students who earn credit in such programs (Reisberg, 1998).

College-Sponsored Enrichment Programs

College-sponsored enrichment programs are designed to serve specific populations of students, including talented, minority, and underprepared or unmotivated students. Most postsecondary institutions in the United States offer such programs. The configuration of the programs varies among institutions, but they usually take the form of precollege summer programs or year-long programs and activities that provide enrichment and motivation for students who are underrepresented (e.g., women and minorities in science and engineering)[9] or those who are not fully served through conventional programs (e.g., gifted and talented students).[10]

Precollege summer programs offer students the opportunity to earn college credit in residential summer school programs while living on college campuses. Students usually attend these programs during the summer following the tenth or eleventh grade. Participants typically take regular college courses along with undergraduates from the host institution and other colleges. These programs are usually designed to provide academic enrichment, foster independence, and promote good work habits.

Specialized Schools

Another vehicle for providing advanced study to secondary students is a specialized school. Most states and many school districts have developed specialized schools that bring together academically talented students and offer them an educational experience geared to their high abilities and their need for peers who share their interests. Specialized schools have proliferated across the country in response to research demonstrating that high-

---

[9]For example, the Summer High School Apprenticeship Research Program (SHARP) Program is a national enrichment and support effort aimed at increasing the numbers of qualified minority students in sciences and engineering by offering internships and mentorships to qualified students. (See the discussion of internships and mentorships later in this chapter.)

[10]The Center for Talented Youth at The John Hopkins University is an example of a program designed to provide academic enrichment to highly gifted students through flexibly paced courses.

ability students develop greater expectations, feel better about themselves, and engage in higher-level processing or discourse when working with other students of similar abilities (Fuchs, Fuchs, Hamlett, and Karns, 1998).

Programs designed to meet the needs of these high-ability learners include governors' schools, both academic year and summer programs; residential and day academies that specialize in mathematics, science, and technology; charter schools;[11] schools-within-a school;[12] and magnet schools.[13] Admission to most of these programs is highly competitive and selective. The configuration of these specialized schools varies markedly from institution to institution. Some of the programs embrace innovative curricula and instructional approaches; others incorporate and/or expand on programs such as AP or IB; while still others use some of the college-level learning options described above.

There are 58 secondary schools that belong to The National Consortium for Specialized Secondary Schools of Mathematics, Science and Technology.[14] In addition, there are hundreds of other specialized schools, some of which focus on mathematics and science, which are not members of that organization.

Distance Learning

Technology has created myriad opportunities to provide advanced study options for students who otherwise might not have access to such programs. As with the other opportunities described in this section, distance learning is a rapidly growing national phenomenon that is configured in a variety of ways, depending on a program's mission and available technology.

---

[11]A publicly funded school that is formed by legislation rather than by the standard school incorporation process. It has the autonomy to make decisions concerning structure, curriculum, and educational emphasis and is held accountable for the academic achievement of its students by means of its charter (www.uscharterschools.org [November 23, 2001]).

[12]A separate and autonomous unit formally authorized by the board of education and/or superintendent that plans and runs its own program, has its own staff and students, and receives its own separate budget. The school-within-a-school usually reports to a district official instead of being responsible to the building principal except in matters of safety; teachers and students typically are affiliated with the school-within-a-school as a matter of choice (Raywid, 1995).

[13]A school or education center that offers a special curriculum capable of attracting substantial numbers of students of different racial backgrounds. A key feature of magnet schools is a specialty curriculum designed to embrace a subject matter or teaching methodology not generally offered to students of the same age or grade level under the same local education agency, such as a science–technology center or a center for the performing arts (Magnet School Assistance Program, Title V, Part A of the Elementary and Secondary Education Act, as amended in 1994).

[14]More information can be found at: http://www.ncsssmst.org/ (November 27, 2001).

For many years, distance learning was used to meet the needs of home schoolers, students seeking independent study options for acceleration or graduation, and those in rural areas who did not have access to enriched educational options. The movement has grown exponentially during the past decade. State departments of education, commercial enterprises, colleges and universities, and high schools are the most frequent sponsors of distance-learning opportunities.

Televised courses were one of the first strategies used for distance learning. For many years, courses were broadcast on network television for adult learners who did not have access to schools. In the past decade, state departments of education have been tapping this resource to provide courses not otherwise available to high school students, particularly in small and rural schools. Although attempts have been made to make televised courses more interactive, they still rely almost exclusively on a lecture format. Teachers conduct classes from electronic classrooms, and students participate by watching the classes at home or at school. Computers, telephones, and fax machines allow students to communicate with the instructor and to ask questions for clarification, but responses are not always immediate. New technology is poised to change this situation. High-speed data networks and online discussions have made communication with telecourse faculty during live broadcasts easier to manage, and the combined use of computers, video cameras, and microphones has created opportunities for live, interactive dialogue between students and faculty that can be heard by other students in different locations. Nonetheless, little is known about the quality of learning that can be supported by televised courses, and the committee notes that further research on this strategy is necessary.

In discussing the viability of using televised courses for the advanced study of science, the committee noted several additional problems. These include providing laboratory experiences primarily by demonstration.[15] The committee believes research is needed to evaluate the effectiveness of this practice in supporting learning with understanding and that alternatives should be investigated if necessary. Another concern is the inability of telefaculty to gain a clear understanding of students' conceptions and misconceptions and to adjust teaching to reflect students' initial understandings. Additionally, there is little opportunity in the context of a televised lecture to encourage the development of students' metacognitive skills.

---

[15]Alternatives to demonstration include the use of regional centers for laboratory work and agreements with high schools and colleges to offer the laboratory component. In these cases, students must report to a central location at specified times. Other alternatives include the use of micro laboratories that can be conducted by students in their homes.

The Education Program for Gifted Youth (EPGY) at Stanford University sponsors a computer-based, multimodel delivery system that exemplifies this approach. The courses use a combination of CD-ROM and Internet technologies to provide students with a multifaceted, highly individualized learning environment. The courses are organized around lectures that are computer-based and multimedia, consisting of voice accompanied by synchronized graphics. The program is designed to allow flexible pacing of instruction. Students who demonstrate ready mastery move quickly through a course, while slower learners receive additional instruction. Formative evaluation of student progress through ongoing data collection and analysis is a key component of the program and is used to adjust instruction for individual students. In all courses, lectures are followed by exercises in which students answer questions that are evaluated by the computer. Additional computer-based instruction and practice are provided to students whose responses to these questions indicate that they need further assistance. In addition, human instructors provide support to these and other students by telephone and electronic mail, as well as through a virtual classroom. To participate in a virtual classroom, students connect via the Internet, using voice and shared whiteboard conferencing software to create a real-time interactive lecture environment.

The committee did not have the opportunity to fully evaluate the Stanford program, but notes that it appears to be a promising model worthy of further evaluation. In evaluating this or other computer-based programs, the focus should be on how well the curricula, instruction, and companion assessment techniques align with the principles of learning with understanding detailed in Chapter 6 of this volume. Student achievement—the ultimate indicator of program effectiveness—should be measured by assessing not only students' command of factual knowledge, but also their conceptual understanding of the subject matter and their ability to apply that knowledge to learning new concepts.

ENRICHMENT ACTIVITIES

Even in schools with strong curricular and instructional resources, educators seek to create activities that will enhance and enrich student learning. With the exception of some national academic and research competitions, most of these activities are the product of collaborations involving individual localities; postsecondary institutions; professional organizations; or research entities, such as the National Aeronautics and Space Administration (NASA) or the National Institutes of Health (NIH). Enrichment activities are typically targeted at high-ability learners, students with strong interests or talent in a particular discipline, and members of groups who are underrepresented in particular occupations.

Internships and Mentorships

Eminent individuals tend to have been profoundly influenced by a single or several mentors or role models (Goertzel, Goertzel, and Goertzel, 1978; Kaufmann, Harrel, Milam, Woolverton, and Miller, 1986; Torrance, 1984). Internships and mentorships can provide students with such experiences.

Internship programs expose students to research and career development opportunities through placement in research facilities or industries. These placements can be during the summer, part time during the school year, or longer term. Research facilities, large government agencies, local colleges, and university scientists all sponsor internships. NIH and NASA both offer research opportunities to high school students. Individual teachers frequently arrange for their students to participate in internships and research activities in local laboratories or universities. The committee learned of many teachers who have marshaled the resources of their communities to provide meaningful experiences for science and mathematics students. We recognize the extraordinary amount of time and energy required to arrange these types of activities and commend the efforts of these individuals.

There are also numerous summer enrichment opportunities that enable students to participate in specialized and challenging programs of advanced study. Some of these programs are designed to address the needs of high-ability learners seeking opportunities to work on problems that are not strictly defined so they can help structure their own learning experiences. An example of this type of program is the nationally recognized Arnold Ross program for advanced mathematics students, held annually at Ohio State University.[20] Another nationally recognized initiative is the Program in Mathematics for Young Scientists at Boston University.[21] Others, such as the University of California's Early Outreach Program, focus on compensatory and motivational activities that encourage and support students in efforts to be successful in more advanced curricula.[22] Many U.S. colleges and universities sponsor this type of program.

---

[20]Additional information about this program is available at http://www.math.ohio-state.edu/ross/ (November 23, 2001).

[21]Additional information about this program is available at http://math.bu.edu/INDIVIDUAL/promys/indice.html (November 23, 2001).

[22]See http://uga.berkeley.edu/apa/APA%20Home/eaop/default.htm (November 23, 2001).

Academic and Research Competitions

Many students participate in activities that require them to develop expertise through self-directed research or intense study of a topical area and then demonstrate their learning by participating in a competition. Some academic and research competitions are geared toward participation by teams of students; others are designed for individual participants. The goal of most academic competitions is to provide a competitive outlet for students who are particularly talented or interested in an area or subject by encouraging them to engage in problem-solving activities that are complex and challenging. Examples of these types of programs include science fairs, mathematics and science Olympiads, the Intel and Duracell/National Science Teachers Association science competitions, inventors' competitions, and bridge-building competitions. External judging is usually a component of these programs. Coaching and mentorship are important aspects of the preparation students receive.

Critics of such competitions cite disparities in the resources available to students and the negative aspects of encouraging competitiveness instead of the cooperation that is more in keeping with the way modern science is conducted in the field. Some worry about the lack of participation by students who have the ability to undertake such work but have not had opportunities in their schools to demonstrate this ability. Thus, these critics say, the competitions reward those who already have access to greater resources and opportunities. Proponents cite the unique opportunity these activities provide for students to engage in problem-solving activities not typically available through classroom curricula.

Alternative Curricular and Instructional Approaches

Students and schools differ in many ways that are important to teaching and learning. Consequently, no single course structure or approach, including those as widely used as AP and IB, can meet the educational needs of every high school student who is ready for advanced study. For example, not all schools have adequate resources (physical, financial, or human) to teach high-quality AP courses, and implementing IB requires a level of schoolwide commitment that not all schools are prepared or able to undertake. Additionally, the goals and objectives of individual schools vary in accordance with their local communities' educational values and beliefs. State educational standards that describe what students who are educated in the state should know and be able to do at particular grade levels play an important role in determining what is taught and the way instruction and curriculum are organized. This variation underscores the need for alternatives to the AP and IB programs.

The committee suggests, however, that before adopting any curriculum for advanced study, those responsible for selecting programs do two things. The first is to evaluate the programs under consideration for alignment with the principles of learning outlined in this and other reports, such as *How People Learn: Brain, Mind, Experience, and School (Expanded Edition)* (National Research Council, 2000b). In so doing, it is important to ensure that the program not only moves students along the learning continuum by increasing their content knowledge, but also fosters a deep conceptual understanding of the subject matter. Second is to assess whether the school has the necessary infrastructure and resources to implement the program successfully, including qualified teachers and adequate time and money to provide ongoing, high-quality professional development opportunities for members of the staff who will be responsible for implementing the program (see Chapter 7, this volume).

CONCLUSION

The two extant national models for advanced study (AP and IB) cannot meet the educational needs of all students. The committee learned of many advanced study alternatives that have been developed by individual schools and school districts, sometimes in conjunction with universities. While the committee applauds local efforts to develop original advanced study programs, we believe such programs are not enough, and additional national programs are needed. This call for more national programs stems from research identifying the benefits that accrue when students and teachers are part of national educational efforts.

In calling for more national programs, the committee wishes to be quite clear that we are not asking for more programs that merely replicate those that already exist. Rather, the committee urges universities, policymakers, and curriculum specialists to encourage the development, evaluation, and dissemination of information about promising alternatives that can help increase access to advanced study for students from diverse backgrounds and communities, as well as those whose learning styles or interests are not adequately addressed by existing national programs.

6

Learning with Understanding: Seven Principles

During the last four decades, scientists have engaged in research that has increased our understanding of human cognition, providing greater insight into how knowledge is organized, how experience shapes understanding, how people monitor their own understanding, how learners differ from one another, and how people acquire expertise. From this emerging body of research, scientists and others have been able to synthesize a number of underlying principles of human learning. This growing understanding of how people learn has the potential to influence significantly the nature of education and its outcomes.

The committee's appraisal of advanced study is organized around this research on how people learn (see, for example, Greeno, Collins, and Resnick, 1996; National Research Council [NRC], 2000b; 2001a; Shepard, 2000). Our appraisal also takes into account a growing understanding of how people develop expertise in a subject area (see, for example, Chi, Feltovich, and Glaser, 1981; NRC, 2000b). Understanding the nature of expertise can shed light on what successful learning might look like and help guide the development of curricula, pedagogy, and assessments that can move students toward more expert-like practices and understandings in a subject area. To make real differences in students' skill, it is necessary both to understand the nature of expert practice and to devise methods that are appropriate to learning that practice.

The design of educational programs is always guided by beliefs about how students learn in an academic discipline. Whether explicit or implicit, these ideas affect what students in a program will be taught, how they will be taught, and how their learning will be assessed. Thus, educational program designers who believe students learn best through memorization and repeated practice will design their programs differently from those who hold that students learn best through active inquiry and investigation.

The model for advanced study proposed by the committee is supported by research on human learning and is organized around the goal of fostering learning with deep conceptual understanding or, more simply, *learning with understanding*. Learning with understanding is strongly advocated by leading mathematics and science educators and researchers for all students, and also is reflected in the national goals and standards for mathematics and science curricula and teaching (American Association for Advancement of Science [AAAS], 1989, 1993; National Council of Teachers of Mathematics [NCTM], 1989, 1991, 2000; NRC, 1996). The committee sees as the goal for advanced study in mathematics and science an even deeper level of conceptual understanding and integration than would typically be expected in introductory courses.

Guidance on how to achieve learning with understanding is grounded in seven research-based principles of human learning that are presented below (see Box 6-1).[1] In Chapter 7, these principles are used as the framework for the design of curricula, instruction, and assessments for advanced study—three facets of classroom activity that, when skillfully orchestrated by the teacher, jointly promote learning with understanding. These principles also serve as the foundation for the design of professional development, for it, too, is a form of advanced learning.

The design principles for curriculum, instruction, assessment, and professional development provide one of the organizing frameworks of the committee's analysis of the AP and IB programs (see Chapters 8 and 9, this volume). While it could be argued that all components of the educational system (e.g., preservice training and leadership) should be included (and we believe they should), our analysis was limited to these four facets. Although this framework was developed to assess current programs of advanced study, it also can serve as a guide or framework for those involved in developing, implementing, or evaluating new educational programs.

SEVEN PRINCIPLES OF HUMAN LEARNING

Principle 1: Principled Conceptual Knowledge

> *Learning with understanding is facilitated when new and existing knowledge is structured around the major concepts and principles of the discipline.*

Highly proficient performance in any subject domain requires knowledge that is both accessible and usable. A rich body of content knowledge about a subject area is a necessary component of the ability to think and

---

[1]The research on which these principles are based has been summarized in *How People Learn: Mind, Brain, Experience and School* (Expanded Edition) (NRC, 2000b).

BOX 6-1   Seven Principles of Learning

1. Learning with understanding is facilitated when new and existing knowledge is structured around the major concepts and principles of the discipline.
2. Learners use what they already know to construct new understandings.
3. Learning is facilitated through the use of metacognitive strategies that identify, monitor, and regulate cognitive processes.
4. Learners have different strategies, approaches, patterns of abilities, and learning styles that are a function of the interaction between their heredity and their prior experiences.
5. Learners' motivation to learn and sense of self affects what is learned, how much is learned, and how much effort will be put into the learning process.
6. The practices and activities in which people engage while learning shape what is learned.
7. Learning is enhanced through socially supported interactions.

solve problems in that domain, but knowing many disconnected facts is not enough. Research clearly demonstrates that experts' content knowledge is structured around the major organizing principles and core concepts of the domain, the "big ideas" (e.g., Newton's second law of motion in physics, the concept of evolution in biology, and the concept of limit in mathematics) (see, for example, Chi et al., 1981; Kozma and Russell, 1997). These big ideas lend coherence to experts' vast knowledge base; help them discern the deep structure of problems; and, on that basis, recognize similarities with previously encountered problems. Research also shows that experts' strategies for thinking and solving problems are closely linked to rich, well-organized bodies of knowledge about subject matter. Their knowledge is connected and organized, and it is "conditionalized" to specify the context in which it is applicable.

If one conceives of advanced study as moving students along a continuum toward greater expertise, then advanced study should have as its goal fostering students' abilities to recognize and structure their growing body of content knowledge according to the most important principles of the discipline. Therefore, curriculum and instruction in advanced study should be designed to develop in learners the ability to see past the surface features of any problem to the deeper, more fundamental principles of the discipline.

Curricula that emphasize breadth of coverage and simple recall of facts may hinder students' abilities to organize knowledge effectively because they do not learn anything in depth, and thus are not able to structure what they are learning around the major organizing principles and core concepts of the discipline. Even students who prefer to seek understanding are often forced into rote learning by the quantity of information they are asked to absorb.

Principle 2: Prior Knowledge

Learners use what they already know to construct new understandings.

When students come to advanced study, they already possess knowledge, skills, beliefs, concepts, conceptions, and misconceptions that can significantly influence how they think about the world, approach new learning, and go about solving unfamiliar problems (Wandersee, Mintzes, and Novak, 1994). People construct meaning for a new idea or process by relating it to ideas or processes they already understand. This prior knowledge can produce mistakes, but it can also produce correct insights. Some of this knowledge base is discipline specific, while some may be related to but not explicitly within a discipline. Research on cognition has shown that successful learning involves linking new knowledge to what is already known. These links can take different forms, such as adding to, modifying, or reorganizing knowledge or skills. How these links are made may vary in different subject areas and among students with varying talents, interests, and abilities (Paris and Ayers, 1994). Learning with understanding, however, involves more than appending new concepts and processes to existing knowledge; it also involves conceptual change and the creation of rich, integrated knowledge structures.

If students' existing knowledge is not engaged, the understandings they develop through instruction can be very different from what their teacher may have intended; learners are more likely to construct interpretations that agree with their own prior knowledge even when those interpretations are in conflict with the teacher's viewpoint. Thus, lecturing to students is often an ineffective tool for producing conceptual change. For example, Vosniadou and Brewer (1992) describe how learners who believed the world is flat perceived the earth as a three-dimensional pancake after being taught that the world is a sphere.

Moreover, when prior knowledge is not engaged, students are likely to fail to understand or even to separate knowledge learned in school from their beliefs and observations about the world outside the classroom. For example, despite instruction to the contrary, students of all ages (including college graduates) often persist in their belief that seasons are caused by the earth's distance from the sun, rather than the sun's tilt on its axis, which affects the amount of solar energy striking the northern and southern regions of the earth as it orbits the sun (Harvard-Smithsonian Center for Astrophysics, Science Education Department, 1987). Roth (1986) similarly found that students continued to believe plants obtain food from the soil, rather than making it in their leaves, even after they had been taught about photosynthesis; this belief persisted since many failed to recognize that the carbon dioxide extracted from the air has weight and makes up most of a plant's mass.

Effective teaching involves gauging what learners already know about a subject and finding ways to build on that knowledge. When prior knowledge contains misconceptions, there is a need to reconstruct a whole relevant framework of concepts, not simply to correct the misconception or faulty idea. Effective instruction entails detecting those misconceptions and addressing them, sometimes by challenging them directly (Caravita and Hallden, 1994; Novak, 2002).

The central role played by prior knowledge in the ability to gain new knowledge and understanding has important implications for the preparation of students in the years preceding advanced study. To be successful in advanced study in science or mathematics, students must have acquired a sufficient knowledge base that includes concepts, factual content, and relevant procedures on which to build. This in turn implies that they must have had the opportunity to learn these things. Many students, however, particularly those who attend urban and rural schools, those who are members of certain ethnic or racial groups (African American, Hispanic, and Native American), and those who are poor, are significantly less likely to have equitable access to early opportunities for building this prerequisite knowledge base (Doran, Dugan, and Weffer, 1998; see also Chapter 2, this volume). Inequitable access to adequate preparation can take several forms, including (1) lack of appropriate courses (Ekstrom, Goertz, and Rock, 1988); (2) lack of qualified teachers and high-quality instruction (Gamoran, 1992; Oakes, 1990); (3) placement in low-level classes where the curriculum focuses on less rigorous topics and low-level skills (Burgess, 1983, 1984; Nystrand and Gamoran, 1988; Oakes, 1985); (4) lack of access to resources, such as high-quality science and mathematics facilities, equipment, and textbooks (Oakes, Gamoran, and Page, 1992); and (5) lack of guidance and encouragement to prepare for advanced study (Lee and Ekstrom, 1987).

Students who lack opportunities to gain important knowledge and skills in the early grades may never get to participate in advanced classes where higher-order skills are typically taught (Burnett, 1995). Consequently, these students may be precluded very early in their school careers from later participation in advanced study—even when they are interested and motivated to enroll. In essence, they are "tracked away." The end result is that many students are denied access to important experiences that would prepare them to pursue the study of mathematics and sciences beyond high school.

Principle 3: Metacognition

Learning is facilitated through the use of metacognitive strategies that identify, monitor, and regulate cognitive processes.

To be effective problem solvers and learners, students need to determine what they already know and what else they need to know in any given situation. They must consider both factual knowledge—about the task, their goals, and their abilities—and strategic knowledge about how and when to use a specific procedure to solve the problem at hand (Ferrari and Sternberg, 1998). In other words, to be effective problem solvers, students must be *metacognitive*. Empirical studies show that students who are metacognitively aware perform better than those who are not (Garner and Alexander, 1989; Schoenfeld, 1987).

Metacognition is an important aspect of students' intellectual development that enables them to benefit from instruction (Carr, Kurtz, Schneider, Turner, and Borkowski, 1989; Flavell, 1979; Garner, 1987; Novak, 1985; Van Zile-Tamsen, 1996) and helps them know what to do when things are not going as expected (Schoenfeld, 1983; Skemp, 1978, 1979). For example, research demonstrates that students with better-developed metacognitive strategies will abandon an unproductive problem-solving strategy very quickly and substitute a more productive one, whereas students with less effective metacognitive skills will continue to use the same strategy long after it has failed to produce results (Gobert and Clement, 1999). The basic metacognitive strategies include (1) connecting new information to former knowledge; (2) selecting thinking strategies deliberately; and (3) planning, monitoring, and evaluating thinking processes (Dirkes, 1985).

Experts have highly developed metacognitive skills related to their specific area of expertise. If students in a subject area are to develop problem-solving strategies consistent with the ways in which experts in the discipline approach problems, one important goal of advanced study should be to help students become more metacognitive. Fortunately, research indicates that students' metacognitive abilities can be developed through explicit instruction and through opportunities to observe teachers or other content experts as they solve problems and consider ideas while making their thinking visible to those observing (Collins and Smith, 1982; Lester et al., 1994;

Schoenfeld, 1983, 1985). Having students construct concept maps[2] for a topic of study can also provide powerful metacognitive insights, especially when students work in teams of three or more (see Box 6-2 for a discussion of concept maps). It is important to note that the teaching of metacognitive skills is often best accomplished in specific content areas since the ability to monitor one's understanding is closely tied to the activities and questions that are central to domain-specific knowledge and expertise (NRC, 2000b).

Principle 4: Differences Among Learners

Learners have different strategies, approaches, patterns of abilities, and learning styles that are a function of the interaction between their heredity and their prior experiences.

Individuals are born with potential that develops through their interaction with their environment to produce their current capabilities and talents. Thus among learners of the same age, there are important differences in cognitive abilities, such as linguistic and spatial aptitudes or the ability to work with symbolic quantities representing properties of the natural world, as well as in emotional, cultural, and motivational characteristics.

Additionally, by the time students reach high school, they have acquired their own preferences regarding how they like to learn and at what pace. Thus, some students will respond favorably to one kind of instruction, whereas others will benefit more from a different approach. Educators need to be sensitive to such differences so that instruction and curricular materials will be suitably matched to students' developing abilities, knowledge base, preferences, and styles. (Annex 6-1 illustrates some of the ways in which curriculum and instruction might be modified to meet the learning needs of high-ability learners.)

Appreciation of differences among learners also has implications for the design of appropriate assessments and evaluations of student learning. Students with different learning styles need a range of opportunities to demonstrate their knowledge and skills. For example, some students work well

---

[2]Concept maps are two-dimensional, hierarchical representations of concepts and relationships between concepts that model the structure of knowledge possessed by a learner or expert. The theory of learning that underlies concept mapping recognizes that all meaningful learning builds on the learner's existing relevant knowledge and the quality of its organization. The constructivist epistemology underlying concept maps recognizes that all knowledge consists of concepts, defined as perceived regularities in events or objects or their representation, designated by a label, and propositions that are two or more concepts linked semantically to form a statement about some event or object. Free software that aids in the construction of concept maps is available at www.cmap.coginst.uwf.edu.

BOX 6-2   **Use of Concept Maps**

Figures 6-1 and 6-2 are examples of actual concept maps constructed by a high school student. Figure 6-1 was made at the beginning of the study of meiosis and shows that the student did not know how to organize and relate many of the relevant concepts. The student equated meiosis with sexual reproduction and was not clear on how meiosis relates to homologous chromosomes. These maps are presented without editing.

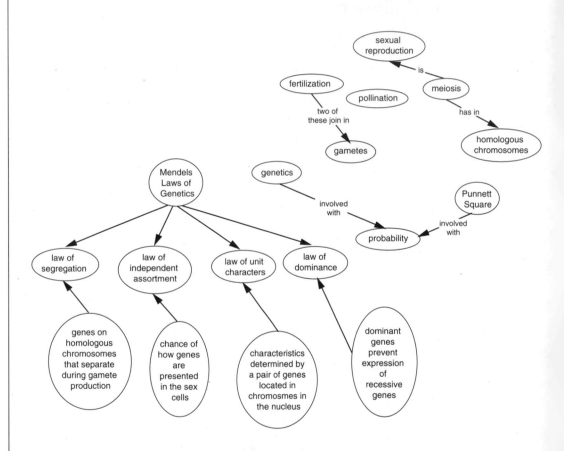

FIGURE 6-1   *Concept map made by an advanced biology student early in the study of meiosis and genetics. Note that several concepts are not integrated into the student's knowledge structure, and he has the misconception that meiosis is sexual reproduction. SOURCE: J. Novak (Jan. 2001) personal correspondence. Used with permission.*

Figure 6-2, a concept map made at the end of the study, reveals an elaborated, integrated understanding of the process. The student now has integrated the meanings of meiosis and sexual reproduction, homologous chromosomes, and other concepts. While some concept meanings still appear a bit fuzzy, the student has clearly made progress in the development of understanding, and his knowledge structure can serve as a good foundation for further study.

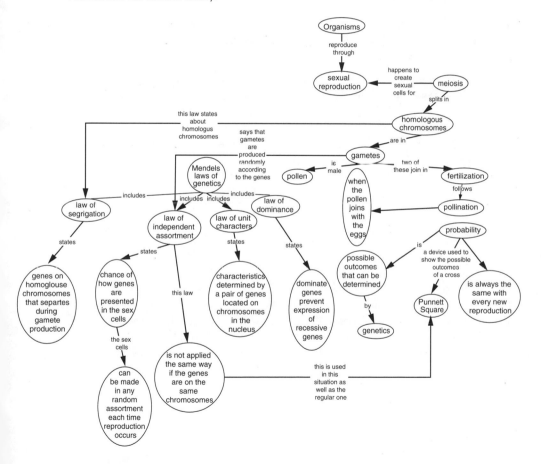

FIGURE 6-2 *Concept map drawn by the same student at the end of the study unit on meiosis. Note that the original misconceptions about the nature of meiosis have been remediated, and more concepts have been integrated into the student's knowledge structure. SOURCE: J. Novak (Jan. 2001) personal correspondence. Used with permission.*

under pressure, while the performance of others is significantly diminished by time constraints. Some excel at recalling information, while others are more adept at performance-based tasks. Some express themselves well in writing, while others do not. Thus using one form of assessment will work to the advantage of some students and to the disadvantage of others (Mintzes, Wandersee, and Novak, 2001; O'Neil and Brown, 1997; Shavelson, Baxter, and Pine, 1992; Sugrue, Valdes, Schlackman, and Webb, 1996).

Principle 5: Motivation

A learner's motivation to learn and sense of self affects what is learned, how much is learned, and how much effort will be put into the learning process.

Humans are motivated to learn and to develop competence (Stipek, 1998; White, 1959). Motivation can be extrinsic (performance oriented), for example to get a good grade on a test or to be accepted by a good college, or intrinsic (learning oriented), for example to satisfy curiosity or to master challenging material. Regardless of the source, learners' level of motivation strongly affects their willingness to persist in the face of difficulty. Intrinsic motivation is enhanced when learning tasks are perceived as being interesting and personally meaningful and are presented at the proper level of difficulty. A task that is too difficult can create frustration; one that is too easy can lead to boredom.

Research has revealed strong connections between learners' beliefs about their own abilities in a subject area and their success in learning about that domain (Eccles, 1987, 1994; Garcia and Pintrich, 1994; Graham and Weiner, 1996; Markus and Wurf, 1987; Marsh, 1990; Weiner, 1985). Some beliefs about learning are quite general. For example, some students believe their ability to learn a particular subject or skill is predetermined, whereas others believe their ability to learn is substantially a function of effort (Dweck, 1989). Believing that abilities are developed through effort is most beneficial to the learner, and teachers and others should cultivate that belief (Graham and Weiner, 1996; Weiner, 1985). The use of instructional strategies that encourage conceptual understanding is an effective way to increase students' interest and enhance their confidence about their abilities to learn a particular subject (Alaiyemola, Jegede, and Okebukola, 1990; Cavallo, 1996).

Cultivating the belief among a broad range of students that the ability to learn advanced science and mathematics is, for the most part, a function of effort rather than inherited talent, ability, and/or intelligence has other benefits as well. For example, the belief that successful learning in advanced study is a matter of effort fosters risk taking in course selection and promotes students' motivation to succeed in challenging situations (Novak and

Gowin, 1984). A belief in the value of effort is especially important for students who are traditionally underrepresented in advanced study. For students to maintain their beliefs about the role of effort in successful performance, teachers and other school personnel must act in ways that do not contradict students' sense that they are capable of understanding science and mathematics and that sustained effort will produce such understanding, even though there may be struggles along the way.

Several recent studies document the power of a high school culture that expects all students to spend time and effort on academic subjects and is driven by a belief that effort will pay off in high levels of academic achievement for everyone, regardless of prior academic status, family background, or future plans. When such norms and expectations are held in common for all students, they define the school's culture. In such settings, remediation of skill deficits takes on a different character, teachers are able and willing to provide rigorous academic instruction to all students, and all students respond with effort and persistence (Bryk, Lee, and Holland, 1993; Lee, 2001; Lee, Bryk, and Smith, 1993; Lee and Smith, 1999; Marks, Doane, and Secada, 1996; Rutter, 1983).

Principle 6: Situated Learning

The practices and activities in which people engage while learning to shape what is learned.

Research on the situated nature of cognition indicates that the way people learn a particular domain of knowledge and skills and the context in which they learn it become a fundamental part of what is learned (Greeno, 1993; Lave, 1991). When students learn, they learn both information and a set of practices, and the two are inextricably related. McLellan (1996, p. 9) states that situated cognition "involves adapting knowledge and thinking skills to solve unique problems . . . and is based upon the concept that knowledge is contextually situated and is fundamentally influenced by the activity, context, and culture in which it is used." Learning, like cognition, is shaped by the conventions, tools, and artifacts of the culture and the context in which it is situated.

Because the practices in which students engage as they acquire new concepts shape what and how the students learn, transfer is made possible to the extent that knowledge and learning are grounded in multiple contexts (Brown, Collins, and Duguid, 1989). Transfer is more difficult when a concept is taught in a limited set of contexts or through a limited set of activities. When concepts are taught only in one context, students are not exposed to the varied practices associated with those concepts. As a result, students often miss seeing the concepts' applicability to solving novel problems encountered in real life, in other classes, or in other disciplines. It is only by encountering the same concept at work in multiple contexts that students can develop a deep understanding of the concept and how it can be used, as well as the ability to transfer what has been learned in one context to others (Anderson, Greeno, Reder, and Simon, 1997).

If the goal of education is to allow learners to apply what they learn in real situations, learning must involve applications and take place in the context of authentic activities (Brown et al., 1989). J. S. Brown and colleagues (1989, p. 34) define authentic activities as "ordinary practices of a culture"—activities that are similar to what actual practitioners do in real contexts. A. L. Brown and colleagues (1993) offer a somewhat different definition: given that the goal of education is to prepare students to be lifelong learners, activities are authentic if they foster the kinds of thinking that are important for learning in out-of-school settings, whether or not those activities mirror what practitioners do. Regardless of which definition is adopted, the importance of situating learning in authentic activities is clear. Collins (1988) notes the following four specific benefits: (1) students learn about the conditions for applying knowledge, (2) they are more likely to engage in invention and problem solving when learning in novel and diverse situations and settings, (3) they are able to see the implications of their knowledge, and (4) they are supported in structuring knowledge in ways that are appropriate for later use.

Teachers can engage learners in important practices that can be used in different situations by drawing upon real-world exercises, or exercises that foster problem-solving skills and strategies that are used in real-world situations. Such an approach provides language, activities, and procedures that can acculturate students into the community of scholars and lifelong learners. Problem-based and case-based learning are two instructional approaches that create opportunities for students to engage in practices similar to those of experts. Technology also can be used to bring real-world contexts into the classroom. The committee emphasizes that with all of these approaches, care must be taken to provide multiple opportunities for students to engage in activities in which the same concept is at work; otherwise learning could become overly contextualized.

Principle 7: Learning Communities

Learning is enhanced through socially supported interactions.

Learning can be enhanced when students have the opportunity to interact and collaborate with others on instructional tasks. In learning environments that encourage collaboration among peers, such as those in which most practicing scientists and mathematicians work, individuals build communities of practice, have opportunities to test their own ideas, and learn by observing others. Research demonstrates that opportunities for students to articulate their ideas to peers and to hear and discuss others' ideas in the context of the classroom is particularly effective in bringing about conceptual change (Alexopoulou and Driver, 1996; Carpenter and Lehrer, 1999; Cobb, Wood, and Yackel, 1993; Kobayashi, 1994; Towns and Grant, 1997; Wood, Cobb, and Yackel, 1991). Social interaction also is important for the development of expertise, metacognitive skills, and formation of the learner's sense of self.

The social nature of learning has important implications for the consequences of the ways in which students are grouped for instruction. For example, students who are placed in low-track classes often have less time to collaborate and interact around instructional tasks. Research indicates that teachers in low-track science and mathematics classes spend more time than teachers in higher-track classes on routines, and more frequently provide seatwork and worksheet activities that are designed to be completed independently (Oakes, 1990). Additionally, teachers in higher-track classes often orchestrate more frequent and varied opportunities for students to participate in small-group problem-solving activities than are provided by teachers in lower-track classes, who tend to focus on behavior management and on maintaining control during learning activities. Some might contend that teachers in both types of classes are responding to the needs of their students. However, teachers must strike a balance between providing the structure that is often appropriate for low-ability students and the active engagement that allows these students to learn at deeper levels.

Newmann and Wehlage (1995) identify teaching strategies that promote intellectual quality and authenticity. One of the most powerful strategies is the "substantive conversation," in which students engage in extended conversational exchanges with the teacher and/or peers about subject matter in a way that builds an improved or shared understanding of ideas or topics. The authors stress that such subject matter conversations go far beyond reporting facts, procedures, or definitions; they focus on making distinctions, applying ideas, forming generalizations, and raising questions. According to the results of research by Gamoran and Nystrand (1990), the opportunities for such substantive engagement are far fewer in low-track than in higher-track classes.

CONCLUSION

The seven principles of learning set forth in this chapter are not ends in themselves. Their usefulness lies in the guidance they provide for the design of curriculum, instruction, assessment, and professional development for advanced study that fosters in students a deep conceptual understanding of a domain. The next chapter articulates design principles for advanced study that draw on these principles of learning.

ANNEX 6-1

CHARACTERISTICS OF HIGH-ABILITY LEARNERS AND IMPLICATIONS FOR CURRICULUM AND INSTRUCTION

Differences among learners have implications for how curriculum and instruction should be structured.[3] Provided below is an example of how a better understanding of learning can assist teachers in structuring their curricula and instruction more appropriately to meet the needs of a particular group of students. Different strategies would most likely be used to meet the needs of other students, although there might be some overlap.

Characteristic: High-ability learners display an exceptionally rich knowledge base in their specific talent domain. Within that domain, they tend to achieve formal operational thought earlier than other students and to display advanced problem-solving strategies. High-ability learners are also able to work with abstract and complex ideas in their talent domain at an earlier age.

Implication: High-ability learners are ready to access the high school mathematics and science curriculum earlier than other students. Thus the high school mathematics and science sequence should be offered to them beginning in middle school.

Characteristic: High-ability students pick up informally much of the content knowledge taught in school, and as a result, that knowledge tends to be idiosyncratic and not necessarily organized around the central concepts of the discipline.

Implication: Assessment of what the learner has already mastered through diagnostic testing is critical. Instruction needs to build on what is already known and on previous experiences, filling in the gaps and correct-

---

[3]The information in this section is drawn from research on gifted and talented learners (see, for example, Association of the Gifted and Talented, 1989; Berger, 1991; Boyce et al., 1993; Dark and Benbow, 1993; Feldhusen, Hansen, and Kennedy, 1989; Johnson and Sher, 1997; Maker, 1982; VanTassel-Baska et al., 1988; Tomlinson, 1995; VanTassel-Baska, 1998).

ing misconceptions. It also must help the student organize his or her knowledge around the central ideas of the discipline. A full course in a content area often is not needed; either it could be skipped, with gaps being filled in as needed, or the curriculum compacted. "The proper psychology of talent is one that tries to be reasonably specific in defining competencies as manifested in the world, with instruction aimed at developing the very competencies so defined" (Wallach, 1978, p. 617).

Characteristic: High-ability learners learn at a more rapid rate than other students and can engage in simultaneous rather than only linear processing of ideas in their talent domain.

Implication: The pace at which the curriculum is offered must be adjusted for these learners. The curriculum also must be at a more complex level, making interdisciplinary connections whenever possible. That is, the curriculum should allow for faster pacing of well-organized, compressed, and appropriate learning experiences that are, in the end, enriching and accelerative.

Characteristic: Many high-ability students will have mastered the content of high school mathematics and science courses before formally taking the courses, either on their own, through special programs, or through Web-based courses.

Implication: Opportunities for testing out of prerequisites should be provided. Many high-ability students could be placed directly in an AP science course, skipping the typical high school–level prerequisite, or begin the IB program earlier than is typical.

Characteristic: High-ability students often can solve problems by alternative means and not know the underlying concept being tapped by a test item (e.g., can solve an algebra problem but not know algebra).

Implication: Assessments should not be solely in multiple-choice format; students must be able to show their work in arriving at a solution.

Characteristic: The motivation of high-ability students to achieve often becomes diminished because of boredom in school, resulting in underachievement.

Implication: Because one facet of effective teaching involves assessing the student's status in the learning process and posing problems slightly exceeding the level already mastered (Hunt, 1961), it is important to provide curricula for high-ability students that are developmentally appropriate for them. Doing so will not only meet the intellectually talented student's educational needs, but also facilitate his or her development of good study skills, more realistic self-concepts, and achievement motivation. Growth in achievement motivation and self-efficacy arises out of challenge and satisfaction in mastering tasks that appropriately match capabilities.

Characteristic: The capacity for learning of high-ability students is underestimated and thus becomes underdeveloped, especially if learning criteria lack sufficient challenge, and curriculum is not adequately knowledge rich and rigorous.

Implication: Curriculum must be targeted at developing especially deep and well-organized knowledge structures that with time will begin to approximate those of experts. Doing so will foster cognitive development, higher-level thinking skills, and creativity. The depth of the curriculum should allow gifted learners to continue exploring an area of special interest to the expert level. Curricula for these students should enable them to explore constantly changing knowledge and information and develop the attitude that knowledge is worth pursuing in a global society.

Characteristic: High-ability children are advanced in their critical and creative thinking skills. They tend to spend much more time up front (i.e., metacognitively) than in the execution phase of problem solving.

Implication: The basic thinking skills to be developed in high-ability students are critical thinking, creative thinking, problem finding and solving, research, and decision making. Those skills should be mastered within each content domain.

Characteristic: High-ability students prefer unstructured problems in which the task is less well defined. They also like to structure their own learning experiences. They do not require careful scaffolding of material or step-by-step learning experiences to master new material or concepts; in fact, they become frustrated with such approaches.

Implication: Opportunities to identify and solve problems should be provided. Interdisciplinarity, greater in-depth exploration of areas of interest, and autonomous learning should be encouraged. Meaningful project work in content areas, in which real-world products are generated, is appropriate as it allows students the opportunity to create on their own and to apply and expand ideas learned in class. To facilitate such work, curricula should encourage exposure to, selection of, and use of specialized and appropriate resources.

Characteristic: High-ability students have the capacity to make connections easily among disparate bodies of knowledge and to deal effectively with abstractions and complexity of thought.

Implication: Curricula ought to emphasize providing students with a deep understanding of the important concepts of a discipline and how they are organized, as well as identify important pathways between disciplines so that separate facets of knowledge are understood as being integrated. Curricula should allow for the development and application of productive thinking skills to instill in students the capacity to reconceptualize existing knowledge and generate new knowledge.

Characteristic: Eminent persons tend to have been profoundly influenced by a single individual, such as an educator. Students in the top mathematical/science graduate programs have reported research experiences during high school at unusually high levels. Those who are precocious in creative production tend to exhibit outstanding achievement in adult life.

Implication: Mentorships, internships, or long-term research opportunities should be provided for advanced students.

Characteristic: High-ability students who become productive adults in a domain have passed through that domain's specific stages. Doing so took them much time and sustained effort, with the talent development process having begun well before secondary school.

Implication: Accelerated learning experiences are critical, given that the development of talent proceeds from practice and mastery of increasingly more difficult and complex skills at an individual rate, and mastery of a domain's knowledge base and the concomitant reorganization of cognitive structures are both necessary for creativity.

Characteristic: High-ability students develop greater expectations, feel better about themselves, and engage in higher-level processing or discourse when working with other students of similar ability.

Implication: High-ability students need the challenge and stimulation of being together for at least part of every school day, with expectations set high enough to challenge their potential ability to meet them.

7

Designing Curriculum, Instruction, Assessment, and Professional Development

The previous chapter describes seven principles that support learning with understanding. This chapter explores the implications of those principles for the intentional and systemic design of four key elements of the educational system—curriculum, instruction, assessment, and professional development—to promote learning with understanding within the context of advanced study. It is critical to recognize that programs for advanced study share many of the objectives of other programs in the same discipline; these design principles, therefore, also apply to the design and development of mathematics and science courses at all levels.

While each of the four key elements is addressed separately here, in practice they work together synergistically and need to be aligned in mutually supportive ways. Without such alignment and interdependence, deep conceptual understanding is more difficult to achieve. For example, if teachers focus on teaching "big ideas" but the related assessments measure students' knowledge of discrete facts, it is impossible to know the extent to which students genuinely understand core concepts. The systemic and dynamic relationship among the four elements also means that changes in one element affect and require changes in the others.

In addition, it is essential to recognize the critical role of the learning environment in fostering learning with understanding. The learning environment of the school and the classroom in which these components of educational programs interact affects the degree to which teachers can integrate curriculum, instruction, and assessment to promote learning with understanding (National Research Council [NRC], 2000b).

CURRICULUM

A curriculum for understanding is intentionally designed around the organizing principles and essential concepts of the domain and provides opportunities for in-depth exploration in a variety of contexts (design principles for curriculum are summarized in Box 7-1). Such a curriculum emphasizes depth of understanding over breadth of coverage. It is designed to provide genuine opportunities for high-quality instruction and multiple points of entry into mathematics and science (Au and Jordan, 1981; Brown, 1994; Heath, 1983; Tharp and Gallimore, 1988).

Research reveals that experts' knowledge is organized around core concepts or organizing principles that guide their thinking in their area of exper-

BOX 7-1 Principles of Curriculum for Understanding

A mathematics or science curriculum for advanced study that promotes learning with understanding:

- Structures the concepts, factual content, and procedures that constitute the knowledge base of the discipline around the organizing principles (big ideas) of the domain.
- Links new knowledge to what is already known by presenting concepts in a conceptually and logically sequenced order that builds upon previous learning within and across grade levels.
- Focuses on depth of understanding rather than breadth of content coverage by providing students with multiple opportunities to practice and demonstrate what they learn in a variety of contexts.
- Includes structured learning activities that, in a real or simulated fashion, allow students to experience problem solving and inquiry in situations that are drawn from their personal experiences and real-world applications.
- Develops students' abilities to make meaningful applications and generalization to new problems and contexts.
- Incorporates language, procedures, and models of inquiry and truth verification that are consistent with the accepted practice of experts in the domain.
- Emphasizes interdisciplinary connections and integration and helps students connect learning in school with the issues, problems, and experiences that figure prominently in their lives outside of the classroom.

tise; expert knowledge is not simply a list of facts and formulas (Chi, Feltovich, and Glaser, 1981; Kozma and Russell, 1997; NRC, 2000b; see also Chapter 6, this volume). Therefore, in designing a curriculum for understanding, the key concepts and processes of the discipline should be clearly identified, explicated, and organized in a coherent fashion around the big ideas (Mintzes, Wandersee, and Novak, 1998; National Council of Teachers of Mathematics [NCTM], 1995; NRC, 1996). In addition, the interrelationships among topics should be clearly articulated to provide a framework teachers can use in developing and setting goals for their students' learning (American Association for the Advancement of Science [AAAS], 2001).

The organization of curriculum plays a critical role in helping students reconstruct misconceptions and see connections between what they are currently learning and what they have learned before. Curriculum for understanding represents more than a collection of activities or bits of information: it provides for the holistic performance of meaningful, complex tasks in increasingly challenging environments (Resnick and Klopfer, 1989). A curriculum for understanding takes the shape of topical strands that are highly interconnected in ways that are consistent with the knowledge structure used by experts in tackling complex tasks in their discipline (Marin, Mintzes, and Clavin, 2000).[1]

The deep disciplinary understanding of experts encompasses a vast amount of knowledge, but generally only a subset of that knowledge is used in the solution of any given problem. Experts not only have acquired extensive and deep knowledge and conceptual understanding, but also are skilled at discerning, identifying, and retrieving knowledge that is relevant to the solution of a particular problem. Their knowledge is organized into meaningful patterns and structures and is conditionalized (situated), meaning that what they know is accompanied by a specification of the contexts in which it is useful (Glaser, 1992; Simon, 1980). Many curricula and instructional materials, however, are not designed to help students conditionalize their knowledge. For example, textbooks are more likely to tell students how to do something than to help them understand the conditions under which doing it will be useful (Simon, 1980, p. 92). Having students work in laboratory settings is a familiar strategy for helping them develop conditionalized knowledge that supports problem solving. Well-designed laboratory experiences also encourage students to apply their knowledge and skills to concrete, real-world problems or novel situations (Resnick, 1994).

---

[1]See also the proceedings of From Misconceptions to Constructed Understanding, the Fourth International Misconceptions Seminar, at http://www.mlrg.org/proc4abstracts.html (November 27, 2001).

Students presented with vast amounts of content knowledge that is not organized into meaningful patterns are likely to forget what they have learned and to be unable to apply the knowledge to new problems or unfamiliar contexts (Haidar, 1997). Curriculum for understanding provides ample opportunity for students to apply their knowledge in a variety of contexts and conditions. This helps them transfer their learning to new situations and better prepares them for future learning (Bransford and Schwartz, 2000). Providing students with frequent opportunities to apply what they learn in multiple contexts requires a reallocation of instructional time. Allowing time for in-depth learning means decisions must be made about what knowledge is of most worth. For this reason, the curriculum needs to specify clearly the appropriate balance between breadth and depth of coverage in terms of student learning outcomes.

It is well accepted that students draw on their families, communities, and cultural experiences to create meaning and understanding. When curriculum is designed to build on students' experiences, teachers are able to engage students' prior knowledge, expose and restructure their knowledge and remediate misconceptions, and enhance motivation to learn. If students are able to draw on their cultural, social, and historical experiences in problem-solving situations, they are more likely to deepen their understanding. This can be accomplished by design through structured activities that, in real or simulated fashion, allow students to experience problem solving and inquiry in situations drawn from their personal experiences.

An effective curriculum allows for incorporating socialization into the discourse and practices of academic disciplines and provides frequent opportunities for students to apply the modes of inquiry and truth verification strategies and processes characteristic of each domain. An appreciation of the distinctive features of disciplines, however, should not lead to their isolation from each other or from the everyday world. Rather, strong curriculum design emphasizes interdisciplinary connections, integration, and authenticity in the relationship between learning in and out of school. These features not only make learning more challenging, exciting, and motivating, but also help students develop their abilities to make meaningful connections by applying and transferring knowledge from one problem context to another. The emphases of a curriculum for supporting learning with understanding are presented in Table 7-1.

INSTRUCTION

Instruction in advanced courses in mathematics and science should engage students in a variety of learning activities that are purposefully designed to connect with what they already know and motivate them to work

TABLE 7-1   Characteristics of Curriculum for Student Understanding

Less Emphasis on	More Emphasis on
Lists of topics to be covered	Underlying disciplinary principles and processes sequenced to optimize learning
Isolated concepts presented in relation to a single context or topic with no connection to other topics	Continuity and interdisciplinary integration through emphasis on the relationships of unifying concepts and processes to many topics
Individual teachers working in isolation	Collaborative teams including content and pedagogy experts
Coverage of as many topics as possible in a limited and fixed amount of time	Understanding of concepts in expanded and more flexible time periods
Example: A curriculum guide specifies that 8 percent of the advanced biology course should include topics related to cell energy, including cellular respiration and photosynthesis. The teacher schedules 1 week for a unit on cellular respiration. During this time, students carry out a variety of activities and laboratory exercises in class and complete out-of-class assignments. At the end of the week they take a unit test. The class goes on to the next unit, photosynthesis.	**Example:** A curriculum specifies four statements of essential knowledge about the production and utilization of energy in cells that are critical to building an understanding of the processes of photosynthesis and respiration. Prior relevant knowledge possessed by students is assessed using quizzes or student concept maps. The teacher schedules 3 days for activities that focus on this knowledge. A rubric is written so that both teacher and students know how the knowledge will be demonstrated. Students carry out a variety of activities in class and complete out-of-class assignments. At the same time, they must demonstrate their knowledge of each of the four specified outcomes before they can receive credit for the unit. Students continue to work on essential knowledge and present evidence when they are ready, even as activities for the next unit may be beginning.
Curriculum developed for one course at a time without articulation among the levels of schooling	Curriculum that is well articulated between the elementary grades and between high school and college and makes recognized connections with other disciplines
A rigid, prescribed, static curriculum	Curriculum that can be adapted to meet the diverse needs of students and situations
No relationship between NRC's *National Science Education Standards*/NCTM's *Principles and Standards for School Mathematics* and programs for advanced study or college courses	Standards-driven changes in courses, leading to advanced high school and introductory college courses through modification of content and pedagogy at the advanced course and college levels

SOURCES: Adapted from ACS (1997); NRC, (1996); and NSTA, (1996).

toward developing deeper understanding. Instruction should focus students on the central concepts and fundamental principles of the discipline. It also should assist them in constructing a framework for organizing new information as they explore concepts in depth and in a variety of contexts and develop problem-solving strategies common to the discipline (Novak, 1991). The design principles for instruction are summarized in Box 7-2.

BOX 7-2 Principles of Instruction for Understanding

Teaching for conceptual understanding in advanced mathematics and science courses:

- Maintains students' focus on the central organizing themes and underlying concepts of the discipline.
- Is based on careful consideration of what students already know, their ideas and ways of understanding the world, and the patterns of practice they bring with them into the classroom.
- Focuses on detecting, making visible, and addressing students' often fragile, underdeveloped understandings and misconceptions.
- Reflects an understanding of differences in students' interests, motivations, preferences, knowledge, and abilities.
- Is designed to provide the appropriate degree of explicitness for the situation and the abilities of the learners.
- Recognizes students' preferences for and varying abilities to process different symbol systems, such as language (written and spoken), images, and numerical representations, by employing multiple representations during instruction.
- Engages students in worthwhile tasks that provide access to powerful mathematical and scientific ideas and practices; moves students to see past the surface features of problems to the deeper, more fundamental principles; and develops their conceptual understanding and skills.
- Structures learning environments in which students can work collaboratively to gain experience in using the ways of thinking and speaking used by experts in the discipline.
- Orchestrates classroom discourse so that students can make conjectures, present solutions, and argue about the validity of claims, thus helping them explore old understandings in new ways, reveal misconceptions, and generalize and transfer their learning to new problems or more robust understandings.
- Provides explicit instruction in metacognition as part of teaching in the discipline.
- Uses various kinds of formal and informal formative assessments to monitor students' understanding and target instruction effectively.
- Creates expectations and social norms for the classroom that allow students to experience success and develop confidence in their abilities to learn.

The selection of instructional strategies and activities should be guided by knowledge of learners and should recognize and build on individual differences in students' interests, understandings, abilities, and experiences. Instruction should take into account common naive concepts held by students, as well as the effects of their cultural and experiential backgrounds on their learning. It also should reflect the teacher's own strengths and interests and consideration of available local resources. Activities and strategies should be continually adapted and refined to address topics arising from student inquiries and experiences.

It is important for instruction in advanced courses in mathematics and science to engage students in inquiry using a variety of activities and strategies, including experimentation, critical analysis of various sources of information, and the application of technology in problem solving. In this way, students combine knowledge in the domain with reasoning and thinking skills as they are engaged collaboratively in asking questions, constructing, testing and analyzing explanations, communicating the explanations, and considering alternatives (Townes and Grant, 1997).

One of a teacher's primary responsibilities is to select and develop significant and meaningful problems, learning experiences, projects, and investigations for students. Learning experiences are worthwhile when they represent concepts and procedures; foster skill development, reasoning, and problem solving; and help students make connections among mathematical and scientific ideas and to real-world applications (NCTM, 1991). Such experiences prompt the learner to see past the surface features of a problem to deeper, more fundamental principles. They "lend themselves to multiple solution methods, frequently involve multiple representations, and usually require students to justify, conjecture, and interpret" (Silver and Smith, 1996, p. 24). The design of such tasks is complex, requiring teachers to take account of students' knowledge and interests, of the ways students learn particular mathematical or scientific ideas, and of common points of confusion and misconceptions about those ideas (Borko et al., 2000).

Accomplishing this complex endeavor requires a qualified teacher. The National Board for Professional Teaching Standards (NBPTS) describes a qualified teacher as one who effectively enhances student learning and demonstrates the high level knowledge, skills, abilities, and commitments reflected in the following five core propositions:[2]

- Teachers are committed to students and their learning.
- Teachers know the subjects they teach and how to teach those subjects to students.

---

[2]See http://www.nbpts.org (November 22, 2001).

- Teachers are responsible for managing and monitoring student learning.
- Teachers think systematically about their practice and learn from experience.
- Teachers are members of learning communities.

To promote understanding, explicit instruction in metacognition should be integrated into the curriculum. Thus, instruction should create tasks and conditions under which student thinking can be revealed so that students, with their teachers, can review, assess, and reflect upon what they have learned and how. Additionally, teachers should make their reasoning and problem-solving strategies visible to students whenever possible (Collins and Smith, 1982; Lester et al., 1994; Schoenfeld, 1983, 1985).

Effective instruction in advanced courses should involve building and nurturing a community of learners. A community of learners encourages students to take academic risks by providing opportunities for them to make mistakes, obtain feedback, and revise their thinking while learning from others with whom they are engaged in inquiry and cooperative problem-solving activities.

To nurture the capacity of students to generalize and transfer their learning to new problems, teachers must help students explore old understandings in new ways. To this end, teachers must draw out misconceptions in order to challenge and displace them (Blumenfeld, Marx, Patrick, Krajcik, and Soloway, 1997; Caravita and Hallden, 1994; Jones, Rua, and Carter, 1998; NRC, 2000b; Pearsall, Skipper, and Mintzes, 1997;).

Since intrinsic motivation is self-sustaining, instruction should be planned so as to maximize the opportunity for developing a strong intrinsic motivation to learn. Students benefit when they can experience success and develop the confidence of a successful learner—one who has the tools to ask relevant questions, formulate problems and reframe issues, and assess his or her own knowledge and understanding (Alaiyemola, Jegede, and Okebukola, 1990; Stipek, 1998). Table 7-2 illustrates the emphases of instructional practices to support learning with understanding.

ASSESSMENT

Educational assessments can be designed for any number of purposes, from conducting large-scale evaluations of multiple components of educational programs to measuring individual students' mastery of a specified skill. Understanding assessment results requires that the user draw inferences from available data and observations that are supported by the assessment. Three key concepts related to assessments—reliability, validity, and fairness—underlie a user's ability to draw appropriate inferences from the

TABLE 7-2 Characteristics of Instruction for Student Understanding

Less Emphasis on	More Emphasis on
Presenting scientific knowledge through lecture, text, and demonstration, with activities centered on the teacher	Guiding students through active and extended inquiry and facilitating student-centered learning
The same learning experiences for all students	Appropriate matching of strategies and learners based on awareness of individual student's prior knowledge, abilities, and interests
Strategies that have students working alone	Strategies that incorporate collaboration among students and foster the development of classroom learning communities
"One-size-fits-all" instructional strategies	Multiple strategies designed to enhance understanding
Establishing blocks of time and designing lessons such that all students are required to learn the same thing in the same way at the same rate	Flexible scheduling and learning experiences that provide students with enough time, space, resources, guidance, and feedback for learning
Students doing numerous, often simplistic and unconnected laboratory activities and being exposed to many different procedures	Students conducting extended investigations and inquiry and having opportunities to progress through cycles of assessment and revision
Focusing on elaborate, equipment-intensive laboratory exercises	Focusing on interactions between students and materials, as well as teacher–student and student–student interactions
Laboratory exercises in which students are provided with all relevant background and procedures and are asked to follow the steps, fill in the data, and answer a few questions, after which the class moves on	Laboratory and inquiry experiences in which students are challenged to formulate questions that can be answered experimentally, propose and support hypotheses, plan procedures, design data tables and data analyses, evaluate and discuss results, and repeat experiments with modifications
Teachers monitoring laboratory work to ensure that the steps of the procedure are being followed correctly	Teachers acting as facilitators for laboratory experimentation; advising students on what essential measurements must be taken; discussing sample sizes; suggesting equipment that is available for use during the experiment; coaching students in techniques and protocols; and, within the limits of safety, allowing students to make mistakes and try again
Example: The teacher's lecture centers on presenting and explaining rate expressions and factors that affect forward and reverse reactions. K_{eq} calculations are shown. The teacher demonstrates color changes in a reversible reaction. LeChatelier's principle is reviewed, and students predict equilibrium shifts on the basis of hypothetical changes in reactants, products, and conditions. Student misconceptions about the nature of equilibrium remain uncovered and unchallenged.	**Example:** The teacher poses a question: "If the rate of a forward reaction is faster than the rate of a reverse reaction, will the system ever come to equilibrium?" Students are asked to construct a model for such a system, in which particles can be moved between two containers at different rates, and to use this model to collect data needed to answer the question. The common student misconception that equilibrium means equal amounts in each container is challenged as students develop an understanding of the principle of equilibrium.

SOURCES: Adapted from ACS (1997); NRC (1996); NSTA (1996).

results. A brief discussion of each is provided in Box 7-3 (for further detail see, American Educational Research Association [AERA]/American Psychological Association [APA]/National Council on Measurement in Education [NCME], 1999; Feldt and Brennan, 1993; Messick, 1993; NRC, 1999b).

Assessment is a critical aspect of effective teaching and improved education (NBPTS, 1994; NCTM, 1995; NRC, 2001a; Shepard, 2000). It is important to note, however, that assessment does not exist in isolation, but is closely linked to curriculum and instruction (Graue, 1993). Thus as emphasized earlier, curriculum, assessment, and instruction should be aligned and integrated with each other, and directed toward the same goal (Kulm, 1990; NCTM, 1995; Shepard, 2000). In advanced mathematics and science, that goal is learning with understanding.

This section reviews design principles for two types of assessments: those that measure student achievement at the end of a program of study, such as AP Physics, and those that are used by teachers to provide feedback to students, guide instruction, and monitor its effects throughout the course of study (see Box 7-4 for a summary of the design principles for assessment). To guide instruction, teachers need assessments that provide specific

BOX 7-3 Reliability, Validity, and Fairness

Reliability generally refers to the stability of results. For example, the term denotes the likelihood that a particular student or group of students would earn the same score if they took the same test again or took a different form of the same test. Reliability also encompasses the consistency with which students perform on different questions or sections of a test that measure the same underlying concept, for example, energy transfer.

Validity addresses what a test is measuring and what meaning can be drawn from the test scores and the actions that follow (Cronbach, 1971). It should be clear that what is being validated is not the test itself, but each inference drawn from the test score for each specific use to which the test results are put. Thus, for each purpose for which the scores are used, there must be evidence to support the appropriateness of inferences that are drawn.

Fairness implies that a test supports the same inferences from person to person and group to group. Thus the test results neither overestimate nor underestimate the knowledge and skills of members of a particular group, for example, females. Fairness also implies that the test measures the same construct across groups.

BOX 7-4 Principles of Assessment for Understanding

The following principles of assessment can be applied both to assessments designed to assist learning (curriculum-embedded or formative assessments) and those designed to evaluate student achievement at the end of a unit of study (summative assessments). Effective assessments for measuring students' learning with understanding in advanced mathematics and science are:

• Based on a model of cognition and learning that is derived from the best available understanding of how students represent knowledge and develop competence in a domain.

• Designed in accordance with accepted practices that include a detailed consideration of the reliability, validity, and fairness of the inferences that will be drawn from the test results (see Box 7-3). This is especially important when the assessment carries high stakes for students, teachers, or schools.

• Aligned with curriculum and instruction that provide the factual content, concepts, processes, and skills the assessment is intended to measure so the three do not work at cross-purposes.

• Designed to include important content and process dimensions of performance in a discipline and to elicit the full range of desired complex cognition, including metacognitive strategies.

• Multifaceted and continuous when used to assist learning by providing multiple opportunities for students to practice their skills and receive feedback about their performance.

• Designed to assess understanding that is both qualitative and quantitative in nature and to provide multiple modalities with which a student can demonstrate learning.

information about what their students are learning and what they do and do not understand. Of primary importance if a test is to support learning is that students be given timely and frequent feedback about the correctness of their understandings; in fact, providing such feedback is one of the most important roles for assessment. There is a large body of literature on how classroom assessment can be designed and used to improve learning and instruction (see for example, Falk 2000; Shepard 2000; Wiggins, 1998; Niyogi, 1995). Concept maps, such as those discussed in Box 6-2 in Chapter 6, are one example of an assessment strategy that can be used to provide timely and informative feedback to students (Edmondson, 2000; Rice, Ryan, and Samson, 1998).

End-of-course tests are too broad and too infrequently administered to provide information that can be used by teachers or students to inform decisions about teaching or learning on a day-to-day basis. The power of such tests lies in their ability to depict students' attainment of larger learning goals and to provide comparative data about how the achievement of one student or one class of students compares with that of others.[3] Ultimately, end-of-course tests are often used to shape teachers' instructional strategies in subsequent years. Thus, the content of the tests should be matched to challenging learning goals and subject matter standards and serve to illustrate what it means to know and learn in each of the disciplines.

Because advanced study programs in the United States are strongly influenced by high-stakes assessment, the committee is especially concerned with how this form of assessment can be structured to facilitate learning with understanding. It is well known that such assessments, even coming after the end of instruction, inevitably have strong anticipatory effects on instruction and learning. Thus if high-stakes assessments fail to elicit complex cognition and other important learning outcomes, such as conceptual understanding and problem solving, they may have negative effects on the teaching and learning that precede them. In designing such assessments, then, both psychometric qualities and learning outcomes should be considered.

If end-of-course tests are to measure important aspects of domain proficiency, test makers need to have a sophisticated understanding of the target domain. They must understand the content and the process dimensions that are valued in the discipline and then design the test to sample among a broad range of these dimensions (Millman and Greene, 1993). Doing so is complicated, however, by the fact that an assessment can only sample from a large universe of desirable learning outcomes and thus can tap but a partial range of desirable cognitions. Consequently, concerns will always arise that a particular assessment does not measure everything it should, and therefore the inferences drawn from it are not valid. Similarly, the selection of tasks for an assessment may be criticized for measuring more than is intended; an example is word problems on mathematics tests that require high levels of reading skill in addition to the mathematics ability that is the target of the assessment. To ensure the validity of inferences drawn from tests, a strong program of validity research must be conducted on all externally designed and administered tests. The higher the stakes of the test, the more critical is this research and the more frequently it must be reviewed (AERA/APA/NCME, 1999).

---

[3]In the case of such tests as the AP and IB examinations, the results are used additionally to guide decisions about college placement and credit.

Test design and construction includes consideration of which forms of complex thinking fairly reflect important aspects of domain proficiency. Assessments that invoke complex thinking should target both general forms of cognition, such as problem solving and inductive reasoning, and forms that are more domain-specific, such as deduction and proof in mathematics or the systematic manipulation of variables in science. Because metacognition is such an important component of experts' performance, both classroom-based and end-of-course assessments should be designed to evaluate students' use of metacognitive strategies (NRC, 2001a).

Given that the goals of curriculum and assessment for advanced study are to promote deep understanding of the underlying concepts and unifying themes of a discipline, effective assessment should reveal whether students truly understand those principles and can apply their knowledge in new situations. The ability to apply a domain principle to an unfamiliar problem, to combine ideas that originally were learned separately, and to use knowledge to construct new products is evidence that robust understanding has been achieved (Hoz, Bowman, and Chacham, 1997; Perkins, 1992).

Meaningful assessment also includes evidence of understanding that is qualitative and quantitative in nature, and provides multiple modalities and contexts for demonstrating learning. Using multiple measures rather than relying on a single test score provides a richer picture of what students know and are able to do. The characteristics of assessments that support learning with understanding are presented in Table 7-3.

TEACHER PROFESSIONAL DEVELOPMENT

One of the most important factors influencing student achievement, if not the most important, is teacher expertise (see Shepard, 2000; National Commission on Mathematics and Science Teaching for the 21st Century, 2000; National Center for Education Statistics [NCES], 2000a; Darling-Hammond, 2000). Thus, the key to implementing the committee's vision of learning with deep conceptual understanding is having highly skilled teachers who can effectively put into practice the strategies suggested earlier in the discussion of instruction for understanding. This observation is particularly true when one is implementing well-structured external programs that build on the regular curriculum already in place at a school. Most teachers, even those regarded as excellent, would have to change their beliefs and practices significantly to teach in a manner consistent with the committee's conceptual framework (Haidar, 1997; Jones et al., 1998; Ryder, Leach, and Driver, 1999; Schoon and Boone, 1998; Southerland and Gess-Newsom, 1999). Such change cannot occur unless teachers are given ample opportunity and support for continual learning through sustained professional development, as

TABLE 7-3   Characteristics of Assessment for Understanding

Less Emphasis on	More Emphasis on
Summative examinations—unit tests and the final examination	Formative assessments—ongoing assessment of teaching and learning
High-stakes tests that impact college entrance and placement and drive unintended program change	Learning assessments that drive program changes in the direction of the goal for advanced studies
Assessments that measure students' ability to recall facts	Assessments that evaluate understanding and reasoning
Assessment as something that is done to students and that provides information to teachers about students	Students participating in developing and analyzing the results of assessments
Private communication of students' ideas and understandings to the teacher/examiner	Classroom discourse including argument and explanation of students' ideas and understandings
Example: During a unit on cell structure, biology students participate in lecture/discussions, complete reading assignments, use electron micrographs to examine cell ultrastructure, and conduct related practical investigations involving microscopic examination of a variety of cell types and scale drawings. At the end of the unit laboratory write-ups are collected, and a unit test is administered.	**Example:** Students participate in varied assessment activities throughout the unit. A brief oral examination tests understanding of a reading assignment. A teacher uses a check sheet during microscope work to assess skills. Laboratory data records are evaluated individually as the students are working on the investigations. A short multiple-choice test on identifying and naming cell parts is given, marked, and discussed. Students prepare a concept map illustrating the relationship between cell structure and function and are asked to explain their thinking to a small group. The group gives feedback, and each student performs a self-assessment of the quality of his or her concept map. The class develops a rubric that will be applied to a unit examination essay question comparing prokaryotic and eukaryotic cell structures. A unit test, of which the essay is one component, is given.
Assessing discrete, easily measured information	Assessing what is most highly valued—deep, well-structured knowledge
Example: A multiple-choice question asking students to select the weak base given a set of chemical formulas.	**Example:** A free-response question involving this scenario: The student is given four 0.10 M solutions labeled A, B, C, D; a conductivity probe; and a pH probe. One of the solutions is a weak acid, one a strong acid, one a weak base, and another a strong base. The student is asked to characterize each solution, describing both the method developed to solve the problem and the results.
Student dependence on using algorithms	Students communicating thought processes
One right or wrong answer	Partial credit for various subtasks and many possible paths to a successful outcome
Unintended uses of results	Clear relationships between the decisions and the data

SOURCES: Adapted from ACS (1997); NRC (1996); NSTA (1996).

well as the opportunity to try out and reflect upon new approaches in the context of their own classrooms (Putnam and Borko, 1997).

Because the standards and frameworks driving reform efforts do not provide specific guidelines for teaching, the implementation of reform visions, including that described in this report, poses a considerable challenge for teachers and school administrators responsible for curriculum and instruction. Moreover, the changes demanded of teachers are not a simple matter of learning new teaching strategies: "Learning to practice in substantially different ways from what one has oneself experienced can occur neither through theoretical imaginings alone nor unguided experience alone" (Darling-Hammond, 1999a, p. 227). Thus the success of current reform efforts—in secondary mathematics and science, as well as other curricular areas—in fostering learning with understanding depends on creating opportunities for teachers' continual learning and providing sufficient professional development resources to exploit these opportunities (Darling-Hammond, 1996, 1999b; Sykes, 1996).

Unfortunately, current professional development for U.S. teachers can be described only as inadequate:

> Sadly and short-sightedly, however, professional development is too often treated not as a necessity but as a luxury item on the school budget. Many people erroneously believe that teachers are not working unless they are standing in front of a classroom. In fact, preparation time, individual study time, as well as time for peer contact and joint lesson planning, are vital sources of both competence and nourishment for all teachers. But teachers are granted precious little time for any of these activities. . . . High quality professional development ought to be the lifeblood of American teaching; instead, it is used only to provide the occasional transfusion. (National Commission on Mathematics and Science Teaching for the 21st Century, 2000, p. 27)

> Nothing has promised so much and been so frustratingly wasteful as the thousands of workshops and conferences that led to no significant change in practice when teachers returned to their classrooms. (Fullan, 1991, p. 315)

To teach advanced mathematics or science well, teachers need to know their subjects deeply and extensively, know their students and understand how they learn, and know the pedagogical techniques specific to their subjects. These three domains of professional knowledge form the core content of professional development for teachers (NCTM, 2000; Schulman, 1986). Teachers use this knowledge to listen carefully to students and examine their work in order to identify understandings and misunderstandings and frame appropriate learning activities for each student (NCTM, 1991; NRC, 1996). Box 7-5 summarizes the design principles for professional development of teachers.

BOX 7-5 Principles of Effective Professional Development

Effective professional development for teachers of advanced study in science and mathematics:

- Focuses on the development of teachers' subject matter knowledge, knowledge of students, and subject-specific pedagogical knowledge.
    - Emphasizes deep conceptual understanding of content and discipline-based methods of inquiry.
    - Provides multiple perspectives on students as learners.
    - Develops teachers' subject-specific pedagogical knowledge.
- Treats teachers as active learners who construct their own understandings by building on their existing knowledge and beliefs.
- Is grounded in situations of practice.
- Takes place in professional communities where teachers have the opportunity to discuss ideas and practices with colleagues.
- Uses with teachers' instructional strategies and assessment practices that teachers are expected to use with students.
    - Is most effective when teachers take an active role.
    - Is an ongoing, long-term effort spanning teachers' professional lives.

Professional development should emphasize more than the fundamental facts, concepts, and procedures of a discipline. It also should help teachers understand the particular methods of inquiry in their discipline, know discipline-specific ways to reason and communicate, and understand the relationships of the discipline to other school subjects and to societal issues (NCTM, 1991; NRC, 1996).

Professional development should also help teachers understand students as learners by providing opportunities to examine students' thinking about mathematics and science. Excellent professional development addresses such issues as how students think and behave, what they already know and believe, and what they find interesting. Issues of race, gender, age, and socioeconomic background also are germane, as is an understanding of students' common preconceptions and misconceptions. In addition, teachers should expect to receive a strong foundation of pedagogical content knowledge from effective professional development. Such knowledge might include instructional and classroom organization strategies, materials and resources (including technology), alternative ways to represent concepts and strategies or assess student understanding, and methods of fostering classroom discourse and communication.

High-quality professional development treats teachers as teachers should treat their students, including acknowledging that learning is an active process wherein learners construct new understandings based on what they already know and believe. There is considerable evidence that existing knowledge and beliefs play an important role in how teachers learn to teach, how they teach, and how they think about teaching in new ways (Cohen and Ball, 1990; Prawat, 1992; Putnam and Borko, 1997). If professional development is to support meaningful change in teaching and teachers, it must address teachers' existing knowledge and beliefs, just as teachers are expected to address prior knowledge in their students in order to promote learning with understanding. What teachers know and believe will influence their interpretation and enactment of new ideas for teaching.

Moreover, professional development instructors are role models who contribute to teachers' evolving visions of what and how to teach. Although they ought to model the kinds of practices they expect teachers to use in their own classrooms, all too often teacher educators, like K–12 educators, revert to what they know best—the ways they were taught themselves. The result is professional development activities that promote traditional views of schooling and uninspired, didactic teaching methods.

Because knowledge is integrally connected with the contexts in which it is acquired and used, teacher learning ought to be situated in practice. There are numerous ways to accomplish this, with advantages for different components of teacher learning (Putnam and Borko, 1997). One approach is to conduct professional development at the schools—and largely in the classrooms—where participants teach. Doing so enables the teacher and staff developer to work together to interpret classroom events in light of various ideas about teaching, learning, and subject matter. A second approach is to have teachers bring experiences from their classrooms, such as samples of students' work or videotapes of classroom activities, to workshops. Away from the classroom, teachers have opportunities to develop a reflective perspective on teaching by considering different points of view on their own teaching practice and that of others. Other activities, such as detailed study of the discipline, may best occur away from the classroom. Settings such as summer workshops free teachers from the daily demands of having to think about the immediate needs of their students and classrooms.

A combination of experiences situated in different settings may be the most powerful way to foster meaningful change in teachers' thinking and practice (Putnam and Borko, 1997). The recommendations of the National Commission on Mathematics and Science Teaching for the 21st Century (2000) provide one model for multifaceted professional development. Central to the commission's recommendations are summer institutes designed to address pressing needs, such as enhancing teachers' subject matter knowledge, introducing new teaching methods, and integrating technology into teaching. Also recommended are ongoing inquiry groups. Teachers need to form learning communities in which they can explore problems of practice that occur during the school year and engage in continuing discussion to enrich their knowledge of subject matter, students, and teaching.

Professional development, as characterized here, typically occurs in professional communities, not in isolation. This model is consistent with a view of cognition as developing within a social context that provides the language, concepts, and modes of thought with which people make sense of the world. If teachers are to be successful in developing new practices, they need opportunities to participate in, as McLaughlin and Talbert (1993, p. 15) put it, "a professional community that discusses new teacher materials and strategies and that supports the risk taking and struggle entailed in transforming practice." Through their participation in such professional communities, as well as through other means of communication, such as books, professional journals, and electronic networks, teachers come to understand and think in ways that are common to those communities while also helping the thinking of the community to develop and change.

Because learning is a developmental process that takes time and hard work, teachers' professional development needs to continue throughout their careers, and teachers need to accept responsibility for their own learning and growth. If teachers view themselves as agents of change, responsible for improving teaching and learning in their schools, they may be more likely to take advantage of high-quality professional development. Professional development, in turn, should support and encourage teachers in accepting such responsibilities.

In sum, tomorrow's students will have very different needs from those of today as a result of new knowledge in the various disciplines, new technologies, and new workplace demands. To meet those needs, teachers must constantly revise their practice and reflect on teaching and learning. To this end, teachers need professional development that provides opportunities for them to expand their knowledge, to experiment with new ideas about teaching and learning, to receive feedback about their teaching, and to work with others to effect positive changes in mathematics and science education (NCTM, 1991; NRC, 1996; Putnam and Borko, 1997). Lifelong learning experiences can provide teachers with the opportunity to continually consider and contribute to the evolving knowledge base of teaching and learning (NRC, 1996). Table 7-4 summarizes the emphases of professional development programs that promote understanding.

TABLE 7-4   Characteristics of Effective Teacher Professional Development

Less Emphasis on	More Emphasis on
Sporadic learning opportunities	Continuous ongoing, connected learning experiences
Transmission of knowledge and skills by lecture	Inquiry into teaching and learning
Isolation of teachers, classrooms, and disciplines	Interdisciplinary inquiry that extends beyond the classroom
Separation of science/mathematics content knowledge and teaching knowledge	Discipline-specific pedagogy
Separation of theory and practice	Integration of theory and practice in school settings
Individual learning, as teachers of an advanced subject are physically and temporally isolated from other teachers of the same advanced subject	Collegial and collaborative learning in a professional community and time for teachers to interact during the school day and year
Teacher as technician and consumer of knowledge	Teacher as reflective practitioner and producer of knowledge
Teacher as target of change	Teacher as source and facilitator of change
Reliance on external or internal expertise only	Mix of internal and external expertise
Fragmented, one-shot workshops	Long-term, coherent plans incorporating 1- to 2-week summer institutes with follow-up during the school year

SOURCES: Adapted from ACS (1997); NRC (1996); NSTA (1996).

FROM FRAMEWORK TO ADVANCED STUDY PROGRAMS

The development of educational programs that foster learning with conceptual understanding, as outlined in this chapter, could be seen as idealization that cannot be achieved in practice; the committee sees it as an imperative. The changes in education proposed here represent a significant departure from current practice in most schools and from most of the preparation and professional development that teachers and school administrators have received. Implementing such changes will not require reforming, but rather transforming the entire social and institutional context for learning, including school culture, leadership practices, and pedagogical practice. The more aligned the institutional and social context for learning is with the committee's conceptual framework for analyzing and designing advanced study, the more likely it is that the innovations we advocate will be sustained over time and enhance student achievement.

The committee has come to a sobering conclusion: given what is now known about human learning, transformation of advanced study is imperative. Accordingly, the committee presents in this report a framework and a set of guidelines for assessing and designing advanced study. This framework was constructed on the basis of current knowledge about how people learn and about the nature of subject matter expertise. Advanced study programs that are aligned with this framework and the attendant principles will foster deep, robust conceptual understanding. They also will make such deep learning accessible to a broader range of students, because the principles of learning and of program design set forth here (1) recognize multiple ways of thinking and (2) support a wide range of perspectives and practices in the school curriculum. The complex, authentic, multidimensional learning opportunities that could be designed following the committee's model could make it possible for all children to discover and use their unique strengths to engage in learning at a deep conceptual level.

8

Analysis of the AP and IB Programs Based on Learning Research

In this chapter, what is known about how people learn, especially the principles of learning presented in Chapter 6, is used as a lens for analyzing and assessing the Advanced Placement (AP) and International Baccalaureate (IB) programs in mathematics and science. In Chapter 9, this analysis is extended with respect to the design principles of curriculum, instruction, assessment, and professional development presented in Chapter 7. The analysis highlights some major strengths and shortcomings in the programs as currently implemented in U.S. high schools and indicates directions for change that would help bring the program elements into closer alignment with the principles of learning set forth in Chapter 6 and with the goals of advanced study. Although the analysis is often critical, the committee recognizes that these advanced programs challenge some of the nation's most talented and highly motivated students and some of its most capable and creative high school teachers to accomplish more than is generally expected of a high school education. Both programs have provided models of high expectations for students and of recognized and valued external assessments of student achievement. Regular and even honors courses are often not sufficiently challenging for many of the best students in the sciences and mathematics.

The AP and IB programs are dynamic and were moving toward significant change even as the present study was being conducted, as exemplified by the report of the Commission on the Future of the Advanced Placement Program (CFAPP) (2001) and the revision of the IB Experimental Sciences curriculum, discussed in Chapters 3 and 4, respectively. Both programs are being adapted to serve broader purposes than those for which they were originally designed. Sometimes, however, the programs are misused through no fault of their developers, as discussed in Chapter 10.

Another set of caveats is in order. Neither the College Board nor the International Baccalaureate Organisation (IBO) articulates the principles of learning on which its program is based. This is understandable, as both programs were created well before the nature of human cognition and learning became the focus of intensive research or the potential for using this research to inform the design of educational programs was emphasized. Nonetheless, now that research is providing a clearer picture of how people learn, it is important to use this information to consider how to improve the programs' courses, assessments, and professional development activities.

Systematic information is lacking about the AP and IB programs as they are actually implemented in U.S. high schools, including the instructional strategies used in individual classrooms, the structure of the syllabi in different schools, the quantity and quality of the facilities available, the preparation of teachers who teach the courses, and the ways in which students are prepared prior to advanced study.[1] What is known, however, is that there is wide variation among teachers and schools. Yet data on the nature of this variation and its effect on student learning are scant, as is information about the cognitive processes elicited by the AP and IB assessments. Because important data about the programs have not yet been published by either the programs or independent researchers, the committee focused its analysis on what the programs say they do, using available program materials such as course guides, released examinations, teacher manuals, program goals and mission statements. and expert testimony from program officials and experienced AP and IB teachers.[2]

The discussion in this chapter is organized around the seven principles of learning set forth in Chapter 6 and is based on the evidence noted above, as well as the findings of the four panels that conducted in-depth appraisals of the AP and IB programs in mathematics, biology, chemistry, and physics for this study.[3] The analysis is focused on determining the extent to which the AP and IB curricula in science and mathematics and the associated instruction and assessments are aligned with the principles of learning and goals for advanced study outlined in previous chapters. This analysis (and that of Chapters 9 and 10) serves as the foundation for the recommendations offered in Chapter 11 for improving advanced study in general and the AP and IB programs in particular. In presenting these analyses, we emphasize that AP and IB are different programs designed for different purposes, and

---

[1]The College Board is beginning to undertake some new research related to how the AP courses are implemented in schools. See www.collegeboard.org/ap/research/index.html (November 28, 2001). The IBO has also established a research committee to oversee studies on the nature of learning in IB classrooms. See www.ibo.org (February 8, 2002).

[2]The College Board and the IBO provided the committee with a considerable range of program materials, such as mission statements; course outlines; teacher guides; sample syllabi; released examinations; scoring rubrics; and research results from studies conducted under the auspices of their researchers, as well as by independent researchers.

[3]A summary of the panels' findings and recommendations is given in Appendix A; and the full panel reports are available online at www.nap.edu/catalog/10129.html.

therefore that findings related to one program do not necessarily apply to the other.

PRINCIPLED CONCEPTUAL KNOWLEDGE

A vital goal of advanced study is to help students progress from novice understanding toward deeper understanding of the fundamental content and unifying concepts of a discipline and toward greater expertise in the processes of inquiry and problem solving. Because they lack an organizing structure, novices tend to approach problems by seeking formulas or algorithms they have used in the past, by focusing on surface features of the problems, or by relying on their intuitions and preconceptions. Experts, on the other hand, think in terms of core concepts and underlying principles in approaching and solving problems. The evidence gathered for this report indicates that, in constructing their programs, AP and IB do not make adequate use of what is known about differences in the ways in which experts and novices structure knowledge. The committee's findings in this area are based on several key observations about the programs.

Breadth Versus Depth

According to the mathematics panel, the breadth of coverage in AP Calculus is appropriate. The curriculum for the IB Mathematical Methods Standard Level (SL) and Mathematics Higher Level (HL) courses, however, encompasses an introduction to elementary calculus (similar to the AP program's AB-level calculus course) and additional areas of study that the teacher selects from among available options. The small number of hours suggested for study of each topic (20 hours for Mathematical Methods SL and 50 hours for Mathematics HL according to the IBO's 1998 course descriptions) leads to the concern that students study each topic only at a procedural level.

The inclusion of too much content is a major issue in the sciences, especially the AP sciences. The 2-year format of the IB HL science courses makes the issue of breadth of content coverage less of a concern for these courses. However, the 1-year IB SL science courses suffer from some of the same shortcomings as the AP science courses in this regard.

The content that is expected to be taught and ultimately assessed in the final examinations for many of the AP and IB HL science courses is quite broad. According to the findings of the biology, physics, and chemistry panels, most teachers, especially AP teachers, find they have insufficient time for more than superficial coverage of some topics before moving on to others. These three science panels are unanimous in expressing their concern that, in an effort to prepare students for an examination by covering all of the topics on the course outline, teachers may place undue emphasis on the presentation and memorization of disconnected facts.

In the science disciplines, both AP and IB materials emphasize concepts, key ideas, and unifying themes. However, the biology, chemistry, and physics panels emphasize that this commitment is largely unrealized in the programs' assessments. Although the science panels find that the examinations do not adequately assess depth of conceptual understanding and place disproportionate emphasis on recall, the panels are encouraged by the fact that the College Board is moving toward making improvements in this area. The 2002–2003 AP biology course description states, "Questions on future AP Biology Examinations can be expected to test students' ability to explain, analyze, and interpret biological processes and phenomena more than their ability to recall specific facts" (College Entrance Examination Board [CEEB] 2001a, p. 7). Although the IB examinations sample the range of assessment statements included in the syllabus for each course, the science panels cite as weaknesses what they consider to be undue emphasis on factual knowledge and failure to target misconceptions and adequately measure conceptual understanding.

In their review of the influence of external tests on the curricula provided in the schools of several nations, Madaus and Airasian (1978) conclude that "most studies have found that the proportion of instructional time spent on various objectives was seldom higher than the predicted likelihood of their occurrence on the external exam" (p. 21). Since both AP and IB courses are designed to prepare students for high-stakes, end-of-course assessments, an instructional focus on "big ideas" will likely remain unrealized until these assessments focus on key concepts in each domain, as has occurred to a considerable extent in AP calculus.

When an advanced course occupies only a single year, as in the AP program, the broad scope of the curriculum and the demands of the assessments can create a conflict between two goals: providing the broad base of content knowledge that is perceived to be necessary for the exam, and promoting conceptual understanding that provides the framework for future learning and application of knowledge. Program developers can continue to address this issue by devising focused curricula and by working to equip teachers to make judgments that support depth of understanding.

Organizing Complex Content

A second observation of the committee and the panels is that the topic outlines for AP and IB science courses sometimes provide insufficient guidance to teachers about how to organize the enormous amount of recommended content around important central ideas. The course objectives are not uniformly structured to reflect the organizing themes of the discipline; each objective is presented in isolation, rather than as part of a larger network. Yet it is precisely this network—the connections among objectives—that is important (National Research Council [NRC], 2000b).

In biology, for example, although the AP course description explicitly addresses principles and themes, teachers are merely given a brief, open-ended framework for conceptual knowledge using themes that cut across different topics and must organize the content themselves. The committee is concerned that students, given the sheer volume of material with which they are confronted in a typical AP biology course, may be unable to use the organizing themes effectively, even when they know what those themes are. Being able to state a theme or memorize a statement is a far cry from understanding it.

The IB Biology Guide, like the guide for all of the IB experimental sciences, identifies "essential principles of the subject" that are common to both the SL and HL courses in a discipline, but the assessment statements used to define what should be taught are grouped by topic rather than thematically. Here also teachers are expected to organize and integrate the material on their own. While it is important not to specify course designs too rigidly, further guidance on organizing the recommended content might produce more consistent results—especially when teachers are undergoing changes in their practice.

In contrast, in the opinion of the mathematics panel, the topics in the AP calculus syllabi are appropriate and well connected. In its current formulation, AP calculus pays careful attention to the central concept of function and to connecting the common ways (numerical, graphical, analytical, and verbal) of representing functions. There is likewise careful attention to developing the main concepts of differentiation and integration, including several interpretations of and applications for each.

Examinations and Conceptual Learning

The AP and IB examinations could be improved if they required students to demonstrate a deeper level of conceptual understanding to earn passing grades. Two of the panels (calculus and chemistry) attribute this problem, of limited depth, at least for AP, in part to the relatively predictable nature of many items on the respective examinations. This characteristic allows or even encourages teachers to instruct students on how to answer particular types of questions, a practice that might not occur if tests consisted of widely varied items whose solutions required the integrated application of key principles.

For example, the mathematics panel is concerned that teachers may be encouraged to focus on teaching their students specific problem types instead of engaging them in modeling and problem-solving activities that would lead to greater understanding of the underlying concepts of the subject. As a result, students could compute a right answer in a limited range of situations but be unable to explain why their solution is correct. Students who do not understand the concepts underlying procedures will have difficulty using mathematics to solve unexpected problems or applying their knowledge in other disciplines, such as physics or economics, or in real-world settings.

The mathematics panel notes that the AP examination has improved under the new syllabus. The effort to promote conceptual understanding by asking nonstandard questions and requiring verbal explanations is an excellent step in the right direction. The fact that there is now a wider variety of applications of integration (and not from a prescribed list) encourages students to think about the meaning of an integral. The panel recognizes and applauds the fact that that the College Board is taking such steps to encourage more modeling activities (applications) and to make its tests less predictable (see, for example, CEEB, 2001b). The mathematics panel notes that many problems on the IB mathematics examinations could also be solved procedurally if students were taught to do so or if they had solved enough practice problems. The panel concludes, however, that there is such a broad range of topics that it would be difficult for students to do well on the examination as a whole without understanding the underlying concepts. Indeed, the panel's analysis of the IB examinations suggests that considerable conceptual understanding is required for students to do well. It appears, however, that opportunities are missed throughout the exam to connect procedural knowledge with conceptual knowledge; this emphasis on procedural knowledge could lead to superficial instruction in IB classrooms.

The science panels call for final assessments that are better tests of conceptual understanding, with less emphasis on students' ability to remember discrete facts, formulas, and procedures. The inclusion of novel tasks that require the application of key principles could encourage teachers to focus on students' development of conceptual understanding and ability to make interdisciplinary connections. The use of a wider range of assessment strategies also might encourage effective instruction (Rice, Ryan, and Samson, 1998). The science panels note that both AP and IB are taking positive steps in this direction. For example, some AP science examinations ask students to design experiments and to demonstrate their solutions to problems. Doing well on this task requires that students have significant prior experience with designing experiments to solve a variety of problems. Teachers thus have an excellent incentive to engage students more regularly in these types of activities.

PRIOR KNOWLEDGE

Research on cognition has strongly confirmed the importance of prior knowledge for all aspects of thinking and learning. One reason prior knowledge is important is almost self-evident: new knowledge is built on what learners already know. Thus before entering AP or IB courses, students need a solid knowledge base.[4] To focus the curriculum and instruction appropriately (a critical factor in maintaining student motivation, as well as in developing understanding), teachers need a clear idea of the depth of knowledge, skills, and experiences their students bring to the classroom.

Prerequisites

Both the AP and IB programs provide fairly detailed information about the necessary prerequisite knowledge and skills in mathematics.[5] However, neither the College Board nor the IBO clearly specifies the competencies students must master in advance in the sciences. In both mathematics and the sciences, the College Board suggests (but does not require) that students complete a previous course or combination of courses before enrolling in AP sciences. Schools are free to adhere to these suggestions or not. Statements about the need for such courses are of limited value for several reasons. First, similarly titled courses vary widely in content and rigor, so students may not have the necessary background even if they follow this advice. Second, some students acquire the knowledge and skills necessary for success through independent study or related experience, not through traditional course taking. Finally, even when prerequisites are clearly specified, it may be difficult to ensure that students have met them.

The IBO does not specify any prerequisites for the experimental sciences. IB HL courses are taught over 2 years. Therefore, the IBO does not believe it necessary to specify prerequisite courses for the experimental sciences, assuming that a 2-year course of study provides ample opportunity for students to both build a solid foundation in the discipline and pursue advanced work. However, these courses also are built on prior knowledge to some extent, and this is worth specifying.

Identifying the prerequisite student knowledge and skills needed for success in each course is of considerable importance to schools in providing adequate preparatory experiences (tools for gauging student mastery of these skills would also be useful). A clear articulation of the body of necessary

---

[4]Interestingly, it has been shown that good science instruction in grades 1 and 2 can strongly influence learning throughout the high school years (Novak and Musonda, 1991; Sneider and Ohadi, 1998).

[5]The IBO calls these skills "presumed knowledge."

prior knowledge could help teachers and counselors advise students about their readiness to take specific AP or IB courses, and appropriate assessments could help them identify areas of weakness that should be addressed before advanced study begins. The programs attempt to provide this information to varying degrees. However, identifying the full range of prerequisite content knowledge, conceptual understanding, and skills is a complex task requiring the combined efforts of experts from the science disciplines, cognitive psychologists, master teachers, and staff from the advanced study programs. The committee believes that the benefits for student learning are well worth the effort. At the same time, while this task is important, it is also essential that prerequisites not become barriers to participation for students from particular ethnic or socioeconomic groups (see Chapters 2 and 10, this volume).

An alternative to the use of more testing to measure readiness for advanced study might be to adopt a developmental approach, such as that devised by the Australian Council for Educational Research. Central to this approach are models of learning known as progress maps, which provide a sequential description of skills and knowledge indicating both the goal and the steps necessary to achieve it. Readiness for AP or IB courses could be calibrated with a position on such a map (as cited in NRC, 2001a, p. 181). Use of such an approach also might be beneficial for students seeking to prepare themselves for advanced work through independent study.[6]

The American Association for the Advancement of Science's (AAAS) Project 2061 program for science literacy recently produced an atlas of learning maps that indicate the interrelationships among science concepts. Although limited in scope at present, these maps provide a useful set of guidelines for building upon science concepts as students advance through school (AAAS, 2000). Adapting aspects of these maps could assist experts in developing appropriate measures of prior knowledge and readiness for advanced study.

Coordination of Courses

The fact that students need to acquire certain prerequisite knowledge and skills before participating in advanced study implies that greater attention should be paid to across-grade curricular and instructional planning. If advanced study is viewed as an extension of the regular curriculum, it follows that students' success in such programs depends on knowledge and skills acquired much earlier.

---

[6]To date, progress maps have been developed primarily for elementary and middle school mathematics and science. If they are to be useful for the purpose proposed here, teams of experts will be required for their development. Examples of progress maps can be found at www.acer.org/.

For example, the study of calculus logically builds on foundational knowledge acquired in previous courses in mathematics. Yet the mathematics panel points out that there are not enough checks in the system to ensure that students have mastered the algebra, trigonometry, and precalculus concepts and skills necessary for success in calculus and in courses beyond. The performance of many AP calculus students is undermined by the fact that they do not learn precalculus thoroughly, or learn adequately how to solve problems and think mathematically. This situation is not a defect of the AP calculus course per se, but of the system in which it is embedded.

An example of prior foundational knowledge is the periodicity of trigonometric functions, such as sine and cosine. While these are not calculus concepts, an understanding of these functions is needed in the study of calculus. If these ideas are learned poorly or not at all in previous coursework, the calculus teacher must devote valuable instructional time to their development, or some students will experience difficulty.

The science panels argue that a syllabus for a year-long advanced course that also serves as an introduction to the discipline allows too little time for students to develop the depth of conceptual understanding that should be the fundamental goal of advanced science courses. Thus they unanimously recommend that students study the biology, chemistry, or physics that is suggested for grades 9–12 in the *National Science Education Standards* (NRC, 1996) before enrolling in advanced high school courses in those disciplines.[7] At the same time, to ensure that students who complete introductory courses do not face excessive redundancy in subsequent courses requires active coordination among teachers at different grade levels.

Implications of Prior Knowledge for Instruction

Because prior knowledge is so important to students' ability to understand new material, care must be taken to structure advanced courses around a coherent curriculum. That is, the presentation of topics must be sequenced so that the concepts and processes imparted to students gradually become more complex (AAAS, 2000). Neither the AP course descriptions (see for example, CEEB, 2001b, p. 8) nor the more detailed IB program guides provide guidance on sequencing concepts or topics. In fact, the IB Chemistry Guide notes that the order in which topics are presented on the course outlines does not constitute a recommended sequence: "It is up to the individual teachers to decide on an arrangement which suits their circumstances"

---

[7] All of the panels agree that there are exceptions to this general rule. For example, particularly precocious students or those who have had significant experiences outside of the classroom related to the discipline might be able to skip the first course.

(IBO, 2001b, p. 35).[8] Similar statements are included in IB program guides for mathematics, biology, and physics (IBO, 2001a, p. 5; IBO, 2001c, p. 9). This flexibility can be a strength in the hands of good teachers because they can adjust their activities in response to what their students understand. On the other hand, less-experienced AP or IB teachers may try to follow college textbooks too closely, and according to the chemistry panel, their doing so could contribute to the problem of excessive breadth.

Misconceptions and Formative Assessment

One important subset of prior knowledge involves misconceptions and naive theories, as discussed in Chapter 6. Even well-performing students often retain and use deeply flawed prior beliefs. The AP and IB programs could address this problem in several ways. First, using emerging research on student misconceptions, they could include in their course guides information about typical misconceptions that students may already harbor or that may arise during study of each of the topics included in the courses. There is considerable research and detailed description of the common types of misconceptions held by learners in mathematics and physics (see for example, Driver, Squires, Rushworth and Wood-Robinson; 1994; Gabel, 1994; Minstrell, 2000b). Information might be provided in the teachers' guides about these common misconceptions, as well as strategies that could be used to address them. Second, a focus on detecting and addressing common misconceptions in content areas could be built into professional development programs. Third, items could be included in the AP and IB final assessments that would reveal common misconceptions, thus focusing teachers on the goal of identifying and remediating misconceptions that persist even after instruction. While the AP physics examination now does this to some extent, the mathematics panel notes that AP calculus examinations miss opportunities to include questions that address common student misconceptions, such as those that arise in attempting to understand the derivative, slope fields, and functions.

One effective strategy for identifying student misconceptions, especially those that endure after instruction, is the use of curriculum-embedded (formative) assessment, which enables teachers and students to set intermediate goals for learning and to select appropriate materials and tasks for pursuing those goals. Formative assessment can also provide information about students' preconceptions and misconceptions, thereby informing subsequent instructional choices (see, for example, Kozma and Russell, 1997; Mestre, 1994; Minstrell, 2000a; NRC, 2001a). The College Board and the IBO could

---

[8]Similar statements are found in AP course guides and teacher's guides.

develop or help teachers develop the tools needed for this purpose. Although some excellent teachers apply this strategy already, it probably cannot be presumed that most do so.

The IBO helps teachers integrate formative assessments of students' practical (laboratory) work and portfolios into instruction on an ongoing basis. However, it does not provide guidance on the development or structure of other forms of ongoing assessment. The AP program provides no explicit guidance on the structure or development of classroom-based assessments, although course guides and teachers' guides mention the usefulness of such measures. The panel's appraisal of professional development materials provided by the AP and IB programs indicates that classroom assessment receives limited attention.

Lacking appropriate interim assessments, many teachers use previously released final examination questions throughout the school year to measure student achievement. This strategy may be useful for predicting students' performance on the AP or IB examinations or providing practice with the test format and item types, but it is of little use as a tool for identifying misconceptions or appraising students' conceptual understanding because the test items are not designed for this purpose. AP and IB teachers also would benefit from professional development opportunities directed toward improving their knowledge of common misconceptions and assisting them with the development of activities or formative assessments that could be used to detect and address those misconceptions. Experienced teachers of advanced study would be needed to staff such workshops.

METACOGNITION

Advanced study courses present a significant opportunity for providing students with instruction in metacognition, or self-monitoring of learning (Mintzes, Wandersee, and Novak, 2000). Research has shown that strong metacognitive skills are characteristic of experts in any field, as well as of effective school-age learners, and that they are developed most effectively in the context of a discipline. For example, White and Frederickson (1998) demonstrate that teaching students metacognitive strategies in physics improves their understandings of the concepts of that discipline. Similarly, Schoenfeld (1983, 1984, 1991) shows that a metacognitive approach to instruction improves students' heuristic methods for mathematical problem solving.

Minimally, AP and IB course materials should recognize proficiency in metacognition as a goal of advanced study. Teachers should elicit metacognitive activity in classroom discourse by posing questions and modeling reasoning. In addition, suitable opportunities for students to demonstrate metacognitive strategies should be built into curricular materials and assessments. The goal should be to help students become proficient in monitoring their own thinking and learning.

Although the AP course outlines and professional development programs for mathematics and science teachers currently pay little explicit attention to metacognition, the teachers' guides suggest that teachers help students develop skills that are important components of metacognitive strategies. For example, according to the teacher's guide for AP chemistry (Mullins, 1994, p. 8), "It would be unreasonable to expect that all AP students come into the class with strong analytical and critical thinking skills; therefore the AP teacher must strive to strengthen these skills within the students. A process of problem solving should be continually modeled and reinforced." Likewise, the teacher's guide for AP calculus (Kennedy, 1997, p. 48) suggests that "teacher modeling of questioning and exploration, multiple approaches to problem solving, correct use of terminology, clarity of work, and openness to the ideas of others are all essential." The committee views these suggestions as positive steps toward addressing the important role of metacognition. However, the statements in the teacher's guides are isolated, and the committee believes the importance of metacognition currently is substantially underrepresented in both the teacher's guides and the types of questions students encounter on the final AP examinations in science. As is the case for principled conceptual knowledge, an instructional emphasis on metacognition will not be realized until that emphasis is reflected in the assessments.

The committee views as promising the fact that in future AP calculus examinations, students will be required to justify and explain their solutions to all calculator problems. Scoring rubrics will consider both the correctness of the solution and whether the reasons for using the selected procedures are justified. Given the strong influence of the assessments on the content and structure of curriculum and instruction, it is likely that AP calculus teachers will provide frequent opportunities for students to make their thinking visible. The committee commends the AP calculus development committee for its attention to this important principle of learning and encourages other AP development committees to follow suit.

The IB program also provides significant opportunities for students to learn and develop metacognitive skills. As discussed in Chapter 4, the IB Theory of Knowledge course[9] is designed to provide students with knowledge about cognitive processes and strategies, practice in using those strategies, and opportunities to evaluate the outcomes of their efforts. "It encour-

---

[9]This course is a requirement for students seeking an IB Diploma (see Chapter 4, this volume, for other requirements).

ages students to become aware of themselves as thinkers, to become aware of the complexity of knowledge, and to recognize the need to act responsibly in an increasingly interconnected world" (IBO, 2000b, p. 3).

DIFFERENCES AMONG LEARNERS

The existence of differences among learners and the extraordinary complexity of such differences have implications for how educational programs are structured, how students are taught, and how learning is assessed. They are also relevant to teacher professional development.

Research on how students differ in knowledge representation and expression is difficult work that is not yet complete. Nonetheless, programs such as AP and IB can begin to address student variations by building corresponding variability into their curricula and assessments and by addressing learner differences as part of their professional development opportunities for teachers. While variety will not ensure a perfect match of instruction or curriculum to the preferences or abilities of each student, it will likely provide many more students with opportunities to learn in ways best suited to their strengths, at least some of the time.

AP or IB teachers who creatively mix pedagogical approaches with sensitivity to the profile of learners in particular classes are likely to reach a broad range of students with varying learning modes and may motivate more students as well. The IB program guides for the experimental sciences recognize the importance of this tenet by indicating that there is no single best approach to teaching IB courses and that teachers should provide a variety of ways of acquiring information that can be accepted or rejected by each student, allowing different routes through the material (IBO, 2001a, 2001b, 2001c, p. 11). A combination of approaches is also likely to result in students learning the same concepts in multiple ways, a strategy that is conducive to building deep understanding. An example of such a strategy is the current "rule of four" emphasis in calculus, which suggests that students, with the help of their teachers, see the links among four representations of mathematics: numerical, graphical, symbolic, and verbal.

Using Differences Among Learners in Assessment

As discussed in Chapter 6, students with different learning styles may need different ways to demonstrate their knowledge and skills. For example, some students work well under pressure, while the performance of others is significantly diminished by time constraints. Some students express themselves well in writing, while others do not. Using one form of assessment will work to the advantage of some students and to the disadvantage of others. Research (see, for example, Linn, 2000; Mintzes et al., 2000; NRC, 2001a) also indicates that the use of different measures administered over a period of time will offer a more accurate picture of what students know than any single measure can provide (Linn and Hsi, 1999). Using information gathered from multiple sources shows respect for the diversity among learners.

The internal assessment that is part of all of the IB experimental science courses and the portfolio that is part of the IB mathematics courses are examples of how large-scale assessment can incorporate the results of different types of measures into a final evaluation of student achievement. However, the scores earned on the internal assessment and the portfolio are not reported separately, but are combined with scores earned on the written final examination and contribute only a fraction of the student's total score. Therefore, some information is lost that might be useful in providing a fuller picture of students' capabilities.

The AP reporting levels of 1 to 5 do not differentiate well among students at higher levels of achievement. A score of 5 putatively represents a commendable level of proficiency, but it fails to capture just how proficient a student is or what a student knows qualitatively. At all levels of achievement on the AP assessments, the score by itself does not speak to what students actually understand. For example, a student who earns a 3 on an AP biology examination might know a great deal about a few topics or less about many things. A student who earns a score of 1 might either know little or have failed to make an effort on the examination. The physics panel addresses this issue at length, indicating that two students who earn scores of 5 can have vastly different levels of understanding. Scores on the 2000 AP Physics B examination that result in a 5 range from 104 to 180. The panel states unequivocally that students at the higher end of the score range are far more competent than those at the lower end. Institutions receiving student scores could benefit from information that reflects this difference. The committee notes that even students who achieve a score of 5 could have serious gaps or inconsistencies in their understanding, and these gaps ought to be revealed as well.

With some planning and effort, the College Board could do much better in assigning qualitative meaning to summary scores.[10] One possibility is that a numerical summary of performance—say a score of 4—could be linked to a description of what students who earn that score are likely to understand.

---

[10]The committee notes that the reporting structure of an assessment cannot be modified without considering whether the test can support the inferences that will be drawn from the reported scores. If they cannot, changes may have to be made in the test itself. This requires long-range planning and changes that must be made at the test development stage.

It also may be possible to review the specific responses of examinees and evaluate them for gaps in understanding, or to provide subscores for specific skill and knowledge areas. Currently, most AP examinations do not include enough items targeting the same concept or skill to allow development of a meaningful subscore for individuals.[11] An exception is the AP Calculus BC exam, which already provides a useful subscore indicating proficiency on the AB section of the material. To develop useful subscores on other exams, the assessments might have to cover less material more deeply or include more items. Reducing the breadth of material covered on the assessments could potentially accomplish two important goals: providing more meaningful and useful information about student performance, and reducing the breadth of content teachers are expected to cover and students are expected to learn in AP classes.

MOTIVATION

Learners' academic motivation influences their choices about which tasks to undertake, the persistence with which they pursue these tasks, the level of effort they expend, and their thoughts about the usefulness of the tasks and their performance on them. Eccles and colleagues (Eccles, Wigfield, and Schiefele, 1998) organized research about motivation into three broad questions students might ask themselves when confronted with a new task: Can I do this task? Do I want to do this task and why? What do I have to do to succeed on this task? These questions are used below to frame an analysis of the ways in which the AP and IB programs help or impede students in developing and maintaining their motivation in advanced study programs.

Believing in the Possibility of Success

Factors that contribute to students' sense that they can be successful in AP or IB courses have been discussed earlier in this report. These factors include students' positive beliefs about their own competence, their expectations for success or failure, their sense of control over the outcomes, their belief that others think they are competent, their belief that support of various kinds is available if they need it, and a strong sense that what they have learned before is adequate preparation for the challenges they will face in AP or IB. The IBO's Middle Years Programme and the College Board's Vertical Teams, Equity 2000, and Pathways Programs are designed to help students believe they can be successful in AP and IB courses.

---

[11]Currently the College Board provides aggregate subscore information to teachers of classes in which five or more students sit for the examination. The IBO provides similar feedback to its teachers.

Deciding to Enroll in an Advanced Course

Many able high school students and others take AP and IB courses because they seek opportunities to challenge themselves academically—opportunities that might otherwise not be available in high school courses. Others select these courses because they believe extrinsic rewards will accrue to them for doing so. These rewards include, for example, a potential advantage in the college admission process at competitive colleges,[12] opportunities for academic recognition, the possibility of earning college credit, and the possibility of placing out of introductory college courses.[13] Most students, however, are motivated by a combination of internal and external factors.

Some students take these courses because their parents want them to do so. Parents' reasons may include those mentioned above, as well as beliefs that AP and IB courses are taught by better teachers and produce more learning, that there are fewer discipline problems in these courses, and that students will have greater access to resources and opportunities in these courses than in others. Peers also exert a strong influence on students' decisions on whether to enroll. Students who are members of peer groups that value AP or IB participation are probably more likely to enroll even when they are not personally interested in a course. This observation may have serious implications for able students who attend schools where their peers do not value academic achievement. Still others take AP and IB classes because no other options exist in their high schools. This is particularly the case in mathematics: students who complete precalculus often have no other choice but to take AP or IB calculus if they want to continue with mathematics.[14]

Investing Effort for Success

Even when students are prepared to take AP or IB courses and have determined that they want to do so, they still must ask themselves whether

---

[12]Responses to a survey of college admission officers conducted by the committee clearly indicate that student perceptions in this area are accurate and that the more selective a college is in terms of admission, the more important it is that a student participate in AP and IB courses if their high school offers such courses (see Chapter 2, this volume).

[13]The committee conducted a survey of biology and mathematics departments at a sample of colleges and universities to ascertain how AP test scores are used for placement and credit (see Chapter 2, this volume).

[14]In September 1986, the Mathematical Association of America and the National Council of Teachers of Mathematics released a joint statement advocating that calculus courses taken in high school be at the college level, in other words, at the level of AP or IB. The statement was published in *Calculus for a New Century* (Steen, 1988).

they are willing to expend the effort required for success. Researchers have begun to examine the relationships among motivation, cognition, and the social context in which learning takes place. The results of some of this work suggest that educational programs designed in accordance with the principles of learning described in this report can enhance students' motivation to engage in advanced study even when considerable effort is involved. Research also has shown that when computers, teachers, and peers are integrated as learning partners, not only does greater achievement result, but also more positive affective changes occur (Canas, Ford, Novak, Hayes, and Reichherzer, 2001; Linn and Hsi, 1999).

Motivation and the Final Examination

It is interesting to note that a far larger percentage of IB than AP students take the final examinations.[15] The IBO promotes the idea that IB courses prepare students for success in college and in real life. The examinations, students are told, are an integral part of the course and are the best way for them to demonstrate to themselves and others that they have achieved competence. In contrast, AP materials focus primarily on the usefulness of AP test scores for college credit and placement. If students lose interest in earning credit or placement or the colleges at which they plan to matriculate do not accept AP credits,[16] they may choose not to sit for the examinations.

The College Board is concerned about the number of students who do not take the AP examinations and is considering ways to address this issue (CFAPP, 2001). All four of the panels and the committee believe that sitting for the examinations should become an integral part of AP courses (see Chapter 11). Otherwise, students will miss an important opportunity to validate their performance, colleges and universities will lack information that can be highly useful in deciding on appropriate placements, and AP will be less credible as a rigorous program for high school students.

LEARNING COMMUNITIES

Learning is mediated by the social environment in which students interact with others. Although students also learn individually, research indicates

---

[15]Virtually all IB students take the examinations (Campbell, 2000). In contrast, only two-thirds of AP students sit for the examinations. (This is an overall estimate provided by the CFAPP [2001], but the committee does not know the extent to which this figure varies across disciplines. It may be, for example, that almost everyone who takes AP U.S. history sits for the examination, but only 25 percent of AP chemistry students do so, or vice versa.)

[16]Students generally receive acceptance to college prior to the May AP examination dates.

that learners benefit from opportunities to articulate their ideas to others and listen to and challenge each other's ideas, and in so doing reconstruct their thinking. Teamwork and collaborative investigations similar to those in which professional scientists engage help students refine important concepts and principles and apply them in real-world contexts. Students build on the learning of others through interaction. For example, students who are using an ineffective problem-solving strategy can learn by observing others who are using more productive methods.

The panels see learning communities as an important avenue for students to develop advanced understanding in their disciplines. The panels recognize the importance of discourse to both student construction of understanding and scientific discovery (Dunbar, 1995). They are concerned, however, that the push to cover too much content during the course of a school year can discourage teachers from permitting students to engage in lengthy discussions, ask questions, make conjectures, and challenge each others' ideas. The science panels' reviews of the broad scope of AP and IB course outlines, sample course syllabi, school scheduling options, and their own experiences lead them to believe that in many (but not all) AP and IB science classrooms, a lecture format is used extensively. Lectures can be an efficient tool for transmitting information, but they are not very useful for eliciting students' misconceptions, helping them understand the conditions for which principles are valid, or providing them with opportunities to practice skills and receive feedback. Traditional lecture formats limit the ability of students to be active participants in their own learning because they cannot control the pace of the information that is being presented, and interaction between lecturer and learner is limited at best.

The science panels are also concerned that students' opportunities to engage in collaborative work with peers in the laboratory components of science courses may be limited by the brevity of the periods within which the laboratories must be offered in today's high schools. They note that most college students engaged in the same courses have laboratory periods that are 2 to 3 hours long. The panels commend the College Board for advocating longer laboratory periods (CEEB, 2001a, 2001c, 2001d), but are skeptical about the frequency with which schools are able to implement this suggestion because of other scheduling constraints. The science panels note that a reduction in the breadth of science curricula could allow more time for collaboration and inquiry.

The panels note approvingly that the internal assessment criteria for IB experimental science courses require teachers to structure the classroom and laboratory environments so that students have opportunities to acquire and develop skills in working with a team. It is likely that both the AP and IB programs could make more deliberate use of interactions in promoting students' understanding of science and mathematics through such strategies as group case studies, project-based science activities, and use of technology that facilitates discourse (Ryder, Leach, and Driver, 1999). Finally, it may be noted that although class time is limited, collaboration can be encouraged outside of class on homework and other assignments, at the discretion of the teacher.

LEARNING IN CONTEXT

The situative perspective recognizes that learning occurs best in the context of performing problem-oriented tasks analogous to those encountered in real work environments. Active, inquiry-based learning should therefore be a major component of the learning environment.

There are many instructional techniques teachers can use to situate learning, such as case-based or problem-based instruction and simulations. However, as mentioned in Chapter 6, care must be taken with all of these approaches to provide multiple opportunities for students to engage in activities in which the same concept is at work; otherwise learning could become overly contextualized, and students might not be able to discern its usefulness in solving different types of problems. The IB program recognizes this: "Students need to be exposed repeatedly to the application of basic concepts to new situations. This can be done through examples used in the classroom, by homework assignments which provide a variety of appropriate situations requiring skills beyond recall of information, and by tests and examinations which use questions similar to those used in the IB examination" (IBO, 1999a, p. 401). There are two primary reasons, however, why multicontext learning is unlikely to occur in AP and IB classrooms: there is a great deal of material to cover in preparation for the examinations, and the AP and IB assessments do not measure students' understanding of underlying principles in unfamiliar contexts frequently enough.

In the real world, problems are not organized neatly into discipline-specific packages. Thus from the situative perspective, advanced study teachers should provide opportunities for students to explore the interdisciplinary connections relevant to complex tasks. Doing so not only makes learning more interesting and motivating, but also develops students' capacity to generalize their learning. In this regard, the mathematics panel concludes:

> The AP program does not make a sufficient attempt to connect calculus with other fields in a realistic way. There is a tendency to use applications of rather ritualistic and formulaic kinds, and of limited difficulty. The test concentrates on a few prescribed applications (e.g., determination of volumes) or gives applications that consist largely of interpretation of symbols or computations in a new context. Its problems have a "whiff" of application, but they are often jarringly unreal at a deeper level.[17]

---

[17]See the panel's report at www.nap.edu/catalog/10129.html.

While the IB external assessment lacks realistic connections to other disciplines, the IB portfolio, which was added to the mathematics program in 2000, includes a modeling exercise that emphasizes interdisciplinary connections with science. The committee and the mathematics panel applaud this new emphasis and encourage the IBO to expand this emphasis to the external assessment. The IB science courses include interdisciplinary topics in some of the topic options and in the required Group 4 interdisciplinary project (see Chapter 4, this volume, for more information about the IB Group 4 Project). In addition, the selection of curricular options in IB experimental science courses is based on resources that are available locally. For example, an IB chemistry curriculum in a school with access to a university's analytical laboratory might include higher physical organic chemistry or modern analytical chemistry. Similarly, a curriculum in a school located in an area where there are chemical manufacturing plants could include the Chemical Industries option. Thus students develop knowledge that is situated in the relationships, practices, and tools of a community. The AP science curricula do not encourage links to other science disciplines, probably as a result of the independent development of each AP course.

The laboratory components of AP and IB science courses can provide excellent opportunities for teachers to situate learning in activities that reflect the kinds of thinking and problem solving in which scientists engage. The physics panel notes that experimental work in advanced courses should provide experience with the ways scientists use experiments, both for gathering data to build theoretical models and for exploring the applicability of these models to new situations. Although both the AP and IB programs emphasize the central role laboratory experiences should play in students' learning, the science panels note that the potential for helping students learn how science is conducted is not realized to an optimal extent in either program. For example, the biology panel notes that the AP required biology laboratories tend to be more "cookbook" (i.e., a set of prescribed procedures) than inquiry-based and consequently do not replicate the ways scientists work. The physics panel is similarly concerned about the "cookbook" nature of many physics laboratories commonly used in schools. In these laboratories, students do not have adequate opportunities to make the kinds of decisions scientists make from the conception of an experiment to the critical review of its results.

Another aspect of situated cognition as related to laboratory work is the ability to use instrumentation. The science panels note that skilled use of instrumentation is an important aspect of the context in which scientific discovery occurs. Through the use of authentic activities, including laboratory work and the skilled use of appropriate instrumentation, the situated nature of learning is respected. Students are less likely to memorize words or phrases that hold no meaning except for helping them obtain high exam scores or grades. Instead, learning can be embedded in more authentic contexts and realistic activities, using tools appropriate to the subject. The biology panel notes that the AP biology laboratory exercises do not require much instrumentation. The physics panel indicates that neither AP nor IB curricula reflect the growing use of computer modeling for the study of physics.

IB science and mathematics assessments, as a function of the internal assessment[18] and portfolio[19] components, respect the situated nature of learning better than do AP assessments.[20] This is because the AP examinations rely exclusively on a single assessment that uses only multiple-choice and free-response questions to measure student achievement. The chemistry panel contends that paper-and-pencil assessments, such as the AP examinations, are not sufficient to measure students' understanding of laboratory methods or interpretation of laboratory data. The biology and physics panels concur. The mathematics panel, while appreciative of the portfolio component of the IB mathematics courses, does not believe the portfolio alone eliminates the need to include on the final examinations questions that require students to use their knowledge and skills to solve real and unfamiliar problems.

CONCLUDING REMARKS

This chapter has presented an analysis of programs for advanced study through the lens of research on learning, as summarized in Chapter 6. The focus has been on the themes of conceptual learning, prior knowledge, differences among learners, motivation, learning communities, and the context of learning. In general, although the programs have important strengths, they do not yet effectively utilize what is known about how people learn. In many instances, they insufficiently emphasize conceptual learning that uses inquiry-based methods, nor do they adequately take into account the importance of prior knowledge (including student preparation in earlier courses). Some of the courses are too broad to allow mastery. Most could do more to help students gain the ability to apply their learning in unfamiliar situations.

---

[18]The internal assessments in the experimental sciences are focused on the candidates' skills in laboratory investigation, which include planning, data collection and processing, evaluation of procedures and results, and manipulative skills and personal skills, which include working with a team (IBO, 2001a, 2001b, 2001c, pp. 20–22).

[19]The purpose of the mathematics portfolio is to "provide candidates with opportunities to be rewarded for mathematics carried out under ordinary conditions, that is, without the time limitations and stress associated with written examinations" (IBO, 1998b, p. 47).

[20]As discussed in Chapter 4, the IB internal assessment allows teachers to evaluate students as they use their knowledge and skills to solve real problems in settings other than testing.

Although the analysis here has included examples from the four disciplines on which this study is focused, the discussion has been fairly general. Readers who are interested in one of the disciplines in particular will find an in-depth assessment in the corresponding panel report. Readers are encouraged to peruse these reports individually or to examine the summary of their findings presented in Appendix A.

Chapter 9 examines the AP and IB programs from a different but related point of view: the four elements of educational programs—curriculum, instructional methods, ongoing and end-of-course assessments, and opportunities for teacher preparation and professional development. The discussion in that chapter considers the extent to which these elements of the AP and IB programs nurture deep conceptual understanding among students—the committee's view of the primary goal for advanced study.

9

Analysis of AP and IB Curriculum, Instruction, Assessment, and Professional Development

This chapter reviews the AP and IB curricula and associated instructional strategies, assessments, and professional development opportunities to identify those features that are consistent with the design principles set forth in Chapter 7. Also examined are the ways in which the four program elements interact to support or undermine students' attainment of the deep conceptual understanding that is the goal of advanced study. In presenting this analysis, the committee acknowledges that there are many teachers in the United States who, by virtue of their experience and pedagogical skills, are able to overcome many of the program deficiencies discussed. We also recognize, however, that an improved program would only serve to enhance the capabilities of these teachers. Additionally, for the many teachers who are not as skilled or experienced, it is important that the curricula and related assessments and teacher preparation for these courses be aligned more completely with what is known about learning to ensure high standards and quality instruction for all AP and IB students.

CURRICULUM

Depth Versus Breadth

The committee's analysis of the AP and IB programs reveals some fundamental characteristics that are incompatible with a curriculum designed to foster deep conceptual understanding. The first major discrepancy, which applies equally to AP and IB, relates to the "less is more" concept in curriculum design. The idea is simple: only if a curriculum is not overly broad in terms of the number of topics to be studied is it possible to study topics in sufficient depth to develop deep conceptual understanding. This idea is consistent with national standards in mathematics and science for grades K–12 (American Association for the Advancement of Science [AAAS], 1993; National Council of Teachers of Mathematics [NCTM], 2000; National Research Council [NRC], 1996). While the written materials produced by the College Board and the International Baccalaureate Organisation (IBO) acknowledge the importance of depth and focus, the daunting scope of the curriculum guides and the associated assessments in some subject areas sends a very different message. One notable exception is the revised AP calculus syllabus, which reflects an appropriate balance between breadth and depth.

Curriculum Development

AP course outlines (and assessments) are designed to mirror the content of typical college-level introductory courses (see Chapter 3, this volume). AP courses are intended to be an acceptable substitute for the introductory courses offered at more than 2,000 colleges and universities. Because AP courses cannot duplicate all of these college offerings, AP development committees try to make the courses maximally similar to as many of their college counterparts as possible. If one makes the commonsense assumption that college-level courses vary substantially in quality, such an approach will limit the development of high-quality AP courses. *Average* and *excellent* are incompatible. By focusing on average rather than exemplary programs, the development process results in an almost certain regression to the mean. A far better goal for the development of AP courses would be to design them in accordance with the principles articulated in this report. Further, suggested instructional strategies should reflect the range of best practices in both high school and college courses instead of emulating college courses across a range of quality and content. Throughout the development process, the goal of fostering learning with deep conceptual understanding must always be pursued.

AP course content is determined using data supplied by college and university department officials who respond to a survey distributed by the College Board. According to College Board officials, the response rate to these surveys is rather low—approximately 40 percent. Thus the responses of a small number of college and university departments may have an undue influence on what is taught in advanced courses across the nation. Designing AP courses to reflect a typical college course also means that until curricular changes become common in introductory college courses, these changes will not be included in AP. On the other hand, because IB courses are developed differently (see Chapter 4, this volume), they can be more responsive than AP courses to changes in the disciplines.

The committee notes that in the 1990s, the College Board began experimenting with other development strategies. In 1994, 23 nationally recognized experts in the area of calculus reform were brought together to work with the development committee in redesigning the AP calculus curriculum. The give and take and varying perspectives of these experts helped create a course that did not simply replicate a typical college course, but reflected current consensus on best practices in mathematics teaching and curriculum design.[1] The collaborative model used to develop AP calculus offers insight into how course development procedures could be modified to improve programs. The best possible outcome is that a focus on quality will result in university and AP courses having reciprocal effects on one another.

Variability

As noted earlier in this volume (see Chapters 3, 4, and 8), AP and IB courses in the same discipline vary from school to school and even from classroom to classroom. Individual teachers are given substantial leeway in implementing AP or IB courses in their classrooms. While flexibility in curricula is an attractive feature for many experienced teachers, allowing them to be creative in their instructional approaches, the result is that college and university faculty face the same problems as AP and IB teachers in being unable to determine what incoming students know and are able to do.

Research on the nature and effectiveness of various practices in AP and IB classrooms is scant. Little is known, except anecdotally, about how AP and IB classrooms are organized, how the courses are implemented, and how they relate to existing school and district curricular offerings. School differences also affect how a course is implemented. The length of class periods, available facilities, and existing state standards, for example, all help shape the courses differently in each locality. Research is needed to understand these differences and their effects on student learning and achievement.

INSTRUCTION

Both the AP and IB programs depart significantly from the committee's framework for designing effective programs for advanced study by failing to address the element of instruction adequately. Neither the College Board nor the IBO gives sufficient attention to identifying and modeling aspects of

---

[1]For a complete history of the reform of AP calculus, see http://apcentral.collegeboard.com/article/0,1281,150-155-0-8019,00.html (February 2, 2001).

instruction that foster learning with understanding. Further, neither program presents explicit models of the nature and range of excellent teaching in AP or IB classrooms. Sample syllabi, Internet discussion groups, professional development activities, and other resources provided by the College Board and the IBO are of varying quality, represent limited perspectives on excellent instruction, and do not adequately take into account variability among students and schools.

Because both AP and IB courses are designed to prepare students for external, standardized final examinations, instruction in AP and IB classrooms is typically directed toward that goal. Unfortunately, the broad scope of the AP and IB curricula, the significant number of examination questions that appear to require only rote learning, and the predictability of the questions included on some examinations may lead teachers to focus their attention on presenting information and teaching problem types, rather than facilitating active student involvement in learning.

Worthwhile Tasks

One of the primary responsibilities and challenges facing teachers of AP and IB courses is the selection and development of worthwhile problems, exercises, tasks, projects, and investigations that can simultaneously develop conceptual understanding, prepare students for successful performance on the examination, and address the varying abilities and preferences of students in the classroom. Currently, AP and IB materials provide little assistance for meeting this challenge.

Promotion of High-Quality Instruction

High-quality instruction in AP and IB science and mathematics courses depends on the availability of qualified teachers. The committee found that neither the College Board nor the IBO has clearly defined the preparation and qualifications of AP or IB teachers; doing so could contribute significantly to the quality of instruction in the programs.

Schools and districts also have an important role to play in promoting high-quality instruction in AP and IB classrooms; the College Board and the IBO cannot do it alone. High-quality instruction depends on many things, such as adequate instructional resources and laboratory facilities; a structure that allows enough time for instruction; ongoing availability of high-quality professional development opportunities; and support from administrators, parents, and educational policymakers.

Most important, schools and districts must recognize that effective teaching in AP and IB classrooms requires time. Advanced study teachers, like other effective teachers, need time to remain abreast of changes in their subject areas and in the pedagogy related to their disciplines. AP and IB teachers need time to prepare their classes, carefully grade and comment on student work, and engage in collaboration and lesson planning with other teachers (see Chapter 2, this volume). For example, Ma (1999) indicates that teachers in China spend more time preparing lessons than teaching them. Time for collaborative planning is an important part of teachers' school hours in China. In the United States, teachers average approximately 13 minutes of planning time for every instructional hour (Darling-Hammond, 1999b; National Commission on Teaching and America's Future, 1996).

ASSESSMENT

AP and IB courses are designed to prepare students for standardized final examinations. Teachers select curriculum materials and gear instruction to prepare their students for success on these examinations, and students focus their learning on the concepts and content they believe they will encounter on the assessments. It is important, therefore, to better understand whether these assessments are aligned or in conflict with the principles of learning with understanding and the design principles of assessment.

Examination Design and Development

As noted earlier (see Chapter 3, this volume), AP examinations are designed by development committees for each of the disciplines in consultation with statisticians and psychometricians to create examinations that meet accepted standards for technical quality (American Educational research Association [AERA]/American Psychological Association [APA]/National Council on Measurement in Education [NCME], 1999).[2] Thus, the development process incorporates the judgments of both disciplinary and psychometric experts. IB examinations are designed differently, in a manner similar to that which might be used by teachers who have a sophisticated understanding of their discipline (see Chapter 4, this volume). Thus, the development of IBO assessments depends heavily on the expertise and professional judgment of master teachers and less on psychometric calibrations. These differences between the two programs' assessments should be considered in light of the ways students' examination scores will be used and the kinds of inferences users expect to support with the scores.

---

[2]Readers who are interested in a more detailed discussion of test construction are referred to other sources (see, for example, AERA/APA/NCME, 1999; Millman and Greene, 1989).

Support for Inferences Drawn from Assessment Results

As noted in Chapter 6, validity research is a vital component of any high-quality assessment program. Validity involves what an examination measures and the meaning that can be drawn from the scores and the actions that follow (AERA/APA/NCME, 1999; Cronbach, 1971). For each purpose for which the scores are used, there must be evidence to support the inferences drawn. In the case of AP, for example, the College Board wants users to draw the inference that students' performance on AP examinations is indicative of their mastery of material taught in a typical college course in the subject. The IBO wants users to draw the inference that students who earn an IB Diploma through their performance on six IB examinations[3] are adequately prepared for postsecondary work in many countries.

"The process of validation involves accumulating evidence to provide a sound scientific basis for the proposed score interpretations" (AERA/APA/NCME, 1999, p. 9). The AP Technical Manual describes two common interpretations of AP scores: (1) a good AP grade indicates that the student would benefit from entering a course more advanced than the usual first-year course, and (2) an AP grade indicates that the student should receive credit for a college course that he or she has not taken.[4] The IBO does not describe the appropriate interpretations of IB grades other than to say that they reflect students' mastery of course content that is designed to prepare them for postsecondary learning.

Given these desired interpretations, validation studies for the AP and IB assessments should include systematic evaluation of such factors as whether the right skills and knowledge are being measured and in the right balance; whether the cognitive processes required by the test are representative of the ways knowledge is used in the discipline; the extent to which the test measures students' knowledge of the broader construct that is the target of instruction, as opposed to their knowledge of specific test items; whether the scoring guidelines focus on student understanding; and whether the test scores accurately represent different levels and kinds of understanding.

The committee's analyses of the test items and the course syllabi on which the tests are based yielded information about content coverage. However, no data were available for evaluating whether the tests measure important cognitive skills. This is because neither program has systematically gathered data to document that test items on its examinations measure the skills they purport to measure. In making determinations about the validity of

---

[3]There are additional requirements for an IB Diploma (see Chapter 4, this volume).
[4]See www.collegeboard.org/ap/techman/chap5/ (November 28, 2001).

inferences, it is necessary to know, for example, that test items intended to measure problem solving do in fact tap those skills and do not just elicit memorized solutions or procedures. There are a number of ways to collect such data. For example, cognitive laboratories might be conducted during which examinees would "think aloud" as they responded to test questions. Information from such laboratories gives test developers insight into the thought processes used by students to derive answers to test questions.

Validity evaluation should consist of more than a haphazard set of research studies. A sound validity evaluation should integrate "various strands of evidence into a coherent account of the degree to which existing evidence and theory support the intended interpretations of test scores for specific uses" (AERA/APA/NCME, 1999, p. 17). Yet the committee's analysis indicates a surprising lack of information about what the AP and IB assessments actually measure. To date, neither program has implemented a strong program of validity research. The committee found only a few validity studies conducted with AP or IB data. For example, Morgan and Ramist (1998) examine college course-taking patterns for AP students; Morgan and Maneckshana (2000) compare performance in advanced-level courses for AP and non-AP students; and Eugene Carson reports on a small study at Virginia Polytechnic Institute and State University that compared the overall grade point averages of IB students with those of AP students and students who participated in neither program.[5] While these studies may be useful, they do not represent pieces of an integrated research program (see Chapter 10, this volume, for a discussion of these studies).

Consequential Validity of AP and IB Assessments

Very little evidence is available for evaluating the consequential validity[6] of the AP and IB assessments. With regard to this aspect of validity, relevant questions might include whether typical examinees become more or less interested in the domain as a result of their experience and whether they are more or less likely to pursue further study than those who do not sit for the examination. In the context of this report, one might ask how students who participate in AP and IB fare in college relative to other students and what the effect is on colleges of the ever-increasing numbers of students entering postsecondary institutions with college credit earned on AP or IB examinations. Equity concerns should also be considered, that is, whether the assessment unintentionally produces inequities of achievement or attitude in either the short or long term. While Morgan and Ramist (1998) begin to

---

[5]Available at http://www.rvcschools.org [August 2000]..

[6]Consequential validity refers to the consequences or uses of assessment results.

address some of these questions, additional studies are needed. Information about the consequential effects of AP and IB assessments are especially important as these programs expand and become a more significant component of U.S. education.

PROFESSIONAL DEVELOPMENT

A common theme of the four panel reports that also emerged throughout the committee's deliberations is the crucial importance of professional development for enhancing teachers' content knowledge in their subject areas. As noted in Chapter 7, this volume, a strong grounding in subject matter knowledge is fundamental to good teaching and should be a primary goal of professional development activities. It is unrealistic to ask teachers to cultivate a deep, principle-based understanding among their students unless they themselves have such understanding. However, the ideal role of professional development for advanced study goes far beyond ensuring that teachers know their subject areas well. Effective professional development also enhances teachers' subject-specific pedagogical knowledge and provides them with multiple perspectives on students as learners. It is grounded in situations of practice; takes place in professional communities; actively involves teachers; and is an ongoing, long-term component of their professional lives. The committee believes that without well-designed and ongoing professional development, it is difficult for teachers to provide high-quality instruction that is aligned with curriculum and assessment to support the goal of learning with understanding. The committee notes that neither AP nor IB professional development opportunities are sustained and that teacher participation in both programs is voluntary.

The mathematics and science panels note that the summer programs offered by AP are highly variable in focus and organization, as well as in quality. The mathematics panel expresses concern that many AP and IB mathematics teachers have insufficient professional development opportunities to derive both mathematical content and pedagogical knowledge or to receive help in implementing modifications to the programs. Having reviewed a significant sampling of AP summer institute materials (1998–2000), the panel finds that many of the workshops did not adequately address substantive issues relevant to teaching calculus. The science panels note that few of the AP workshops, even those that emphasized laboratory experiences, focused on inquiry.[7] The panels commend the IBO for its professional development activities related to internal assessments that focus on inquiry.

---

[7]Inquiry includes laboratory investigation, but also a broad array of information gathering, appraisal, and testing of ideas toward the goal of understanding science deeply.

The College Board and the IBO are just beginning to fully develop vehicles for establishing professional communities of learners among geographically separated teachers. The primary means being used are discussion groups and databases that can be accessed on the Internet. However, the committee notes that both the College Board and the IBO have regional organizations for teachers. Some are more active than others, and each provides different types of activities. For example, the IBO has a vibrant group in Florida that runs its own conferences, and the College Board, through its regional offices (notably in the southwest), provides opportunities for teachers in the regions to work with colleagues in professional development activities throughout the school year. Nonetheless, there are too few opportunities for teachers to interact with colleagues on issues important to teaching. This is especially true in high schools where AP or IB teachers in a particular discipline may be the only members of their departments who teach these courses.

The National Commission on Mathematics and Science Teaching for the 21st Century (2000, pp. 27–28) provides some suggestions that could become part of AP and IB Web-based efforts. These include the creation of (1) an online professional journal that would encourage teachers of advanced mathematics and science to engage in publishable research and to share new teaching strategies with colleagues, both nationally and internationally; (2) a dedicated database of teaching ideas, plans, and other resources; (3) an interactive online resource for conversations, meetings, and idea sharing; and (4) interactive videos for observing good teachers and critiquing teachers' own efforts, for mentoring, and for online instruction. Research is needed to determine the effectiveness of such Web-based mechanisms for teacher professional development.

CONCLUSION

The committee has advocated the use of a model that can help sponsors of advanced study programs make decisions on how their programs can best improve in the years ahead. This model includes both principles of learning and design principles for curriculum, instruction, assessment, and professional development. The committee believes that if programs of advanced study, such as AP and IB, were to place principles of learning at the center of their own implicit models, the programs would improve in quality and effectiveness with regard to fostering deep understanding. Program quality would also be enhanced if the programs were to recognize the systemic and mutually interactive nature of curriculum, instruction, assessment, and professional development. With care, persistence, and a strong guiding model, advanced study programs could become worthy beacons for all of American education.

10

Uses, Misuses, and Unintended Consequences of AP and IB

This chapter examines a number of ways in which the Advanced Placement (AP) and International Baccalaureate (IB) programs and their assessment results are used. Some of these uses are appropriate and intended by the program sponsors; others are not. Unintended uses are making these programs high stakes in terms of their consequences for students, for teaching and learning, and for schools.

HIGH STAKES

In 1998, *Newsweek* published a list (Mathews, 1998a) entitled "The 100 Best High Schools in America."[1] This list, which ranks public high schools according to the number of AP and IB tests taken, divided by the number of graduating seniors, was drawn from the book *Class Struggle: What's Wrong (and Right) with America's Best Public High Schools* (Mathews, 1998b). The ostensible purpose of the list, now published annually for Washington area schools in the *Washington Post*, is to quantify the level of challenge high schools provide to their students. The author of the list acknowledges that such rankings have their limitations, but believes it is better to have such a tool, even one that may be misleading, than to have no means of comparing schools and motivating parents and students to demand more from their schools (Mathews, 1998b).

The practice of ranking schools by the number of AP or IB tests administered, as *Newsweek* does, or using students' scores on AP or IB exams for evaluating teachers or comparing the quality of teachers and schools, as some parents, school administrators, or policymakers may do, is making these programs high stakes in ways the program developers never intended.

---

[1]The list does not include public schools that admit more than half of their student body through a competitive process that includes examinations or other academic criteria.

Such misuses of AP and IB assessments are both educationally inappropriate and counter to the Standards for Educational and Psychological Testing (American Educational Research Association [AERA]/American Psychological Association [APA]/National Council on Measurement in Education [NCME], 1999). Moreover, neither the College Board nor the International Baccalaureate Organisation (IBO) has to date provided sufficient guidance to counter many of these misuses. This section considers some of the unintended consequences of these practices.

Effects on Students

Making decisions about the effectiveness of teachers or the quality of their teaching primarily on the basis of AP or IB test scores may have unintended consequences for students. For example, if teachers are evaluated on the basis of AP or IB test results, they may discourage certain students from taking AP or IB courses because they believe those students will not perform well, or they may counsel students for whom they anticipate a low grade to skip the final examination. Such practices can deny students the opportunity to try an AP or IB course or to validate what they have learned in comparison with nationally or internationally established standards.

Effects on Teaching and Learning

Teachers who are evaluated on the basis of student test results are more likely to teach to the test than to teach what they deem important (see, for example, Koretz, 1988, 1996; Koretz, Linn, Dunbar, and Shepard, 1991; Linn, Graue, and Sanders, 1990; Shepard, 1990; Shepard and Cutts-Dougherty, 1991). The committee acknowledges that the nature of the AP and IB programs makes teaching to the test the norm; the test specifications are the curriculum (see Chapter 3, this volume). However, the committee does not believe the AP and IB tests reviewed for this study sampled broadly and deeply enough across the full range of content knowledge, conceptual understanding, processes, and skills valued in the respective disciplines to make teaching to the test an appropriate strategy for developing the level of conceptual understanding that should be the goal of advanced study.

Therefore, the panels and the committee view teaching to AP and IB tests as potentially interfering with teaching what is truly important for enhancing student learning. For example, the mathematics panel notes that the AP and IB examinations have overemphasized procedure and underemphasized application and conceptual understanding. The chemistry panel also identifies a lack of contextual problems in the AP examinations. The biology and physics panels find that both the AP and IB assessments cover too much content, and the chemistry panel decries the lack of attention to important interdisciplinary connections. The biology and chemistry panels note a lack of test items that measure laboratory skills on the AP examinations, and the physics panel indicates that neither AP nor IB assessments require students to apply what they learn in class to solve new or novel problems. In sum, teaching to AP and IB tests for the purpose of raising test scores can lead to superficial coverage of a broad base of content knowledge, to teachers ignoring the importance of meaningful inquiry-based and laboratory experiences (AP only), and to students feeling that what they are learning in school has little application to the real world.

Effects on Teachers

Inferences about teacher quality and effectiveness cannot be supported by data drawn solely, or even primarily, from AP and IB test scores. One important reason for this is that students come to AP and IB classrooms with different levels of skill and mastery of content that make it difficult to determine the effects of a single teacher's work on student achievement in any particular year. A well-prepared group of students might, for example, earn high scores on their AP or IB final examinations even if the quality of the teaching in their class was low. Similarly, an underprepared group of students might do quite poorly on AP or IB assessments because of their previous preparation, despite the valiant efforts of a highly qualified and dedicated AP or IB teacher. Although this is the case for all subjects, it appears to be especially true for advanced mathematics because of the hierarchical and sequential nature of the subject.

Effects on Schools

Ranking Schools by the Number of AP or IB Tests Taken

Policymakers and others often rely on numbers, rankings, comparisons of standardized test results, and other quantifiable data to draw conclusions about the state of education in the United States. The media report these data as valid and scientific, and the public uses them as a basis for making important decisions and judgments.

For example, the annual list described at the beginning of this chapter has been used by many as a measure of overall school quality. The list has taken on a life of its own. It is now so important to be included among the top 100 schools on the list that some competitive high schools not included have posted disclaimers on their Web sites indicating why this is the case.[2]

---

[2]An example is City Honors High School in Buffalo, New York; see http://cityhonors.buffalo.k12.ny.us/city/news/1999-00/0003/news0003newsw/news0003newsw.html (January 11, 2002).

Many others that are listed among the top 100 openly publicize their ranking as a sign of excellence.

Using the number of AP and IB examinations or number of AP and IB courses offered in a school as a measure of school quality also penalizes in the arena of public opinion schools that have chosen, because of different educational values or priorities, to offer other rigorous options to their students. Ignoring the value of these alternative approaches can stifle creativity and innovation in the development of new programs. Such alternative approaches could be as rigorous as AP or IB and also be more suitable to the student body served by a particular school.

Additionally, ranking schools by the proportion of students who take AP or IB examinations ignores the central issue of how many of those students are adequately prepared through high-quality courses to succeed on the exams. The committee notes that among states and school districts where all AP students are required to take the examinations, a notable number of students may not complete the examination or answer test questions conscientiously.

Evaluating School Quality by the Numbers

The fundamental objective of education is to promote the academic growth of each student. Evaluations of school quality should help identify those schools that are accomplishing this goal and those that are not. When assessment scores are used to evaluate schools, efforts must be made to determine whether the scores are indicative of growth (or lack of growth) that is due to the quality of the instructional program, or merely reflect students' home environments, external learning experiences, and available resources. There are many schools that provide high-quality instruction in school districts where resources are scarce whose students continue to grow academically. There are other schools in which test scores are high, but the quality of instruction may not be as good as in schools with lower test scores. The higher assessment scores may be more reflective of the students' other opportunities than of the quality of the school itself. In sum, relying solely, or even primarily, on AP or IB test scores to evaluate school quality reflects a failure to recognize that there are substantive differences in educational institutions across the nation (see Chapter 2, this volume), while also ignoring the varying characteristics of the students who attend these schools.

QUALITY CONTROL

With increasing calls for educational quality and accountability, educators and policymakers alike have turned to AP or IB to improve the quality of their schools and curricula. The pressure to introduce or expand AP or IB offerings in high schools can have a number of unintended consequences. For example, schools that claim to offer advanced study programs may or may not be able to support such programs adequately, and the resulting courses may be far from what is intended by the program sponsors. Ensuring the quality and integrity of the AP and IB programs is a complex endeavor that it is frequently affected by factors beyond the control of either the College Board or the IBO.

Standards and Regulation of Courses

The IBO carefully regulates which schools can offer IB courses and how those courses must be structured. As a result, schools are unable to offer IB courses or the IB Diploma without the imprimatur of the IBO.

In contrast, the College Board has no clear standards for what constitutes an AP course or the schools that offer them. This lack of consistency invites misuse of the AP name. For example, schools have been known to label non-AP courses as AP in an effort to make their students more competitive for admission to college. Others may have instituted AP courses without ensuring that they have the facilities and personnel needed to offer a college-level program. Consequently, all four of the panels call on the College Board to certify or regulate AP programs and teachers.

Curriculum Compression

The committee found that schools' efforts to prepare students for AP and IB science and mathematics courses often help stimulate improvements in the prerequisite courses, and that this is an important and positive effect of these programs. However, there also may be some unintended consequences. For example, some students may be adversely affected when schools compress preparatory courses in order to prepare as many students as possible for AP or IB courses. Compression can occur by reducing coverage of specific subjects in a curriculum to provide adequate time for advanced study or by beginning the high school sequence of courses earlier in a student's career.

To illustrate the point, strong preparation is important in mathematics because of the hierarchical and cumulative nature of the subject. However, the mathematics panel notes that there is considerable anecdotal evidence that some students intending to take calculus are rushed through prerequisite courses without thoroughly learning the preparatory material. Mathematical sophistication takes time to develop, and knowledge of a catalog of mathematical facts and techniques is not sufficient. The mathematics panel notes that most of the students who do poorly in AP or IB calculus did not learn their algebra well enough. These students probably would have been better served by spending more time learning algebra and saving calculus for college. At the same time, there are students who are ready for a rigorous calculus course in high school. Schools need to maintain a delicate balance between meeting the needs of this latter group and pushing too many students into advanced mathematics before they are ready. Achieving this balance is not easily accomplished.

Compression of the curriculum also can occur when students are allowed to skip prerequisite courses and take an AP course as a first course. Among the sciences, AP physics is the course students most frequently select as a first course in the discipline. Data obtained from the College Board (College Entrance Examination Board [CEEB], 2000d) indicate that almost half of all AP physics test takers had had no prior experience with physics before enrolling in the AP course. Thus, the AP course had to cover both a year of high school physics and a year of college physics, making in-depth examination of any topic nearly impossible.

Participation in Examinations

The IBO expects that all students who take IB courses will take the associated examinations. The IBO uses student performance on its examinations to monitor and improve the overall quality of IB programs in different countries and schools. In contrast, the four panels note that the College Board has not developed examination policies or expectations for students' participation in the AP examinations. Because the examinations provide the only external evidence that schools are preparing students in a manner consistent with the College Board's expectations, the panels suggest that a clearly articulated policy is necessary if the College Board is to maintain quality control of the AP name.

Online Courses

As discussed in Chapter 5, advances in technology have made it possible for colleges, universities, technology companies, and other nonprofit and for-profit organizations to create and distribute AP courses and other AP support services, such as professional development for AP teachers, online. Although the reach of these online courses has to date been small relative to other AP opportunities, their potential for growth is unlimited. The biology and chemistry panels are particularly concerned that students who take AP courses online and earn a qualifying score on the examination could earn college credit or placement without having had any hands-on laboratory experience.[3] They call on the College Board to set quality standards for online laboratory components of science courses. It may be noted that, because only authorized schools can provide IB courses, laboratories, and examinations, third-party providers currently cannot offer programs that carry the IB name.

ACCESS AND EQUITY

Disparities in access to AP and IB courses for students who live in inner-city and rural areas are a serious educational and social problem that is discussed throughout this report. However, other students in the United States also lack meaningful access to these courses because their schools deny them the opportunity to enroll.

Limiting Students' Access to AP and IB

Limiting students' access to advanced study occurs in all kinds of educational settings, including the most competitive high schools in America—schools with adequate resources, qualified teachers, and well-prepared students (Mathews, 1998b). These schools, while typically advocating college preparation for everyone, have created layers upon layers of curricular differentiation such that only a select group of students are allowed entrance into certain AP and honors courses; other students are placed in less prestigious courses[4] (Attewell, 2001; Mathews, 1998b; Oakes and Wells, 2001).

In a recent study, Attewell (2001) finds that many high-achieving students from elite high schools are not able to take the AP courses they would have been able to take had they attended less prestigious schools. He attributes this phenomenon to the fact that many elite high schools provide their best students with opportunities to participate in AP and honors courses while denying access to others. He finds further that, as a function of these placement policies, many highly able students who attend elite high schools are less likely than similar students in other high schools to take advanced mathematics or science courses or examinations. Schools limit participation in part, Attewell contends, because restricting access to AP to the strongest students guarantees that the school's overall pass rate on the final examina-

---

[3]Strategies for providing laboratory experiences to online students are discussed in Chapter 5.

[4]Mathews (1998b) estimates that each year, 25,000 interested and adequately prepared students in the United States are told they cannot take AP or IB courses. He further speculates that another 75,000 or more students who have the ability to do well in such courses do not elect to take them because no one encourages them to do so.

tions will be very high, boosting their reputation with the top colleges they care most about influencing.

The committee agrees that AP and IB are not appropriate for all students. Some are not prepared for or do not want to take college-level courses in high school, and such courses are not appropriate for all high school students. However, research shows that there are few rigorous options outside of these classes, especially in high schools with well-developed AP and IB programs (Callahan, 2000). Thus, students who are denied access to or choose not to take these classes are forced to enroll in what are often far less challenging options.

Prerequisites

Prerequisites are frequently used as gatekeepers to regulate enrollment in AP and IB courses. Sometimes this practice is deemed necessary because there is limited space. In other cases, the school simply wants to control which students take the courses to maintain quality (as represented, for example, by high test scores). The committee reviewed more than 100 curriculum guides prepared by individual high schools for their students, parents, and teachers. This review revealed that prerequisite requirements for enrollment in AP or IB courses range from open admission to highly restrictive criteria such as PSAT scores above a certain threshold, all A's in courses leading up to the AP courses, uniformly high teacher recommendations, and evidence of consistently high levels of motivation or excellent work habits. Many of these guides also contain statements to the effect that students who take courses for which they are not recommended must have signed permission from a parent absolving the teacher and the school from responsibility if the student does not succeed. If measures are to be used to extend or restrict access to AP and IB courses, the committee urges that schools demonstrate that their criteria for entry to advanced study are valid predictors of student success.

COLLEGE CREDIT AND PLACEMENT

AP Program

Throughout this report, the committee has challenged the assumption that AP courses uniformly reflect the content coverage and conceptual understanding that is developed in good college courses. We now ask whether students who place out of introductory courses in college on the basis of their AP scores are as well prepared for further study as their peers who take the introductory courses in college.

The College Board has conducted several studies to investigate this question. Recently, Morgan and Ramist (1998) examined the performance of AP and non-AP students in second-level courses in 25 subjects at 21 colleges. These subjects included sciences and mathematics, as well as many others. Breland and Oltman (2001), using data published by Morgan and Ramist (1998), examined the performance in upper-level courses of students who took AP comparative government and politics and AP economics. The conclusion of both of these studies was that students who earned qualifying scores on AP examinations appeared to earn grades in second-level courses that were as good as those earned by students who took the first-level course in college. *However, this conclusion is true only for an overall average.* Further, it was implicitly assumed in these studies that any student with a score of 3 or better on the AP examination would be allowed to take the second-level course. The committee knows from its department survey (see Chapter 2, this volume) that this is not the case. Thus a more precise conclusion for these studies is that *students with qualifying AP scores who were exempted from first-year courses in college appeared, on average,. to earn grades in second-year courses that were no lower than those earned by students who took the introductory courses in college.*

With the assistance of an educational statistician,[5] the committee examined the assumptions, methods, and conclusions of these two studies. This examination revealed that the methodology used in conducting the studies makes it difficult to determine how often and under what circumstances there is a positive advantage for AP students relative to non-AP students in second-level courses. There are two principle reasons for this difficulty:

- The investigators based their conclusions on averages of grades that were computed across classes and institutions to obtain overall averages. No effort was made to control for differences in the types and quality of the institutions involved in the study or for how well the AP courses matched the introductory courses students had placed out of in the different institutions.

- No attempt was made to control for differences among students that could be related to their performance in second-level courses. Examples of such differences include SAT scores (both SAT I and SAT II in the relevant subjects), high school grade point average, whether or not the students intended to major in the subject, and the quality of their overall high school curricula. No evidence is provided in the study reports as to whether stu-

---

[5]The committee's analysis of the College Board studies was conducted by Bert F. Green, professor of psychology, Emeritus, The Johns Hopkins University.

dents with the same credentials, apart from the AP examination score, also could skip the introductory-level courses with the same positive results in the next-level course.

In conclusion, the methodology used by the investigators to gather and analyze their data makes it difficult to determine whether any apparent advantage held by AP students over non-AP students is a function of the colleges they attend, the classes they enter, their own academic backgrounds and abilities, or the quality of the AP courses they took in high school. Further, there is no way to determine, from the data provided, the number of classes among the various colleges in which non-AP students outperformed AP students. It is possible that AP students were at a disadvantage in some classes or at some colleges.[6]

The committee's analysis of the College Board studies indicates that colleges and universities should not automatically award advanced placement to students with specified AP scores and assume that they will be successful.[7] Rather, it is more consistent with the evidence developed by the College Board for colleges to adopt policies that consider students individually and in combination with the requirements of the courses into which they seek placement.

IB Program

The practice of awarding university credit and placement for IB Higher Level (HL) courses dates back to at least 1973, when the National Council on the Evaluation of Foreign Student Credentials recommended that U.S. colleges and universities accept IB HL[8] examination grades for college credit

---

[6]It might have been more useful to treat the study as a meta-analysis, with each class in which there were AP and non-AP students being treated as a datum. In this scenario, each class would furnish an advantage or disadvantage for AP students with respect to their non-AP classmates. If each class were treated as a datum, standard deviations could be reported, and other class-level characteristics, such as size, instructional methodologies, and the degree to which knowledge gained in a first-level class was important for success in the second-year course, could be analyzed with respect to the performance of AP and non-AP students. Perhaps AP students do better only in small classes, or at selective colleges, or when inquiry is emphasized. Perhaps they do not do better when material from first-level courses is emphasized or when there is a poor match between the AP courses and the introductory courses taught at their colleges.

[7]The Morgan and Ramist and Breland and Oltman studies tell us only that on average, students who are exempted from introductory courses get grades that are as good as those of students who take the first course in college. They do not tell us whether AP students at a particular institution who are exempted from that college's introductory courses have the same depth of understanding of a subject area as students who take the first course at that college.

[8]IB HL courses are taken over a 2-year period (see Chapter 4, this volume).

when foreign students present such grades. Since that time, more than 750 colleges have established policies to accept IB HL credits from students worldwide. According to Paul Campbell, associate director of the International Baccalaureate Organisation of North America (IBNA) (personal communication, March 2000), the number of institutions accepting IB examination scores for credit or placement has increased as a result of individual students petitioning colleges on a case-by case, college-by-college basis.

In seeking credit and placement, many students cite evidence that IB HL courses are comparable to similar AP courses for which colleges and universities routinely grant credit and placement. However, the committee could find no systematic studies that have examined the validity of the claim that AP and IB courses are comparable.[9] Additionally, the IBO does not design its courses to be similar to introductory college courses, so it is difficult to determine how comparable the two are. Additionally, we know of no systematic studies that compare how well students who score differently on IB examinations perform in upper-level college courses or whether their performance varies by discipline.[10] It is therefore unclear to what extent advanced placement in upper-level college courses is merited on the basis of IB examination scores alone.

More evidence is needed to understand the consequences for students and colleges of awarding advanced placement for AP or IB examination scores. The evidence appears to support the interpretation that a student who earns a high AP score will earn a good grade in an upper-level course in that discipline. However, no evidence has been developed to demonstrate that students who earn qualifying scores on AP or IB examinations have achieved a depth of understanding of the subject comparable to that obtained by students taking the introductory college-level courses. Consequently, the disadvantages that accrue to AP and IB students who decide not

---

[9]The only study purporting to address the issue of AP and IB comparability was conducted at Case Western Reserve University, where the scores of students who took both AP and IB examinations in the same subject area were compared. The findings indicated that students who scored a 6 or 7 on IB HL examinations scored a 4 or 5 on the AP examination in the same subject area; the reverse was not the case. It may be assumed that all of these students took the IB course and not the AP course since students cannot take an IB examination without having taken the corresponding IB course. The methodology used in the study was not specified.

[10]The committee found a summary of isolated studies that examine the overall performance of IB students in college. Some of these studies were conducted at Virginia Polytechnic Institute and State University, University of Florida, and Marquette University. One study that looked at IB students' performance in upper-level science and mathematics courses revealed that IB students outperformed all other students in terms of overall grade point average and/or grades in upper-level courses (Guild of IB Schools, www.rvcschools.org [August 2000]). However, it is difficult to determine the validity of the study results because information about the methodology used by the investigators is incomplete.

to take an introductory college course in a subject before going on to a second-level course are not known.

CONCLUSION

The potential for misinterpreting and misusing test results and other aspects of the AP and IB programs is high and likely to become higher unless countermeasures are taken. The consequences of such misuses extend to students, teachers, high schools, and institutions of higher education.

The misuse of scores and programs appears less widespread for the IB than for the AP program. This difference likely results from the IBO's maintaining tighter control over its program. In addition, the IB program is offered in far fewer schools in the United States than the AP program, making it more difficult to use data on the former program to draw inappropriate comparative inferences about the quality of schools or teachers. Until the College Board makes a concerted effort to educate the media, policymakers, and the public about correct and incorrect interpretations and uses of its examination results, the kinds of abuses described here, and the consequences associated with them, will almost certainly continue and will probably increase.

As this report demonstrates, advanced study programs have an enormous influence on virtually all other components of the education system in the United States. As the programs are currently structured, some of these influences have worked to improve education. However, serious shortcomings persist. It is incumbent upon all individuals and institutions with a stake in improving advanced study and making it accessible to many more students to do so systematically, collaboratively, and in ways that are consistent with emerging research about learning and effective program design. The next chapter offers a series of recommendations for accomplishing these goals. This set of recommendations emerges from the committee's analysis of existing programs of advanced study; the way these programs influence and are affected by other components of the education system in the United States; and whether the programs' current structures are consistent with the principles of learning and the design principles of curriculum, instruction, assessment, and professional development set forth in this report.

11

Recommendations

Chapters 6 and 7 of this report present a framework for examining programs of advanced study. This framework is based on extensive research on student learning and the implications of that research for the design and integration of curriculum, instruction, assessment, and professional development. In Chapters 8 and 9 this framework is used to analyze the Advanced Placement (AP) and International Baccalaureate (IB) programs; areas in which there is alignment with the principles of learning are highlighted, as are aspects of the programs that deviate from those principles. Chapter 10 provides further analysis through an examination of the uses, misuses, and unintended consequences of the AP and IB programs and examination results.

The present chapter presents a set of recommended actions that could significantly improve existing programs for and approaches to advanced study and serve as the basis for the design of alternatives. Italic type is used to highlight particular groups to which the recommendations are directed. However, given the diversity and decentralized nature of the educational system in the United States, the committee leaves specific implementation strategies to local and state education agencies. Similarly, program developers must also decide how to execute our recommendations within the unique structures of their respective organizations. The committee's first and most important recommendation articulates a principle concerning the goals of advanced study and is addressed to all those involved in developing or teaching advanced study courses.

RECOMMENDATION 1:
THE PRIMARY GOAL OF ADVANCED STUDY

The primary goal of advanced study in any discipline should be for students to achieve a deep conceptual understanding of the

discipline's content and unifying concepts. Well-designed programs help students develop skills of inquiry, analysis, and problem solving so that they become superior learners.

It is not enough for students to achieve familiarity with factual content alone; they need to understand the central ideas of the discipline in order to build a conceptual framework for further learning and apply what they have learned to new situations and to other disciplines. A consequence of this principle is that accelerating students' exposure to college-level material, while appropriate as a component of some secondary advanced study programs, is not by itself a sufficient goal. Except for a small number of highly able students, courses that pursue acceleration as the sole objective may proceed too quickly for many students to develop deep conceptual understanding.

RECOMMENDATION 2: ACCESS AND EQUITY

Schools and school districts must find ways to integrate advanced study with the rest of their program by means of a coherent plan extending from middle school through the last years of secondary school. Course options in grades 6–10 for which there are reduced academic expectations (i.e., those that leave students unprepared for further study in a discipline) should be eliminated from the curriculum. An exception might be made for courses designed to meet the needs of special education students.

Many additional students could benefit from participation in advanced study given improved preparation in earlier years and wider program availability. As documented in Chapter 2, certain racial and ethnic groups (including African American and Hispanic students) are substantially underrepresented among matriculants in advanced courses and among AP test takers, though the causes for this are unclear. A coherent plan that extended across grade levels and schools within a district could enable a higher proportion of potentially qualified students to benefit from advanced study. By treating all students as potential participants while in grades 6–10, schools could help even those who do not eventually enroll in advanced study to emerge with strong foundations in mathematics and science.

The positive effects on student achievement of a high school curriculum that stresses high levels of academic learning for all students have been demonstrated empirically (Lee, 2001; Lee, Burkam, Chow-Hoy, Smerdon, and Geverdt, 1998; Lee, Croninger, and Smith, 1997). The committee therefore recommends that *high schools* eliminate low-level, "dead-end" mathematics and science courses,[1] which do not afford students the opportunity to prepare adequately for advanced study. Additional support will be needed to make this recommended action work for some students.

Access to advanced study is currently limited in many schools, especially those that are located in rural areas, urban centers, and other localities that enroll large proportions of low-income and minority students. *States, school districts, and program developers* (those who design courses for advanced study) must work to expand these opportunities to all schools. Finally, *districts*, with the support of advanced study programs, must provide substantial professional development opportunities for teachers, invest appropriately in laboratory facilities and materials, and develop academic support systems for those students who need them.

RECOMMENDATION 3: LEARNING PRINCIPLES

Programs of advanced study in science and mathematics must be made consistent with findings from recent research on how people learn. These findings include the role of students' prior knowledge and misconceptions in building a conceptual structure, the importance of student motivation and self-monitoring of learning (metacognition), and the substantial differences among learners.

Program developers should collaborate with discipline experts, researchers in pedagogy and cognitive science, and master teachers to examine existing programs and develop new ones. They should ensure that the components of their programs (curriculum, instruction, assessment, and professional development) are consistent with what is known about how people learn and work together to foster students' conceptual understanding.

RECOMMENDATION 4: CURRICULUM

Curricula for advanced study should emphasize depth of understanding over exhaustive coverage of content. They should focus on central organizing concepts and principles and the empirical infor-

---

[1]The committee chose not to cite such courses specifically by name because (1) the decentralized nature of U.S. education means that school districts title their courses in accordance with their own unique curriculum structure, and labeling conventions making it difficult to name with accuracy all the possible courses to which we refer; and (2) similarly titled courses offered in different school districts could be very different (for example, a course called "general chemistry" could provide adequate preparation for advanced study in one district but not in another). The committee chose, therefore, to define low-level courses as those that leave a student unprepared for further study in the discipline.

mation on which those concepts and principles are based. Because science and technology progress rapidly, frequent review of course content is essential.

Curricula should be focused on a reasonable number of concepts that can be studied in depth during the time allotted. Integration of the advanced study curriculum with earlier courses is essential, because building on earlier experiences can contribute to achieving both breadth of knowledge and depth of understanding over a period of years. It may sometimes make sense for advanced courses to extend over multiple school years to allow sufficient time for this process, as occurs in the IB program.

Identifying organizing principles and structuring them appropriately for advanced learners is labor-intensive and requires varied expertise. Therefore, effective curriculum development must be a collaborative effort conducted by teams of experienced teachers working with curriculum specialists and experts in the disciplines, in cognitive theory, and in pedagogy. The teams need to use a systematic approach to the development process that is aligned with the principles of learning set forth in this report and that involves repeated cycles of design, trial teaching with students, evaluation, and revision.

RECOMMENDATION 5: INSTRUCTION

Instruction in advanced courses should engage students in inquiry by providing opportunities to experiment, analyze information critically, make conjectures and argue about their validity, and solve problems both individually and in groups. Instruction should recognize and take advantage of differences among learners by employing multiple representations of ideas and posing a variety of tasks.

While the quality of instruction depends on the knowledge, creativity, and sensitivity of teachers, *program developers* can do much to suggest possible strategies, and *school administrators* need to provide both material resources and opportunities for professional development if high-quality teaching is to be achieved. Effective ways to use the Internet and other electronic resources should be encouraged and evaluated. In general, the committee recommends careful alignment of instruction with the *National Science Education Standards* (NRC, 1996) and the standards proposed by the National Council of Teachers of Mathematics (NCTM, 1991) and the National Board for Professional Teaching Standards (NBPTS, 2001).

RECOMMENDATION 6: ASSESSMENT

Teachers of advanced study courses should employ frequent formative assessment of student learning to guide instruction and monitor learning. External, end-of-course examinations have a different purpose: they certify mastery. Both types of assessment should include content and process dimensions of performance and evaluate depth of understanding, the primary goal of advanced study (see Recommendation 1).

Since end-of-course assessments strongly influence instruction, *program staff* must ensure that these assessments measure students' depth of understanding and their ability to transfer knowledge to unfamiliar situations. Programs should report the results of their end-of-year assessments in sufficient detail so the results are useful to students in evaluating what they have learned, to colleges in advising students accurately on their course options, and to schools and teachers in improving their advanced study courses and programs. Combining the results of several different indicators instead of relying solely or primarily on the results of a single high-stakes examination can provide a more accurate picture of student achievement.

Program staff should assist teachers in developing formative assessments that measure student progress toward desired learning outcomes. While classroom assessment is primarily the responsibility of teachers, programs can favorably affect student progress and increase teacher effectiveness by suggesting appropriate strategies and providing examples.

RECOMMENDATION 7: QUALIFIED TEACHERS AND PROFESSIONAL DEVELOPMENT

Schools and districts offering advanced study must provide frequent opportunities for continuing professional development so teachers can improve their knowledge of both content and pedagogy. National programs for advanced study should clearly specify and monitor the qualifications expected of teachers. Professional development activities must be adequately funded and available to all teachers throughout their teaching careers.

Professionals in most demanding fields require continuing education to maintain and improve their knowledge over time. The same applies to teachers. Professional development should emphasize deep understanding of content and discipline-based methods of inquiry, provide multiple perspectives on students as learners, and develop teachers' subject-specific pedagogical knowledge and skills. It should treat teachers as active learners, build on their existing knowledge, and take place in professional communities where colleagues have the opportunity to discuss ideas and practices.

Many groups can contribute effectively to teacher professional development. Discipline-based *professional associations* should help identify the knowledge and skills required for excellent teaching. *Researchers* should investigate the effects of different levels of teacher professional development on student learning and achievement in advanced study. *University and college science and mathematics departments* and *schools of education* must work collaboratively to develop discipline-specific approaches to teacher preparation and continuing professional development. *States*, in monitoring the quality of local education, should collect and report data on the qualifications of teachers of advanced study. *National programs* of advanced study should assume greater responsibility for assisting schools, districts, and states in developing professional development programs and in upgrading their own programs in the ways suggested in this report.

RECOMMENDATION 8: ALTERNATIVE PROGRAMS

Approaches to advanced study other than AP and IB should be developed and evaluated. Such alternatives can help increase access to advanced study for those not presently served and result in the emergence of novel and effective strategies.

Some small-scale alternatives are described in Chapter 5. However, there is much room for new ideas. *Funding and research agencies* should encourage the development of additional advanced study options and should collect and disseminate information about existing alternatives that might become national models.

Little has been said in this report about the special needs of very high-ability students (the top few percent in mathematics and science). However, the committee urges *funding agencies* to sponsor research related to the learning needs of these exceptional students and to support educators in the development of innovative strategies for meeting those needs.

RECOMMENDATION 9: THE SECONDARY–COLLEGE INTERFACE

9(a): When awarding credit and advanced placement for courses beyond the introductory college level, institutions should base their decisions on an assessment of each student's understanding and capabilities, using multiple sources of information. National examination scores alone are generally insufficient for these purposes.

Legislatures should avoid imposing laws or regulations requiring public colleges and universities to award credit for specified minimum scores on AP or IB examinations. *Offices of college admissions* should emphasize that taking advanced study courses without doing well in them or without taking the exams is insufficient. *Program developers* should clearly discourage anyone from using their programs and assessment results to draw inappropriate inferences about teachers, schools, and communities.

9(b): College and university scientists and mathematicians should modify their introductory courses along lines similar to those proposed in this report for high school advanced study. Departments should carefully advise undergraduates about the benefits and costs of bypassing introductory courses.

It is still common in some introductory college science and mathematics courses to cover large numbers of topics relatively superficially and with little connection to the world in which the topics are applied, thereby encouraging memorization at the expense of developing deep understanding of concepts and principles. These courses need to be brought into alignment with Recommendations 4 through 6, in part because teachers' ideas about how to teach science and mathematics come from their own college experiences.

Many students who participate in secondary advanced study later enroll in introductory college courses. Therefore, these college courses need to evolve so that they will continue to be appropriate for audiences with diverse preparation.

RECOMMENDATION 10: CHANGES IN THE AP AND IB PROGRAMS

10(a): The College Board should abandon its practice of designing AP courses in most disciplines primarily to replicate typical introductory college courses. The committee endorses recent moves by the College Board in this direction. As noted in particular in the report prepared by the calculus panel for this study, the College Board now bases AP calculus on expected outcomes and emerging best practices in college and university courses, rather than on lists of topics to be covered and tested. This approach, embraced by most of the mathematics professional communities, can serve as a model for revisions in other subject areas.

10(b): The College Board and the IBO should evaluate their assessments to ensure that they measure the conceptual understanding and complex reasoning that should be the primary goal of advanced

study. Programs of validity research should be an integral part of assessment design.

10(c): Both the College Board and the IBO should take more responsibility for ensuring the use of appropriate instructional approaches. Specifying the knowledge and skills that are important for beginning teachers and providing models for teacher development are likely to advance teacher effectiveness.

10(d): The College Board should exercise greater quality control over the AP trademark by articulating standards for what can be labeled an AP course, desirable student preparation for each course, strategies for ensuring equity and access, and expectations for universal participation in the AP examinations by course participants. When necessary, the College Board should commission experts to assist with these tasks.[2] These standards should apply whether AP is offered in schools or electronically.

10(e): The College Board and the IBO should provide assistance to schools in their efforts to offer high-quality advanced courses. To this end, the College Board should provide more detailed curriculum, information about best practices for instruction and classroom assessment, and strategies for enhancing professional development opportunities.

10(f): The College Board and the IBO should offer more guidance to educators, policymakers, and the general public concerning proper uses of their examination scores for admission, placement, and teacher evaluation. They should also actively discourage misuse of these scores.

10(g): The College Board and the IBO should develop programs of research on the implementation and effectiveness of their programs. This research should address such questions as the following: What is the preparation of teachers in these programs? What instructional strategies are actually used in practice, as indicated by classroom observation? How effective are the AP and IB professional development activities? How do the programs affect other school offerings and the curricula of the preceding years? How do students who participate in the AP and IB programs fare in college as compared with students lacking this experience? How are their choices of college courses affected? How do students fare who take the

---

[2]The committee notes that the College Board has used this strategy in the past. For example, in 1997 the National Task Force on Minority High Achievement was convened to assist the College Board in outlining recommendations for substantially increasing the number of African American, Latino, and Native American undergraduates who achieve high levels of academic success.

courses but not the exams? What is the impact on colleges of the large numbers of students earning credit through advanced study? Answers to such questions are urgently needed if the programs are to improve. Given the large and growing investment in this segment of secondary education, a substantial research effort is justified. Both *public and private agencies* should be prepared to assist in sponsoring this research. The various parties, including *the agencies and the programs,* should consider how to ensure independent review of the results. The *College Board and the IBO* should develop ways to incorporate the results of this recommended research systematically into the ongoing improvement of their programs.

References

Adelman, C. (1999). *Answers in a toolbox: Academics, intensity, attendance patterns, and bachelor's degree attainment*. Washington, DC: U.S. Department of Education, Office of Educational Research and Improvement.

Alaiyemola, F.F., Jegede, O.J., & Okebukola, P.A.O. (1990). The effect of a metacognitive strategy of instruction on the anxiety level of students in science classes. *International Journal of Science Education, 12*(1), 95-99.

Alexopoulou, E., & Driver, R. (1996). Small group discussion in physics: Peer interaction modes in pairs and fours. *Journal of Research in Science Teaching, 33*(10), 1099-1114.

American Association for the Advancement of Science. (1989). *Science for all Americans: A Project 2061 report on literacy goals in science, mathematics, and technology*. New York: Oxford University Press.

American Association for the Advancement of Science. (1993). *Benchmarks for science literacy*. New York: Oxford University Press.

American Association for the Advancement of Science. (2000). *Atlas of scientific literacy*. Washington, DC: Author.

American Association for the Advancement of Science. (2001). *Atlas of scientific literacy*. Washington, DC: American Association for the Advancement of Science, Project 2061, and National Science Teachers Association.

American Chemical Society. (1997). *Chemistry in the national science education standards: A reader and resource manual for high school teachers*. Washington, DC: Author.

American Educational Research Association. (1999). Class size: Issues and new findings [Special Issue]. *Education Evaluation and Policy Analysis, 21*(2).

American Educational Research Association, American Psychological Association, & National Council on Measurement in Education. (1999). *Standards for educational and psychological testing*. Washington, DC: American Educational Research Association.

American Federation of Teachers. (1999). *Making standards matter*. Washington, DC: Author.

American Federation of Teachers. (2000). *Doing what works: Improving big city school districts*. Washington, DC: Author.

American Federation of Teachers. (2001). *Survey and analysis of teacher salary trends 1999.* Washington, DC: Author.

American Youth Policy Forum. (2000). *High schools of the millennium.* Washington, DC: Author.

Anderson, J.R., Greeno, J.G., Reder, L.M., & Simon, H.A. (1997). Perspectives on learning, thinking, and activity. *Educational Researcher, 29*(4), 11-13.

Association of the Gifted and Talented. (1989). *Standards for programs involving the gifted and talented.* Reston, VA: The Council for Exceptional Children.

Atanda, R. (1999). *Do gatekeeper courses expand education options?* Washington, DC: U.S. Department of Education, National Center for Education Statistics.

Attewell, G. (2001). The winner-take-all high school: Organizational adaptations to educational stratification. *Sociology of Education, 74*(4), 267-296.

Au, K.H., & Jordan, C. (1981). Teaching reading to Hawaiian children: Finding a culturally appropriate solution. In H. Trueba, G.P. Guthrie, & K.H. Au (Eds.), *Culture in the bilingual classroom: Studies in classroom ethnography* (pp. 139-152). Rowley, MA: Newbury House.

Bachman, J.G., & Schulenberg, J. (1993). How part-time work intensity relates to drug use, problem behavior, time use, and satisfaction among high school seniors: Are these consequences or merely correlates? *Developmental Psychology, 29*(2), 220-235.

Ballou, D. (1996). Do public schools hire the best applicants? *The Quarterly Journal of Economics, III*(1), 97-133.

Basham, P. (2001). Home schooling: From the extreme to the mainstream. *Public Policy Sources, The Fraser Institute,* (51).

Benbow, C.P., & Minor, L.L. (1986). Mathematically talented males and females and achievement in the high school sciences. *American Educational Research Journal,* (23), 425-436.

Benbow, C.P., & Stanley, J.C. (1982). Consequences in high school and college of sex differences in mathematical reasoning abilities: A longitudinal perspective. *American Educational Researcher, 19,* 598-622.

Berger, S.L. (1991). *Differentiating curriculum for gifted students.* (ERIC Digest Number E510). Reston, VA: Clearinghouse on Handicapped and Gifted Children.

Berliner, D., & Biddle, B. (1996). *The manufactured crisis: Myths, fraud, and the attack on America's public schools.* Reading, MA: Addison-Wesley.

Blumenfeld, P.C., Marx, R.W., Patrick, H., Krajcik, J., & Soloway, E. (1997). Teaching for understanding. In B.J. Biddle, T.L. Good, & I.F. Goodson (Eds.), *The international handbook of teachers and teaching, volume II* (pp. 819-878). Dordrecht, Netherlands: Kluwer.

Borko, H., Peressini, D., Romagnano, L., Knuth, E., Yorker, C., Wooley, C., Hovermill, J., & Masarik, K. (2000). Teacher education does matter: A situative view of learning to teach secondary mathematics. *Educational Psychologist, 35,* 193-206.

Bottoms, G. (1998). *Things that matter most in improving student learning.* Atlanta, GA: Southern Regional Education Board.

Boyce, L.N., Bailey, J.M., Sher, B.T., Johnson, D.T., Van Tassel-Baska, J., & Gallagher, S.A. (1993). *Curriculum assessment guide to science materials.* Williamsburg, VA: College of William and Mary, Center for Gifted Education.

Bransford, J.D., & Schwartz, D.L. (2000). Rethinking transfer: A simple proposal with multiple implications. In A. Iran-Nejad, & P. D. Pearson (Eds.), *Review of research in education* (volume 24, pp. 61-101). Washington, DC: American Educational Research Association.

Breland, H.M., & Oltman, P.K. (2001). *An analysis of Advanced Placement (AP) examinations in economics and comparative government and politics.* College Board Research Report 2001-4; ETS RR-01-17. New York: College Entrance Examination Board.

Brown, A.L. (1994). The advancement of learning. *Educational Researcher, 23*(8), 4-12.

Brown, A.L., Ash, D., Rutherford, M., Nakagawa, K., Gordon, A., & Campion, J.C. (1993). *Distributed expertise in the classroom.* In G. Salomon (Ed.), *Distributed cognitions: Psychological and educational considerations* (pp. 188-228). Cambridge: Cambridge University Press.

Brown, J.S., Collins, A., & Duguid, P. (1989). Situated cognition and the culture of learning. *Educational Researcher, 18*(1), 32-42.

Bryk, A.S., Lee, V.E., & Holland, P.B. (1993). *Catholic schools and the common good.* Cambridge, MA: Harvard University Press.

Bureau of Labor Statistics. (1999). *Occupational outlook handbook.* Washington, DC: U.S. Department of Labor.

Burgess, R.G. (1983). *Experiencing comprehensive education: A study of Bishop McGregor School.* London: Methuen.

Burgess, R.G. (1984). It's not a proper subject: It's just Newsom. In I. Goodson & S. Ball, *Defining the curriculum.* London: Falmer Press.

Burnett, G. (1995). *Alternatives to ability grouping: Still unanswered questions.* ERIC Digest Number 111. New York: Clearinghouse on Urban Education.

Burton, N.W., Bruschi, B., Kindig, L., & Courtney, R. (2000). *Draft interim report of advanced placement research project—Documentation and evaluation of advanced placement summer institutes: Advanced placement new teacher needs study.* New York: College Entrance Examination Board.

Callahan, C. (2000). *The historical role of Advanced Placement and International Baccalaureate programs for talented students in American high schools.* Paper presented at Committee on Programs for Advanced Study of Mathematics and Science in American High Schools meeting, March 26, Irvine, CA.

Campbell, P. (2000). *International Baccalaureate Programme.* Paper presented to the Committee on Programs for Advanced Study of Math and Science in American High Schools, March 26, Irvine, CA.

Canas, A., Ford, K., Novak, J., Hayes, P., & Reichherzer, T. (2001). Online concept maps: Enhancing collaborative learning by using technology with concept maps. *The Science Teacher, 68*(2), 49-51.

Caravita, S., & Hallden, O. (1994). Re-framing the problem of conceptual change. *Learning and Instruction, 4,* 89-111.

Carnevule, D. (1999). ACLU sues California over unequal access to Advanced Placement courses. *Chronicle of Higher Education, 45*(48).

Carpenter, T.P., & Lehrer, R. (1999). Teaching and learning mathematics with understanding. In E. Fennema, & T.A. Romberg (Eds.), *Classrooms that promote mathematical understanding* (p. 1932). Mahwah, NJ: Erlbaum.

Carr, M., Kurtz, B.E., Schneider, W., Turner, L.A., & Borkowski, J.G. (1989). Strategy acquisition and transfer among German and American children: Environmental influences on metacognitive development. *Developmental Psychology, 25*, 765-771.

Carr, S. (2000). More states create virtual high schools. *The Chronicle of Higher Education, 47*(3), A40.

Carr, S. (2001). South Dakota finds mixed results with online AP courses. *The Chronicle of Higher Education, 47*(37), A40, May.

Cavallo, A.M.L. (1996). Meaningful learning, reasoning ability, and students' understanding and problem solving of topics in genetics. *Journal of Research in Science Teaching, 33*(6), 625-656.

Chi, M.T.H., Feltovich, P.J., & Glaser, R. (1981). Categorization and representation of physics problems by experts and novices. *Cognitive Science*, (5), 121-152.

Choy, S.P., Bobbitt, S.A., Henke, R.R., Medrich, E.A., Horn, L.J., & Lieberman, J. (1993). *America's teachers: Profile of a profession.* (NCES 93-025). Washington, DC: U.S. Department of Education, National Center for Education Statistics.

Cobb, P., Wood, T., & Yackel, E. (1993). *Discourse, mathematical thinking, and classroom practice. Contexts for learning: Social cultural dynamics in children's development.* Oxford, UK: Oxford University Press.

Cohen, D.K., & Ball, D.L. (1990). Relations between policy and practice: A commentary. *Educational Evaluation and Policy Analysis, 12*, 331-338.

College Board. (2000). *Advanced placement program, workshop consultant endorsement policy.* New York: Author.

College Board. (2001). *Advanced placement program, institute endorsement policy.* New York: Author.

College Entrance Examination Board. (1997). *A guide for the recommended laboratory program for Advanced Placement chemistry.* New York: Author.

College Entrance Examination Board. (1999a). *Advanced placement course description, biology, 2000, 2001.* New York: Author.

College Entrance Examination Board. (1999b). *Advanced placement course description, calculus, 2000, 2001.* New York: Author.

College Entrance Examination Board. (1999c). *Advanced placement course description, physics, 2000, 2001.* New York: Author.

College Entrance Examination Board. (1999d). *Advanced placement technical manual 2000.* New York: Author.

College Entrance Examination Board. (2000a). *College and university guide to the Advanced Placement Program.* New York: Author.

College Entrance Examination Board. (2000b). *Released exam 1999, AP chemistry.* New York: Author.

College Entrance Examination Board. (2000c). *2000 National summary reports.* New York: Author.

College Entrance Examination Board. (2000d). *Unpublished responses from student questionnaire administered in May 2000.* New York: Author.

College Entrance Examination Board. (2001a). *Advanced placement course description, biology, May 2002, 2003.* New York: Author.

College Entrance Examination Board. (2001b). *Advanced placement course description, calculus, 2002, 2003.* New York: Author.

College Entrance Examination Board. (2001c). *Advanced placement course description, chemistry, 2002, 2003.* New York: Author.

College Entrance Examination Board. (2001d). *Advanced placement course description, physics, 2002, 2003.* New York: Author.

Collins, A. (1988). *Cognitive apprenticeship and instructional technology.* (Technical Report No. 6899). Cambridge, MA: BBN Labs.

Collins, A., & Smith, E. (1982). Teaching the process of reading comprehension. In D.K. Detterman, & R.J. Sternberg (Eds.), *How and how much can intelligence be increased?* Norwood, NJ: Ablex.

Commission on the Future of the Advanced Placement Program. (2001). *Access to excellence: A report of the Commission on the Future of the Advanced Placement Program.* New York: College Entrance Examination Board.

Council of Chief State School Officers. (1998). *Key state policies on K-12 education: Standards, graduation, assessment, teacher licensure, time and attendance.* Washington, DC: Author.

Council of Chief State School Officers. (1999). *State indicators of science and mathematics 1999: State trends and new indicators from the 1997-98 school year.* Washington, DC: Author.

Cronbach, L.J. (1971). Test validation. In R.L. Thorndike (Ed.), *Educational measurement* (2nd ed.). Washington, DC: American Council on Education.

Damon, W., & Eisenberg, N. (1998). *Handbook of child psychology* (5th ed.). New York: Wiley.

Dark, V.J., and Benbow, C.P. (1993). Cognitive differences among the gifted: A review and new data. In D.K. Detterman (Ed.), *Current topics in human intelligence* (vol. 3, pp. 85-120). New York: Ablex.

Darling-Hammond, L. (1996). What matters most: A competent teacher for every child. *Phi Delta Kappan,* (78), 193-201.

Darling-Hammond, L. (1999a). Educating teachers for the next century: Rethinking practice and policy. In G.A. Griffin (Ed.), *The education of teachers: 98th yearbook of the National Society for the Study of Education* (pp. 221-256). Chicago: University of Chicago Press.

Darling-Hammond, L. (1999b). Target time toward teachers. *Journal of Staff Development,* 20(2).

Darling-Hammond, L. (2000). Teacher quality and student achievement: A review of state policy evidence. *Education Policy Analysis Archives,* 8(1).

Darling-Hammond, L., Wise, A.E., & Klein, S.P. (1999). *A license to teach.* San Francisco, CA: Jossey-Bass.

Dirkes, M.A. (1985). Metacognition: Students in charge of their thinking. *Roeper Review,* 8(2), 96-100.

Doran, B.J., Dugan, T., & Weffer, R. (1998). Language minority students in high school: The role of language in learning biology concepts. *Science Education, 82*(3), 311-331.

Dornbusch, S.M. (1994). *Off the track.* Presidential address at the biennial meeting of the Society for Research on Adolescence, San Diego, CA.

Dossey, J. (1998). Making algebra dynamic and motivating: A national challenge (keynote address). In National Research Council, *The nature and role of algebra in the k-14 curriculum, proceedings of a national symposium* (pp. 17-22). Washington, DC: National Academy Press.

Driver, R., Squires, A. Rushworth, P., & Wood-Robinson, V. (1994). *Making sense of secondary science: Research into children's ideas.* New York: Routledge.

Dunbar, K. (1995). How scientists really reason: Scientific reasoning in real-world laboratories. In R.J. Sternberg, & J.E. Davidson (Eds.), *The nature of insight* (pp. 365-395). Cambridge, MA: The MIT Press.

Dweck, C.S. (1989). Motivation. In A. Lesgold, & R. Glaser (Eds.), *Foundations for a psychology of education.* Hillsdale, NJ: Erlbaum.

Eccles, J.S. (1987). Gender roles and women's achievement related decisions. *Psychology of Women Quarterly, 11*, 135-172.

Eccles, J.S. (1994). Understanding women's educational and occupational choices. *Psychology of Women Quarterly, 18*, 585-610.

Eccles, J.S., & Harold, R. (1996). Family involvement in children's and adolescents' schooling. In B. Booth, & J. Dunn (Eds.), *Family-school links: How do they affect educational outcomes.* Hillsdale, NJ: Erlbaum.

Eccles, J.S., Wigfield, A., & Schiefele, U. (1998). Motivation to succeed. In W. Damon, & N. Eisenberg (Eds.), *Handbook of child psychology, Vol. IV: Social and personality development* (pp. 1017-1095). New York: Wiley.

Edmondson, K. (2000). Assessing science understanding through concept maps. In J. Mintzes, J. Wandersee, & J. Novak (Eds.), *Assessing science understanding* (pp. 19-40). San Diego: Academic Press.

Education Commission to the President of the United States. (2000). *Report of the Web-based Education Commission to the President of the United States.* Washington, DC: Author.

Education Week. (1999). Quality counts 1999. Rewarding results, punishing failure. [Special issue, January].

Education Week. (2000). Quality counts 2000: Who should teach? [Special issue, January].

Education Week. (2001). Quality counts 2001 A better balance: Standards, tests, and the tools to succeed. [Special issue, January].

Ekstrom, R.B., Goertz, M., & Rock, D.A. (1988). *Education and American youth.* Philadelphia: Falmer Press.

Eubanks, S.C. (1996). *The urban teacher challenge: A report on teacher recruitment and demand in selected great city schools.* Belmont, MA: Recruiting New Teachers, Inc.

Falk, B. (2000). *The heart of the matter: Using standards and assessment to learn.* Portsmouth, NH: Heinemann.

Feldhusen, J., Hansen, J., & Kennedy, D. (1989). Curriculum development for GCT teachers. *GCT, 12*(6), 12-19.

Feldt, L.S., & Brennan, R.L. (1993). Reliability. In R.L. Linn (Ed.), *Educational measurement* (3rd ed., pp. 105-147). Washington, DC: American Council on Education.

Ferguson, R.F. (1991). Paying for public education. *Harvard Journal on Legislation*, (28), 465-498.

Ferguson, R.F. (1998). Can schools narrow the black-white test score gap? In C. Jencks, & M. Phillips (Eds.), *The black-white test score gap*. Washington, DC: The Brookings Institution.

Ferguson, R.F., & Ladd, H.F. (1996). How and why money matters: An analysis of Alabama schools. In H.F. Ladd (Ed.), *Holding schools accountable: Performance-based reform in education*. Washington, DC: The Brookings Institution.

Ferrari, M., & Sternberg, R.J. (1998). The development of mental abilities and styles. In D. Kuhn, & R. Siegler (Eds.), *The handbook of child psychology* (5 ed., vol. 2: Cognition, Perception, and Language, pp. 899-946). New York: Wiley.

Flavell, J.H. (1979). Metacognition and cognitive monitoring: A new area of cognitive-developmental inquiry. *American Psychologist, 34*, 906-911.

Frome, P. (2001). *High schools that work: Findings from the 1996 and 1998 assessments*. Washington, DC: U.S. Department of Education, Planning and Evaluation Service.

Fuchs, L.S., Fuchs, D., Hamlett, C.L., & Karns, K. (1998). High achieving students' interactions and performance on complex mathematical tasks as a function of homogeneous and heterogeneous pairings. *American Educational Research Journal, 35*, 227-268.

Fullan, M.G. (1991). *The new meaning of educational change*. New York: Teachers College Press.

Gabel, D. (Ed.). (1994). *Handbook of research on science teaching and learning*. New York: MacMillan.

Gamoran, A. (1987). The stratification of high school learning opportunities. *Sociology of Education, 60*(3), 135-155.

Gamoran, A. (1992). The variable effects of high school tracking. *Sociology of Education, 57*(4), 812-828.

Gamoran, A., & Hannigan, E.C. (2000). Algebra for everyone? Benefits of college-preparatory mathematics for students with diverse abilities in early secondary school. *Educational Evaluation and Policy Analysis, 22*(3).

Gamoran, A., & Nystrand, M. (1990). *Tracking, instruction, and achievement*. Paper presented at the World Congress of Sociology, Madrid, Spain.

Gamoran, A., Nystrand, M., Berends, M., & LePore, P.C. (1995). An organizational analysis of the effects of ability grouping. *American Educational Research Journal, 32*(4), 687-715.

Gandal, M. (1997). *Making standards matter 1997: An annual fifty-state report on efforts to raise academic standards*. Washington, DC: American Federation of Teachers.

Garcia, T., & Pintrich, P.R. (1994). Regulating motivation and cognition in the classroom: The role of self-schemas and self-regulatory strategies. In D. Schunk, & B.

Zimmerman (Eds.), *Self-regulation of learning and performance: Issues and educational application* (pp. 127-154). Hillsdale, NJ: Erlbaum.

Garner, R. (1987). *Metacognition and reading comprehension.* Norwood, NJ: Ablex.

Garner, R., & Alexander, P. (1989). Metacognition: Answered and unanswered questions. *Educational Psychologist, 24,* 143-158.

Glaser, R. (1992). Expert knowledge and processes of thinking. In D. F. Halpern (Ed.), *Enhancing thinking skills in the sciences and mathematics* (pp. 63-75). Hillsdale, NJ : Erlbaum.

Gobert, J.D., & Clement, J.J. (1999). Effects of student-generated diagrams versus student-generated summaries on conceptual understanding of casual and dynamic knowledge in plate tectonics. *Journal of Research in Science Teaching, 36*(1), 39-53.

Goertzel, M., Goertzel, V., & Goertzel, T. (1978). *300 eminent personalities.* San Francisco: Jossey-Bass.

Gonzalez, E.J., O'Connor, K.M., & Miles, J.A. (2001). *How well do advanced placement students perform on the TIMSS advanced mathematics and physics tests?* Chestnut Hill, MA: Boston College, Lynch School of Education, International Study Center.

Goodlad, J.I. (1984). *A place called school: Promise for the future.* New York: McGraw-Hill.

Gourman, J. (1999). *The Gourman report: A rating of undergraduate programs in American and international universities.* New York: Random House.

Graham, S., & Weiner, B. (1996). Theories and principles of motivation. In D.C. Berliner, & R.C. Calfee (Eds.), *Handbook of educational psychology* (pp. 63-84). New York: Macmillan.

Gratz, D.B. (2000). High standards for whom? *Phi Delta Kappan.* May 2000. 81(9).

Graue, M.E. (1993). Integrating theory and practice through instructional assessment. *Educational Assessment, 1,* 293-309.

Greenberg, K.H. (1992). *Research and mediated learning: Implications for program implementation.* Paper presented at the conference on Mediated Learning in Health and Education: Forging a New Alliance, St. Petersburg, FL.

Greeno, J.G. (1993). Number sense as situated knowing in a conceptual domain. *Journal in Research in Mathematics Education,* (22), 170-218.

Greeno, J.G., Collins, A.M., & Resnick, L.B. (1996). Cognition and learning. In D. Berliner, & R. Calfree (Eds.), *Handbook of educational psychology* (pp.15-46). New York: Macmillan.

Greenwald, R., Hedges, L.V., & Laine, R.D. (1996). The effects of school resources on student achievement. *Review of Educational Research, 66*(3), 361-396.

Grissmer, D. (1999). Class size: Issues and new findings [Special Issue]. *Education Evaluation and Policy Analysis, 21*(2).

Haidar, A.H. (1997). Prospective chemistry teacher's conceptions of the conservation of matter and related concepts. *Journal of Research in Science Teaching, 34*(2), 181-197.

Hanushek, E. (1996). A more complete picture of school resource policies. *Review of Educational Research, 66*(3), 397-409.

Hart, P.D. Research Associates. (1999). *Shell Education Survey.* Study #5487. Washington, DC: Author.

Harvard-Smithsonian Center for Astrophysics, Science Education Department (1987). *A private universe (Video).* Cambridge, MA: Science Media Group.

Heath, S.B. (1983). *Ways with words: Language, life, and work in communities and classrooms.* Cambridge: Cambridge University Press.

Hebel, S. (1999). AP courses are new target in struggle over access to college in California. *Chronicle of Higher Education, 46*(14).

Herr, N.E. (1993). The relationship between advanced placement and honors science courses. *School Science and Mathematics, 93,* 183-187.

Hoffman, L. (1998). Overview of public elementary and secondary schools and districts: School year 1996-97. *Education Statistics Quarterly,* NCES No. 98204, September 29.

Hong, L.K. (2001). Too many intrusions on instructional time. *Phi Delta Kappan, 82*(9).

Horn, L., Hafner, A., & Owings, J. (1992). *A profile of American eighth-grade mathematics and science instruction.* Washington, DC: U.S. Department of Education, National Center for Education Statistics.

Horn, L., Nunez, A., & Bobbitt, L. (2000). *Mapping the road to college: First generation students' math track, planning strategies, and context of support.* (NCES 2000-153). Washington, DC: U.S. Department of Education, National Center for Education Statistics.

Hoz, R., Bowman, D., & Chacham, T. (1997). Psychometric and edumetric validity of geomorphological knowledge which are tapped by concept mapping. *Journal of Research in Science Teaching, 34*(9), 925-947.

Hunt, J.M. (1961). *Intelligence and experience.* New York: Ronald Press.

Ingersoll, R.M. (1999). The problem of underqualified teachers in American secondary schools. *Educational Researcher, 28*(2), 26-37.

International Baccalaureate North American. (2000). *International Baccalaureate North American statistical summary—May 2000 examination session.* New York: Author.

International Baccalaureate Organisation. (1997a). *IB guide to the diploma programme, 1997.* Geneva, Switzerland: Author.

International Baccalaureate Organisation. (1997b). *Mathematical methods standard level.* Geneva, Switzerland: Author.

International Baccalaureate Organisation. (1998a). *IB experimental sciences internal assessment clarifications.* Geneva, Switzerland: Author.

International Baccalaureate Organisation. (1998b). *IB mathematics HL diploma programme guide 1998.* Geneva, Switzerland: Author.

International Baccalaureate Organisation. (1998c). *IB mathematics HL.* Geneva, Switzerland: Author.

International Baccalaureate Organisation. (1998d). *Mathematical methods standard level.* Geneva, Switzerland: Author.

International Baccalaureate Organisation. (1998e). *IB further mathematics standard level.* Geneva, Switzerland: Author.

International Baccalaureate Organisation. (1999a). *1999 IB chemistry subject report.* Geneva, Switzerland: Author.

International Baccalaureate Organisation. (1999b). *IB coordinator notes.* Geneva, Switzerland: Author.

International Baccalaureate Organisation. (1999c). *IB diploma grade descriptors group 4.* Geneva, Switzerland: Author.

International Baccalaureate Organisation. (1999d). *IB experimental sciences course revisions.* Geneva, Switzerland: Author.

International Baccalaureate Organisation. (1999e). *Teacher support material: Experimental sciences—internal assessment.* Geneva, Switzerland: Author.

International Baccalaureate Organisation. (2000a). *Experimental sciences chemistry curriculum review report.* Geneva, Switzerland: Author.

International Baccalaureate Organisation. (2000b). *IB theory of knowledge.* Geneva, Switzerland: Author.

International Baccalaureate Organisation. (2000c). *May 2000 chemistry subject report.* Geneva, Switzerland: Author.

International Baccalaureate Organisation. (2000d). *Vade mecum.* Geneva, Switzerland: Author.

International Baccalaureate Organisation. (2001a). *IB diploma programme guide: Biology, 2001.* Geneva, Switzerland: Author.

International Baccalaureate Organisation. (2001b). *IB diploma programme guide: Chemistry, 2001.* Geneva, Switzerland: Author.

International Baccalaureate Organisation. (2001c). *IB diploma programme guide: Physics, 2001.* Geneva, Switzerland: Author.

Johnson, D.T., & Sher, B.T. (1997). *Resource guide to mathematics curriculum materials for high-ability learners in grades k-8.* Williamsburg, VA: College of William and Mary, Center for Gifted Education.

Johnston, R.C. (2000). Rochester plan adds flexibility to high school. *Education Week, 19*(43), 18-19.

Johnstone, D.B. (1993). Enhancing the productivity of learning. *AAHE Bulletin, 46*(4), 3-8.

Johnstone, D.B., & Del Genio, B. (2001). *College-level learning in high school: Purposes, policies, and practical implications.* Washington, DC: Association of American Colleges and Universities.

Jones, L.R., Mullis, I.V.S., Raizen, S.A., Weiss, I.R., and Weston, E.A. (1992). *The 1990 science report card: NAEP's assessment of fourth, eighth, and twelfth graders.* Princeton, NJ: Educational Testing Service.

Jones, L.V., Davenport, E.C., Bryson, A., Bekhuis, T., & Zwick, R. (1986). Mathematics and science test scores as related to courses taken in high school and other factors. *Journal of Educational Measurement, 23*(3), 197-208.

Jones, M.G., Rua, M.J., & Carter, G. (1998). Science teacher's conceptual growth within Vygotsky's zone of proximal development. *Journal of Research in Science Teaching, 35*(9), 967-985.

Jordan, H., Mendro, R., & Weerasinghe, D. (1997). *Teacher effects on longitudinal student achievement: A report on research in progress.* Paper presented at the annual CREATE meeting, Indianapolis, IN.

Kaufman, P., Bradby, D., & Teitelbaum, P. (2000). *High schools that work and whole school reform: Raising academic achievement of vocational completers through the reform of school practice*. Southern Regional Education Board. Berkeley, CA: University of California at Berkeley, National Center for Research in Vocational Education.

Kaufmann, F., Harrel, G., Milam, C.P., Woolverton, N., & Miller, J. (1986). The nature, role, and influence of mentors in the lives of gifted adults. *Journal of Counseling and Development, 64*, 576-578.

Kennedy, D. (1997). *Teachers guide, AP calculus*. New York: College Entrance Examination Board.

Kirst, M.W. (1998). *Improving and aligning k-16 standards, admissions, and freshman placement policies*. Stanford, CA: Stanford University, National Center for Postsecondary Improvement.

Kobayashi, Y. (1994). Conceptual acquisition and change through social interaction. *Human Development, 37*, 233-241.

Koretz, D. (1988). Arriving in Lake Wobegon: Are standardized tests exaggerating achievement and distorting instruction? *American Educator, 12*(2), 8-15, 46-52.

Koretz, D. (1996). Using student assessments for educational accountability. In E.A. Hanushek & D.W. Jorgenson (Eds.), *Improving the performance of America's schools* (pp. 171-196). Washington, DC: National Academy Press.

Koretz, D., Linn, R.L., Dunbar, S.B., & Shepard, L.A. (1991). The effects of high-stakes testing: Preliminary evidence about generalization across tests. Presented at The Effects of High Stakes Testing symposium annual meetings of the American Educational Research Association and the National Council on Measurement in Education, Chicago, April.

Kozma, R.B., & Russell, J. (1997). Multimedia and understanding: Expert and novice responses to different representation of chemical phenomena. *Journal of Research in Science Teaching, 34*(9), 949-968.

Kuehn, P. (2001). Online AP courses are not the answer. *California Star News,* November 15, 2000. Available at www.californiastar.com/courses.html (February 11, 2002).

Kulm, G. (1990). *Assessing higher order thinking in mathematics*. Washington, DC: American Association for the Advancement of Science.

Lave, J. (1991). Situating learning in communities of practice. In L. Resnick, J. Levine, & S. Teasley (Eds.), *Perspectives on socially shared cognition* (pp. 63-83). Washington, DC: American Psychological Association.

Lee, V.E. (2001). *Restructuring high schools for equity and excellence: What works*. New York: Teachers College Press.

Lee, V.E., & Bryk, A.S. (1989). A multilevel model of the social distribution of high school achievement. *Sociology of Education, 62*(3), 172-192.

Lee, V.E., Bryk, A.S., & Smith, J.B. (1993). The organization of effective secondary schools. *Review of Research in Education, 19*, 171-268.

Lee, V.E., Croninger, R.G., & Smith, J.B. (1997). Course-taking, equity, and mathematics learning: Testing the constrained curriculum hypothesis in U.S. secondary schools. *Educational Evaluation and Policy Analysis, 19*(2), 99-121.

Lee, V.E., & Ekstrom, R. (1987). Student access to guidance counseling in high school. *American Educational Research Journal, 24*, 287-310.

Lee, V.E., & Smith, J.B. (1996). Collective responsibility for learning and its effect on gains in achievement for early secondary school students. *American Journal of Education, 104*(2), 103-147.

Lee, V.E., & Smith, J.B. (1999). Social support and achievement for young adolescents in Chicago: The role of school academic press. *American Educational Research Journal, 36*(4), 907-945.

Lee, V.L., Burkam, D.T., Chow-Hoy, T., Smerdon, B.A., & Geverdt, D. (1998). *High school curriculum structure: Effects on coursetaking and achievement in mathematics for high school graduates—An examination of data from the National Education Longitudinal Study of 1988.* (NCES Working Paper No. 98). Washington, DC: U.S. Department of Education, National Center for Education Statistics.

Lester, F.K. Jr., Masingila, J.O., Mau, S.T., Lambdin, D.V., dos Santon, V.W., & Raymond, A.M. (1994). Learning how to teach via problem solving. In D. Aichele, & A. Coxford (Eds.), *Professional development for teachers of mathematics* (pp. 152-166). Reston, VA: National Council of Teachers of Mathematics.

Lichten, W. (2000). Whither advanced placement? *Education Policy Analysis Archives, 8*(29), 1-19.

Linn, M.C., & Hsi, S. (1999). *Computers, teachers, peers: Science learning partners.* Mahwah, NJ: Erlbaum.

Linn, R. (2000). Assessment and accountability. *Educational Researcher, 29*, 4-16.

Linn, R.L., Graue, M.E., & Sanders, N.M. (1990). Comparing state and district results to national norms: The validity of the claims that "everyone is above average." *Educational Measurement: Issues and Practice, 9*(3), 5-14.

Louis, K.S. (1992). Restructuring and the problem of teachers' work. In A. Lieberman (Ed.), *The changing contexts of teaching: Ninety-first yearbook of the National Society for the Study of Education* (pp. 138-156). Chicago: University of Chicago Press.

Lucas, S.R. (1999). *Tracking inequalities: Stratification and mobility in American schools.* New York: Teachers College Press.

Ma, L. (1999). *Knowing and teaching elementary mathematics: Teachers' understanding of fundamental mathematics in China and the United States.* Mahwah, NJ: Erlbaum.

Ma, L., & Willms, J.D. (1999). Dropping out of advanced mathematics: How much do students and schools contribute to the problem. *Educational Evaluation and Policy Analysis, 21*(4), 365-383.

Madaus, G.F., & Airasian, P. (1978). A post hoc technique for identifying between program differences in achievement. *Studies in Educational Evaluation, 4*(1), 1-8.

Maker, C.J. (1982). *Curriculum development for the gifted.* Rockville, MD: Aspen.

Marin, B.L., Mintzes, J.J., & Clavin, I.E. (2000). Restructuring knowledge in biology: Cognitive processes and metacognitive reflections. *International Journal of Science Education, 22*(3), 303-323.

Markow, D., Fauth, S., & Gravitch, D. (2001). *MetLife survey of the American teacher, 2001.* New York: MetLife.

Marks, H.M., Doane, K.B., & Secada, W.B. (1996). Support for student achievement. In F.M. Newmann & Associates (Ed.), *Authentic achievement: Restructuring schools for intellectual quality.* San Francisco: Jossey-Bass.

Markus, H., & Wurf, E. (1987). The dynamic self-concept: A social psychological perspective. *Annual Review of Psychology, 38,* 299-337.

Marsh, H.W. (1990). A multidimensional, hierarchical model of self-concept: Theoretical and empirical justification. *Educational Psychology Review,* (2), 77-172.

Mathews, J. (1998a). 100 best high schools in America. *Newsweek,* March 30.

Mathews, J. (1998b). *Class struggle: What's wrong (and right) with America's best public high schools.* New York: Times Books.

McKnight, C.C., Crosswhite, F.J., Dossey, J.A., Kifer, E., Swafford, J A., Travers, K.J., & Cooney, T.J. (1987). *The underachieving curriculum: Assessing U.S. school mathematics from an international perspective.* Champaign, IL: Stipes.

McLaughlin, M., & Talbert, J.E. (1993). *Contexts that matter for teaching and learning: Strategic opportunities for meeting the nation's educational goals.* Stanford, CA: Stanford University, Center for Research on the Context of Secondary School Teaching.

McLellan, H. (1996). Being digital: Implications for education. *Educational Technology, 36*(6), 5-20.

Messick, S. (1993). Validity. In R.L. Linn (Ed.), *Educational measurement* (3 ed., pp. 13-103). Washington, DC: American Council on Education.

Mestre, J. (1994). Cognitive aspects of learning and teaching science. In S. Fitzsimmons, & L. Kerpelman (Eds.), *Teacher enhancement for elementary science and mathematics: Status, issues, and problems.* Washington, DC: National Science Foundation.

Milgram, R.M. (1989). *Teaching gifted and talented learners in regular classrooms.* Springfield, IL: Charles C. Thomas.

Millman, J., & Greene, J. (1993). The specification and development of tests of achievement and ability. In R.L. Linn (Ed.), *Educational measurement* (3 ed., pp. 335-366). New York: American Council on Education.

Minstrell, J. (2000a). The role of the teacher in making sense of classroom experiences and effecting better learning. In D. Klahr, & S. Carver (Eds.), *Cognition and instruction: 25 years of progress.* Mahwah, NJ: Erlbaum.

Minstrell, J. (2000b). Student thinking and related assessment: Creating a facet-based learning environment. In Committee on the Evaluation of National and State Assessments of Educational Progress. N.S. Raju, J.W. Pellegrino, M.W. Bertenthal, K.J. Mitchell, and L.R. Jones (Eds.) *Grading the nation's report card: Research from the evaluation of NAEP* (pp 44-73). Division of Behavioral and Social Sciences and Education, National Research Council. Washington, DC: National Academy Press

Mintzes, J., Wandersee, J., & Novak, J.D. (1998). *Teaching science for understanding.* San Diego: Academic Press.

Mintzes, J., Wandersee, J., & Novak, J.D. (2000). *Assessing science understanding.* San Diego: Academic Press.

Mintzes, J.J., Wandersee, J.H., & Novak, J.D. (2001). Assessing science understanding in biology. *Journal of Biological Education, 35*(3), 119-124.

Morgan, R., & Maneckshana, B. (2000). *Advanced placement students in college: An investigation of their course-taking patterns and college majors.* New York: College Entrance Examination Board.

Morgan, R., & Ramist, L. (1998). Advanced placement students in college: An investigation of course grades at 21 colleges. *Unpublished Statistical Report No. SR-98-13.* Princeton, NJ: Educational Testing Service.

Mullins, J. (1994). *Teachers guide, AP chemistry.* New York: College Entrance Examination Board.

Murnane, R.J. (1996). Staffing the nation's schools with skilled teachers. In E.A. Hanushek, & D.W. Jorgenson (Eds.), *Improving America's schools: The role of incentives* (pp. 241-258). Washington, DC: National Academy Press.

National Association of Secondary School Principals. (1996). *Breaking ranks: Changing an American institution.* Reston, VA: Author.

National Board for Professional Teaching Standards. (1994). *What teachers should know and be able to do.* Detroit, MI: Author.

National Center for Education Statistics. (1992a). *The 1990 science report: NAEP's assessment of fourth, eight, and twelfth graders.* Washington, DC: U.S. Department of Education.

National Center for Education Statistics. (1992b). *A profile of American eight-grade mathematics and science instruction.* (NCES 92-486). Washington, DC: U.S. Department of Education.

National Center for Education Statistics. (1998). *Pursuing excellence: A study of U.S. twelfth-grade mathematics and science achievement in international context.* (NCES 98049). Washington, DC: U.S. Department of Education.

National Center for Education Statistics. (2000a). *The condition of education 2000.* (NCES 2000-62). Washington, DC: U.S. Department of Education, Office of Educational Research and Improvement.

National Center for Education Statistics. (2000b). *Monitoring school quality: An indicators report.* (NCES 2001-30). Washington, DC: U.S. Department of Education.

National Center for Education Statistics. (2001a). *Digest of education statistics 2000.* (NCES 2001-034. Washington, DC: U.S. Department of Education, Office of Educational Research and Improvement.

National Center for Education Statistics. (2001b). *1998 National Assessment of Educational Progress (NAEP) high school transcript study.* (NCES 2001477). Washington, DC: U.S. Department of Education.

National Commission on Excellence in Education. (1983). *A nation at risk: The imperative for educational reform.* Washington, DC: U.S. Government Printing Office.

National Commission on Mathematics and Science Teaching for the 21st Century. (2000). *Before it's too late: A report to the nation from the National Commission on Mathematics and Science Teaching for the 21st century.* Jessup, MD: Education Publications Center.

National Commission on Teaching and America's Future. (1996). *What matters most: Teaching for America's future.* New York: National Commission on Teaching and America's Future, Teachers College, Columbia University.

National Commission on the High School Senior Year. (2001a). *The lost opportunity of senior year: Finding a better way (preliminary report)*. Washington, DC: Author.

National Commission on the High School Senior Year. (2001b). *Raising our sights: No high school senior left behind*. Washington, DC: Author.

National Council of Teachers of Mathematics. (1989). *Curriculum and evaluation standards for school mathematics*. Reston, VA: Author.

National Council of Teachers of Mathematics. (1991). *Professional standards for teaching mathematics*. Reston, VA: Author.

National Council of Teachers of Mathematics. (1995). *Assessment standards for school mathematics*. Reston, VA: Author.

National Council of Teachers of Mathematics. (2000). *Principles and standards for school mathematics*. Reston, VA: Author.

National Education Goals Panel. (2001). *Promising practices: Progress toward the goals, 2000*. Washington, DC: Author.

National Research Council. (1996). *National science education standards*. National Committee on Science Education Standards and Assessment. Coordinating Council for Education. Washington, DC: National Academy Press.

National Research Council. (1998). *The nature and role of algebra in the k-14 curriculum: Proceedings of a national symposium*. National Council of Teachers of Mathematics and Mathematical Sciences Education Board. Washington, DC: National Academy Press.

National Research Council. (1999a). *Equity and adequacy in education finance: Issues and perspectives*. Committee on Education Finance. H.F. Ladd, R. Chalk, & J.S. Hansen, (Eds.). Commission on Behavioral and Social Sciences and Education. Washington, DC: National Academy Press.

National Research Council. (1999b). *High stakes: Testing for tracking, promotion, and graduation*. Committee on Appropriate Test Use. J.P. Heubert & R.M. Hauser, (Eds.). Commission on Behavioral and Social Sciences and Education. Washington, DC: National Academy Press.

National Research Council. (1999c). *Making money matter: Financing America's schools*. Committee on Education Finance. H.F. Ladd & J.S. Hansen, (Eds.). Commission on Behavioral and Social Sciences and Education. Washington, DC: National Academy Press.

National Research Council. (1999d). *Transforming undergraduate education in science, mathematics, engineering, and technology*. Committee on Undergraduate Science Education. Center for Science, Mathematics, and Engineering Education. Washington, DC: National Academy Press.

National Research Council. (2000a). *Educating teachers of science, mathematics, and technology: New practices for the new millennium*. Committee on Science and Mathematics Teacher Preparation. Washington, DC: National Academy Press.

National Research Council. (2000b). *How people learn: Brain, mind, experience, and school* (Expanded ed.). Committee on Developments in the Science of Learning. J.D. Bransford, A.L. Brown, & R.R. Cocking, (Eds.). Commission on Behavioral and Social Sciences and Education. Washington, DC: National Academy Press.

National Research Council. (2001a). *Knowing what students know: The science and design of educational assessment*. Committee on the Foundation of Assessment. J. Pellegrino, N. Chudowsky, & R. Glaser, (Eds.). Division of Behavioral and Social Sciences and Education. Washington, DC: National Academy Press.

National Research Council. (2001b). *Testing teacher candidates: The role of licensure tests in improving teacher quality*. Committee on Assessment and Teacher Quality. K.J. Mitchell, D.Z. Robinson, B.S. Plake, & K.T. Knowles, (Eds.). Division of Behavioral and Social Sciences and Education. Washington, DC: National Academy Press.

National Research Council. (2002a). *Learning and understanding: Improving advanced study of mathematics and science in U.S. high schools—Report of the content panel for biology*. Available at www.nap.edu/catalog/10365html.

National Research Council. (2002b). *Learning and understanding: Improving advanced study of mathematics and science in U.S. high schools—Report of the content panel for chemistry*. Available at www.nap.edu/catalog/10364html.

National Research Council. (2002c). *Learning and understanding: Improving advanced study of mathematics and science in U.S. high schools—Report of the content panel for physics*. Available at www.nap.edu/catalog/10361html.

National Research Council. (2002d). *Learning and understanding: Improving advanced study of mathematics and science in U.S. high schools—Report of the content panel for mathematics*. Available at www.nap.edu/catalog/10380html.

National Science Foundation. (1999). *Women, minorities, and persons with disabilities in science and engineering: 1998*. (NSF 99-338). Arlington, VA: Author.

National Science Teachers Association. (1996). *NSTA pathways to the science standards (high school)*. Arlington, VA: Author.

National Science Teachers Association. (2000). *Science teacher credentials, assignments, and job satisfaction: Results of a survey*. Arlington, VA: Author.

Newman, F.M., & Wehlage, G.G. (1995). *Successful school restructuring: A report to the public and educators by the Center on Organization and Restructuring of Schools*. Madison, WI: University of Wisconsin-Madison, School of Education, Wisconsin Center for Education Research, Center on Organization and Restructuring of Schools.

Niyogi, N.S. (1995). *The intersection of instruction and assessment: The classroom*. Princeton, NJ: Educational Testing Service.

Noonan, D., Sieder, J.J. & Peraino, K. (2001). Stop stressing me. *Newsweek,* January 29, 137(5).

Novak, J. D. (1985). Metalearning and metaknowledge strategies to help students learn how to learn. In L.H.T. West, & A.L. Pines (Eds.), *Cognitive structure and conceptual change* (pp. 189-209). Orlando, FL: Academic Press.

Novak, J.D. (1991). Clarify with concept maps. *The Science Teacher, 58*(7), 45-49.

Novak, J.D. (1998). *Learning, creating, and using knowledge: Concept maps as facilitative tools in schools and corporations*. Mahwah, NJ: Erlbaum.

Novak, J.D. (2002). Meaningful learning: The essential factor for conceptual change in limited or in appropriate propositional hierarchies leading to empowerment of learners. *Science Education, 86*(4), 548-571.

Novak, J.D., & Gowin, D.B. (1984). *Learning how to learn*. New York: Cambridge University Press.

Novak, J.D., & Musonda, D. (1991). A twelve-year longitudinal study of science concept learning. *American Educational Research Journal, 28*(1), 117-153.

Nystrand, M., & Gamoran, A. (1988). *A study of instruction as discourse*. Madison: University of Wisconsin-Madison, Wisconsin Center for Education Research.

O'Neil, Jr., H.F., & Brown, R.S. (1997). *Differential effects of question formats in math assessments on metacognition and affect*. (CSE Technical Report 449). Los Angeles: University of California at Los Angeles, Center for Research on Evaluation, Standards, and Student Testing, Center for the Study of Evaluation.

Oakes, J. (1985). *Keeping track: How schools structure inequality*. New Haven, CT: Yale University Press.

Oakes, J. (1990). *Multiplying inequalities: Race, social class, and tracking on students' opportunities to learn mathematics and science*. Santa Monica, CA: RAND.

Oakes, J., Gamoran, A., & Page, R.N. (1992). Curriculum differentiation: Opportunities, outcomes, and meanings. In P. Jackson (Ed.), *Handbook of research on curriculum* (pp. 570-608). New York: Macmillan.

Oakes, J., & Guiton, G. (1995). Matchmaking: Tracking decisions in comprehensive high schools. *American Educational Research Journal, 32*(1), 3-34.

Oakes, J., Rogers, J., McDonough, P., Solorzano, D., Mehan, H., & Noguera, P. (2000). *Remedying unequal opportunities for successful participation in advanced placement courses in California high schools*. Unpublished paper prepared for the American Civil Liberties Union of Southern California.

Oakes, J., & Wells, A.S. (2001). The comprehensive high school, detracking, and the persistence of social stratification. Draft manuscript, UCLA.

Office of Educational Research and Improvement. (1999). *The education system in the United States: Case study findings*. Washington, DC: U.S. Department of Education.

Orfield, G., & Paul, F. (1995). *High hopes and long odds: A major report on Hoosier teens and the American dream*. Indianapolis, IN: Indiana Youth Institute.

Paris, S.G., & Ayers, L.R. (1994). *Becoming reflective students and teachers with portfolios and authentic assessment*. Washington, DC: American Psychological Association.

Paul, F. (1995). Academic programs in a democratic society: Structured choices and their consequences. *Advances in Educational Policy, 2*.

Pearsall, N.R., Skipper, J., & Mintzes, J.J. (1997). Knowledge restructuring in the life sciences: A longitudinal study of conceptual change in biology. *Science Education, 81*, 193-215.

Perkins, D.N. (1992). *Smart schools: From training memories to educating minds*. New York: Free Press.

Pintrich, P.R., & Schrauben, B. (1992). Students' motivational beliefs and their cognitive engagement in classroom academic tasks. In D. Schunk, & J. Meece (Eds.), *Student perceptions in the classroom: Causes and consequences* (pp. 149-183). Hillsdale, NJ: Erlbaum.

Porter, A.C., Kirst, M.W., Osthoff, E.J., Smithson, J.L., & Schneider, S.A. (1993). *Reform up close: An analysis of high school mathematics and science classrooms*.

Madison, WI: University of Wisconsin-Madison, School of Education, Wisconsin Center for Education Research, Center on Organization and Restructuring of Schools.

Powell, A.G., Farrar, E., & Cohen, D.K. (1985). *The shopping mall high school: Winners and losers in the educational marketplace.* Boston, MA: Houghton-Mifflin.

Prawat, R.S. (1992). Teachers' beliefs about teaching and learning: A constructivist perspective. *American Journal of Education, 100,* 354-395.

Putnam, R.T., & Borko, H. (1997). Teacher learning: Implications of new views of cognition. In B.J. Biddle, T.L. Good, & I.F. Goodson (Eds.), *The international handbook of teachers and teaching* (vol. II, pp. 1223-1296). Dordrecht, Netherlands: Kluwer.

Raudenbush, S.W. (1984). Magnitude of teacher expectant effects on pupil IQ as a function of the credibility of expectancy induction: A synthesis of findings from 18 experiments. *Journal of Educational Psychology, 76*(1), 85-97.

Raudenbush, S.W., Rowan, B., & Cheong, Y.F. (1993). Higher order instructional goals in secondary schools: Class, teacher, and school influences. *American Educational Research Journal, 30*(3), 523-553.

Raywid, M.A. (1995). Alternatives and marginal students. In M.C. Wang, & M.C. Reynolds (Eds.), *Making a difference for students at risk: Trends and alternatives* (pp. 119-155). Thousand Oaks, CA: Corwin Press.

Reisberg, L. (1998). Some professors question programs that allow high-school students to earn college credits: Proliferation of dual enrollment and increase in Advanced Placement raise doubts about rigor. *The Chronicle of Higher Education, 44*(42).

Resnick, L. (1994). Situated rationalism: Biological and social preparation for mapping. In L. Hirschfeld, & S. Gelman (Eds.), *Mapping the mind: Domain specificity in cognition and culture.* New York: Cambridge University Press.

Resnick, L.B., & Klopfer, L.E. (1989). *Toward the thinking curriculum: Current cognitive research.* Washington, DC: Association for Supervision and Curriculum Development.

Rice, D.C., Ryan, J.M., & Samson, S.M. (1998). Using concept maps to assess student learning outcomes in the science classroom: Must different methods compete? *Journal of Research in Science Education, 35*(10), 1103-1127.

Riley, R.W. (1999). *Annual back-to-school address: Changing the American high school to fit modern times.* The National Press Club, Washington, DC (September 15).

Romo, H., & Falbo, T. (1996). *Hispanic high school graduation: Defying the odds.* Austin, TX: University of Texas Press.

Rosenthal, R., Baratz, S.S., & Hall, C.M. (1974). Teacher behavior, teacher expectations, and gains in pupils' rated creativity. *Journal of Genetic Psychology, 124,* 115-121.

Rosenthal, R. (1987). Pygmalion effects: Existence, magnitude, and social importance. *Educational Researcher, 16*(9), 37-41.

Rosenthal, R., & Jacobson, L. (1968). *Pygmalion in the classroom.* New York: Holt, Rinehart, & Winston.

Rosenthal, R., & Rubin, D.B. (1978). Interpersonal expectancy effects: The first 345 studies. *Behavior and Brain Science, 3,* 377-415.

Roth, K.J. (1986). *Conceptual-change learning, and student procession of science texts.* (The Institute for Research on Teaching, Research Series No. 167.) East Lansing, MI: Michigan State University.

Rothman, F., & Narum, J. (1999). *Then, now, and in the next decade: A commentary on strengthening undergraduate science, mathematics, engineering, and technology education.* Washington, DC: Project Kaleidoscope.

Roy, K.R. (2001). *A district that puts physics first: A Connecticut school district puts Lederman's vision to the test.* In New Horizons in Mathematics and Science Education, *ENC Focus Magazine, 8*(4). [Available at Eisenhower National Clearinghouse, http://www.enc.org].

Rubenstein, R. (1998). Resource equity in the Chicago public schools: A school-level approach. *Journal of Education Finance, 23*(4), 468-489.

Russell, A.B. (1998). *Statewide college admissions, Student preparation, and remediation. Policies and programs: Summary of a 1997 SHEEO survey.* Denver, CO: State Higher Education Executive Officers.

Rutter, M. (1983). School effects on pupil progress: Research findings and policy implications. *Journal of Child Development, 54,* 1-29.

Rutter, M., McNaughan, B., Mortimore, P., & Ouston, J. (1979). *Fifteen thousand hours: Secondary schools and their effects on children.* Cambridge, MA: Harvard University Press.

Ryder, J., Leach, J., & Driver, R. (1999). Undergraduate science student's images of science. *Journal of Research in Science Teaching, 36*(2), 201-219.

Sanders, W.L., & Rivers, J.C. (1996). *Cumulative and residual effects of teachers on future student academic achievement: Research progress report.* Knoxville, TN: University of Tennessee, Value-Added Research and Assessment Center.

Schmidt, B.J., Finch, C.R., & Faulkner, S.L. (1992). *Helping teachers to understand their roles in integrating vocational and academic education: A practitioner's guide.* (MDS-276). Berkeley, CA: University of California at Berkeley, National Center for Research in Vocational Education.

Schmidt, W.H., McKnight, C.C., Cogan, L.S., Jakewerth, P.M., & Hourang, R.T. (1999). *Facing the consequences: Using TIMSS for a closer look at U.S. mathematics and science education.* Dordrecht, Netherlands: Kluwer.

Schneider, B. (1999). The ambitious generation. *Education Week.* April 14, 18(31).

Schoenfeld, A.H. (1983). Problem solving in the mathematics curriculum: A report, recommendation and annotated bibliography. *Mathematical Association of America Notes,* (1).

Schoenfeld, A.H. (1984). Episodes and executive decisions in mathematical problem solving. In R. Lesh, & M. Landau (Eds.), *Acquisition of mathematics concepts and processes.* New York: Academic Press.

Schoenfeld, A.H. (1985). *Mathematical problem solving.* Orlando, FL: Academic Press.

Schoenfeld, A.H. (1987). What's all the fuss about metacognition? In A.H. Schoenfeld (Ed.), *Cognitive science and mathematics education.* Hillside, NJ: Erlbaum.

Schoenfeld, A.H. (1991). On pure and applied research in mathematics education. *Journal of Mathematical Behavior, 10,* 263-276.

Schofield, C. (2000). *Teacher's guide, AP biology.* New York: College Entrance Examination Board.

Schoon, K.J., & Boone, W.J. (1998). Self-efficacy and alternative conceptions of science preservice elementary teachers. *Science Education, 82*(5), 553-568.

Schulman, L.S. (1986). Those who understand: Knowledge growth in teaching. *Educational Researcher, 15*(2), 4-14.

Shaughnessy, M.F. (1998). An interview with Rita Dunn about learning styles. *The Clearing House, 71*(3), 141-145.

Shavelson, R.J., Baxter, G.P., & Pine, J. (1992). Performance assessments: Political rhetoric and measurement reality. *Educational Researcher, 21*(4), 22-27.

Shepard, L., & Cutts-Dougherty, K. (1991). *Effects of high-stakes testing on instruction*. Paper presented at the annual joint meeting of the American Educational research Association and the National Council on Measurement in Education, Chicago, IL.

Shepard, L.A. (1990). Inflated test score gains: Is the problem old norms or teaching the test? *Educational Measurement: Issues and Practice, 9*(3), 15-22.

Shepard, L.A. (2000). The role of assessment in a learning culture. *Educational Researcher, 29*(7), 4-14.

Silver, E.A., & Smith, M.S. (1996). Building discourse communities in mathematics classrooms. *Communication in mathematics*. Reston, VA: National Council of Teachers of Mathematics.

Simon, H.A. (1980). Problem solving and education. In D. T. Tuma, & R. Reif (Eds.), *Problem solving and education: Issues in teaching and research*. Hillsdale, NJ: Erlbaum.

Sizer, T. (1992). *Horace's compromise: The dilemma of the American high school*. Boston: Houghton-Mifflin.

Skemp, R. (1978). Relational understanding and instrumental understanding. *Arithmetic Teacher, 26*(3), 9-15.

Skemp, R. (1979). *Intelligence, learning, and action*. New York: Wiley.

Sneider, C.I., & Ohadi, M.M. (1998). Unraveling students' misconceptions about earth's shape and gravity. *Science Education, 82*(2):265-284.

Southerland, S.A., & Gess-Newsom, J. (1999). Preservice teachers' views of inclusive science teaching as shaped by images of teaching, learning, and knowledge. *Science Education, 83*(2), 131-150.

Springer, K. & Peyser, M. (1998). The rat race begins at 14: Stressed-out kids aiming for top colleges refuse to slow down. *Newsweek*. March 30, 131(13).

Steen, L.A. (Ed.). (1998). *Calculus for a new century: A pump, not a filter, a national colloquium, October 28–29, 1987*. (MAA Notes Series #8). Washington, DC: Mathematical Association of America.

Steinberg, L., & Dornbusch, S.M. (1991). Negative correlates of part-time employment during adolescence: Replication and elaboration. *Developmental Psychology, 27*(2), 304-313.

Stipek, D.J. (1998). *Motivation to learn: From theory to practice* (2 ed.). Boston: Allyn and Bacon.

Sugrue, B., Valdes, R., Schlackman, J., & Webb, N. (1996). *Patterns of performance across different types of items measuring knowledge of Ohm's Law*. (CSE technical report 405.) Los Angeles: University of California at Los Angeles, Center for

Research on Evaluation, Standards, and Student Testing, Center for the Study of Evaluation.

Sykes, G. (1996). Reform of and as professional development. *Phi Delta Kappan, 77,* 465-467.

Tafel, J., & Eberhart, N. (1999). *Statewide school-college (K-16) partnerships to improve student performance.* Denver, CO: State Higher Education Executive Officers.

Tharp, R.G., & Gallimore, R. (1988). *Rousing minds to life: Teaching, learning, and schooling in social context.* New York: Cambridge University Press.

Tomlinson, C.A. (1995). *How to differentiate instruction in mixed-ability classrooms.* Alexandria VA: Association for Supervision and Curriculum Development.

Torrance, E.P. (1984). *Mentor relationships: How they aid creative achievement, endure change and die.* New York: Bearly.

Townes, M.H., & Grant, E.R. (1997). "I believe I will go out of this class actually knowing something": Cooperative learning activities in physical chemistry. *Journal of Research in Science Teaching, 34*(8), 819-835.

Useem, E. (1992). Middle school and math groups: Parent's involvement in children's placement. *Sociology of Education, 65*(4), 263-279.

Van Zile-Tamsen, C.M. (1996). *Metacognitive self-regulation and the daily academic activities of college students.* Buffalo, NY: State University of New York at Buffalo, unpublished doctoral dissertation.

VanTassel-Baska, J. (1998). *Characteristics and needs of talented learners.* In J. VanTassel-Baska (Ed.), *Excellence in educating gifted and talented learners* (3rd ed., pp.173-192). Denver: CO: Love.

VanTassel-Baska, J., Feldhusen, J., Seely, K., Wheatly, G., Silverman, L., & Foster, W. (1988). *Comprehensive curriculum for gifted learners.* Needham Heights, MA: Allyn and Bacon.

Viadero, D. (2001). AP program assumes larger role. *Education Week, 20*(32), April 25.

Vosniadou, S. & Brewer, W.F. (1992). Mental models of the earth: A study of conceptual change in childhood. *Cognitive Psychology, 24*(4), 535–85.

Wallach, M.A. (1978). Care and feeding of the gifted. *Contemporary Psychology, 23,* 616-617.

Wandersee, J.H., Mintzes, J.J., & Novak, J.D. (1994). Research on alternative conceptions in science. In D. Gabel (Ed.), *Handbook of research on science teaching and learning: A project of the National Science Teachers Association* (pp. 177-210). New York: Macmillan.

Weiner, B. (1985). An attributional theory of achievement, motivation and emotion. *Psychological Review, 92*(4), 548-573.

Weiss, I. (1994). *A profile of science and mathematics education in the United States: 1993.* Chapel Hill, NC: Horizon Research.

Welner, K.G. (2001). *Legal rights, local wrongs: When community control collides with educational equity.* Albany, NY: State University of New York Press.

White, B.Y., & Frederickson, J.R. (1998). Inquiry, modeling, and metacognition: Making science accessible to all students. *Cognition and Instruction, 16*(1), 3-118.

White, R.W. (1959). Motivation reconsidered: The concept of competence. *Psychological Review, 66,* 297-333.

Wiggins, G. (1998). *Educative assessment: Designing assessments to inform and improve student performance.* San Francisco: Jossey-Bass.

Wood, T., Cobb, P., & Yackel, E. (1991). Change in teaching mathematics: A case study. *American Educational Research Journal, 28*(3), 587-616.

Wright, S.P., Horn, S.P., & Sanders, W.L. (1997). Teacher and classroom context effects on student achievement: Implications for teacher evaluation. *Journal of Personnel Evaluation in Education, 11,* 57-67.

Zimmerman, B. (1989). A social cognitive view of self-regulated academic learning. *Journal of Educational Psychology, 23,* 614-628.

Appendix A

Overview of Panel Findings and Recommendations

INTRODUCTION

A major goal of this project was to understand advanced study as it is currently implemented in the sciences and mathematics. Accordingly, the National Research Council (NRC) charged the committee with examining advanced study in biology, chemistry, physics, and mathematics (with an emphasis on calculus). The largest advanced study programs for high school students in these disciplines are part of the Advanced Placement (AP) and International Baccalaureate (IB) programs. Because the four subjects are so different, four independent panels of experts in these disciplines were convened to advise the committee.

Panel Composition and Charge

The four panels were assembled using the normal process for appointing all NRC committees: a slate of qualified individuals was identified on the basis of recommendations from a variety of sources and submitted to the NRC for approval. Each panel included an educational researcher with a strong base in the discipline, an accomplished university teacher–scholar in the discipline, and a secondary teacher involved with advanced programs in the discipline. A member of the study committee chaired each panel, and a senior member of the committee's staff provided assistance and expertise at each of the panel meetings. The chair of each panel served as liaison to the committee. The names of the panel members and chairs are listed at the front of this report.

The charge to the panels (reproduced in Annex A-1 at the end of this appendix) included addressing all the major areas under the full committee's charge, including evaluation of the AP and IB programs in light of what is known about cognition and learning and the nature of the particular discipline, identification of major conceptual issues that should serve as curricular foci, means of balancing breadth and depth, interdisciplinary connections, quality of assessments, teaching methodology, comparison with national standards, and preparation of high school students for further study at the college level. The panels were not asked to consider programs other than AP and IB because of time limitations.

Each panel met for two 2-day sessions during the spring and summer of 2000. Prior to each meeting, panel members received general information about the AP and IB programs, as well as materials more specific to their disciplines. These materials included curriculum guidelines; questions from final examinations that had been released by the College Board and the International Baccalaureate Organisation (IBO); and, for the science panels, laboratory manuals used in AP and IB science courses. Panel members also examined other information about research on learning, curriculum, assessment, and teacher education and professional development. Copies of salient national reports, such as *National Science Education Standards* (NRC, 1996) and *Principles and Standards for School Mathematics* (National Council of Teachers of Mathematics, 2000), were provided as well. Panel members also applied their personal knowledge and experience with the two programs in formulating findings and recommendations.

Review and Interpretation of Panel Findings and Recommendations

The chair of each panel assumed responsibility for drafting a report and consulting with panel members to incorporate their suggestions and secure their agreement on the report contents. Each panel report underwent an independent, monitored review by reviewers external to the NRC. The chair of each panel then assumed primary responsibility for preparing the panel's response to review, along with appropriate changes.

The panels' findings and recommendations represent the consensus of the panel members. Reviewers agreed that the findings are well substantiated. The committee acknowledges, however, that different groups of experts might have arrived at somewhat different recommendations regarding desirable changes. In other words, there may be several solutions to some of the problems that were noted.

Since the recommendations of the panels are discipline-specific, the committee did not have the expertise to consider each recommendation in detail. However, the panels' findings were an important part of the evidence used by the committee in analyzing advanced study programs and in reaching agreement on the recommendations presented in Chapter 11 of this report.

As might be expected when four groups of disciplinary experts evaluate educational programs in their subject areas, there are both substantial common elements and significant differences among the panel findings. Problems found to be critical in one discipline are not necessarily important in others. Since each panel undertook its work altogether independently of the others, the common elements are particularly worthy of note. Following a review of some of these common elements, the findings and recommendations of the four panels are presented.[1]

COMMON ELEMENTS IN THE PANELS' FINDINGS

All of the panels find considerable merit in both the AP and IB programs, which provide challenging opportunities for motivated students that might not otherwise be available. The panels also note major deficiencies in both programs that they believe need to be addressed. The AP calculus program is further along in the process of improvement than are the AP science programs.

Research on Learning: All of the panels agree that the AP and IB programs are not yet effectively utilizing what is known about how people learn in developing their courses and their assessments. The science panels also note that the programs are not consistent with national standards such as those presented in *National Science Education Standards* (NRC, 1996). Although the programs emphasize the importance of higher-order learning and thinking, the amount of content to be covered and assessed, particularly in the sciences, tends to encourage rote memorization rather than conceptual learning. The programs do not yet stress the need for teachers to understand and correct students' misconceptions. The science panels note that the AP program misses important opportunities to promote interdisciplinary connections between mathematics and the sciences and between different sciences. At present, the IB program does a somewhat better job of recognizing these linkages through its Group 4 Project and its internal assessments in the sciences.

Examinations: AP and IB curricula are designed to prepare students for successful performance on end-of-course examinations. The content and structure of the examinations, therefore, have a profound effect on what is taught and how in AP and IB classrooms. The science panels agree that the examinations for AP and IB have some deficiencies. Most serious of these is

---

[1]The full report of each panel, including substantial analysis and supporting material, is available online at www.nap.edu/catalog/10129.html. Those interested in a particular discipline should download the corresponding report.

that, in the science panels' judgment, exam questions do not test conceptual understanding adequately, a situation that adversely affects learning to the extent that classroom instruction is guided by the examinations. The mathematics panel indicates that both the AP and IB mathematics assessments require conceptual understanding, but both examinations could focus on assessing such understanding to a greater degree. Making the AP calculus examinations less predictable, for example, would encourage teachers to teach concepts rather than problem types.

Evolution of Course Content and Technology: The biology and chemistry courses in the AP and IB programs do not adequately reflect the evolution of these disciplines over the last two decades. The physics courses also include substantial amounts of older material, but the physics panel does not judge this to be a compelling problem relative to other concerns. Technological advances, especially in the application of computers, are causing major changes in all of the disciplines and generating novel instructional possibilities that are not yet adequately reflected in course content.

Teacher Preparation: All four panels note that neither the College Board nor the IBO has provided clear expectations for teacher preparation, that qualified teachers are in short supply, and that better teacher preparation is a prerequisite for substantial program improvement.

Student Preparation: All of the panels note the potential for inadequate student preparation for advanced study. In some cases preparation time has become compressed to allow time for the advanced programs. Indeed, as the programs have grown, they have affected the entire high school science and mathematics curriculum. Furthermore, a significant number of students are taking AP science courses as the first course in the discipline, particularly in physics. Additional discussion of these issues is presented in Chapters 2 and 10 of this report.

The Secondary–Postsecondary Interface: Finally, all the science panels believe there is insufficient cooperation and communication between high schools and universities with regard to structuring secondary advanced study for students who will enroll in advanced science and mathematics courses when they enter college. The mathematics panel, on the other hand, views cooperation and collaboration between high schools and colleges as a strong point of the AP program. The mathematics panel credits the College Board with facilitating communication among all stakeholders with regard to the teaching of calculus. In all disciplines increased cooperation could lead to improvements in the structure of secondary advanced programs, better teacher preparation and professional development, and college course sequences that are appropriate for students having different experiences in high school.

BIOLOGY PANEL

Principal Findings

Curriculum

Finding: The AP course outline is not up to date, and it overemphasizes environmental, population, and organismic (EPO) biology at the expense of molecular, cell, developmental (MCD) and evolutionary biology. Although similarly out of date, the IB curriculum achieves a more appropriate balance between the EPO and MCD areas. The AP curriculum should include more on the process of science, including the responsible conduct of research, and the core IB curriculum should include more evolutionary biology. The core curricula of both programs should be updated to include concepts from current areas of rapid progress, such as genomics, cell signaling, mechanisms of development, and molecular evolution.

Finding: A major problem with the AP course is that pressure to cover all of biology in less than a year precludes in-depth study and leads to superficial knowledge. In contrast, the IB program allows time for some in-depth study by subdividing the curriculum into core and options, and by allowing 2 years for the Higher Level (HL) course. The AP course needs to include more options, both in the curriculum and on the tests, to make the breadth covered manageable. One solution would be to have two AP courses—one emphasizing EPO and the other MCD biology—both with significant evolutionary emphasis.

Finding: Both AP and IB have stated themes around which the courses are theoretically organized. The eight themes of the AP curriculum mix philosophy and content, with some redundancy in the content themes, but appear to be adequate for their stated purpose. In the IB curriculum, there are only four stated themes, which surprisingly do not include two that appear essential—energy transfer and heredity. Themes in both courses are intended to provide integration of different topics, but the extent to which these themes are used in presenting subject matter generally depends on decisions made by individual teachers. Particularly in AP courses, better integration of topics is needed.

Finding: Meaningful learning in biology must involve inquiry-based laboratory experiences that require students not simply to carry out a technique or learn a laboratory skill, but also to pose questions, formulate hypotheses, design experiments to test those hypotheses, collaborate to make experiments work, analyze data, draw conclusions, and present their analyses and conclusions to their peers.

Finding: There is little evidence of interdisciplinary emphasis in the AP course outline. In contrast, the entire IB program, including its biology component, rests on the importance of interdisciplinary connections in learning. The IB program is exemplary and far superior in this regard. The AP program should consider changes that would promote interdisciplinary learning.

Instruction and Professional Development

Finding: AP courses and to a somewhat lesser extent IB courses generally rely on the traditional transmission–reception mode of instruction rather than a constructivist model in which students develop their own conceptual framework through inquiry-based, problem-centered active learning (as recommended in the *National Science Education Standards* [NRC, 1996]). Both programs need to effect changes in the teaching approaches used.

Finding: The way the AP and to a lesser extent the IB courses are taught is inconsistent with current knowledge in several ways: rapid-fire course coverage at the expense of depth of understanding; continued reliance on the traditional passive-learner, transmission–reception model of learning; failure to specifically target common known misconceptions; limited use of history as a route to understanding in the context of people and society; failure to keep pace with new technological and instrumentation opportunities, such as learning through computer modeling of biological systems and hand-held data collection and analysis equipment for field work; over reliance on multiple-choice and fill-in-the-blank test questions; and limited experiential and inquiry-based learning in the laboratory, including the "persuasion of peers" phase crucial to the scientific process. In general, the application of research-based learning theory to the design of instruction and assessment is lacking.

Finding: A greater emphasis on inquiry-based learning in AP and IB courses might motivate more students to pursue further training in biology and biology-related careers.

Finding: Many teachers at the secondary level are unprepared to teach college-level biology with regard to content knowledge, and many schools that offer AP programs do not have the resources to support adequate laboratory instruction. The College Board should evaluate and certify AP schools and teachers in some manner.

Finding: More in-service preparation and support are needed, and more attention should be paid to pedagogy in manuals and workshops, particularly for AP teachers.

Assessment

Finding: AP and IB final examinations primarily measure rote learning when assessing students' mastery of content knowledge, concepts, and applications. However, in the IB assessment process, evaluation of a portfolio, laboratory notebooks, and other work provides more perspective. The AP exam should include more free-response questions and evaluation of laboratory work, and the examinations for both programs should test more concept knowledge. With regard to application of knowledge to other courses and situations, the AP exam is limited by a lack of interdisciplinary emphasis, while the IB assessments include such applications. As noted above, the AP course and exam would benefit from more interdisciplinary emphasis.

Finding: The perceived need for comprehensiveness and the single high-stakes exam of the AP program in particular encourage teachers to promote rote learning in order to cover all the necessary material.

Finding: Both the AP and IB examinations emphasize assessment of what is easily measured: rote learning of facts and concepts, rather than what is most highly valued—hierarchically structured conceptual knowledge and understanding of scientific processes.

The Secondary–Postsecondary Interface

Finding: University-sponsored outreach programs can be a major resource for high school advanced biology programs and should be encouraged. More communication between high schools and universities—in both directions—would be helpful in fulfilling the needs of both institutions and in developing curricula and assessments.

Finding: There are many concerns with the use of AP and IB scores for granting of advanced placement. Some top-ranked colleges do not accept either AP or IB credit or both. For a variety of reasons discussed above, some AP and IP biology courses are not of high enough quality to be appropriate for college credit. The AP biology course as presently constituted is too EPO-oriented to be an appropriate substitute for a first-year college MCD-oriented biology course.

Finding: Because of the lack of in-depth study in many AP courses, students who place out of first-year college courses may be at a disadvantage later at institutions where the introductory course is taught effectively. The available data on how well the AP courses prepare students for advanced work in the field may be misleading.

Recommendations

Overall Recommendation: The College Board should certify schools and teachers that wish to offer AP biology courses and should provide suitable training opportunities for prospective AP biology teachers. The College Board should also develop procedures for ongoing assessment of AP programs and teachers through regular sampling of student work; such sampling should also be used for assessment of student achievement in addition to the final examinations.

Overall Recommendation: Certification and assessments of both the AP and IB programs by the College Board and the IBO, respectively, should be designed to ensure that changing emphases in standards for teaching, professional development, assessment, and content, as set forth in the *National Science Education Standards* (NRC, 1996), are being implemented. Teacher preparation and in-service workshops in both programs should place more emphasis on pedagogy—how to facilitate student-centered, problem-oriented, inquiry-based learning—and on recent results of research on cognition and learning.

Overall Recommendation: Colleges and universities should be strongly discouraged from using performance on either the AP or IB examination as the sole basis for automatic placement out of required introductory college courses for biology majors and distribution requirements for nonmajors.

Curriculum

Recommendation: Students should in general not be allowed to take AP biology as a first science course in high school. A prior biology course should be a prerequisite for AP biology, and a prior chemistry course should be strongly urged as well. In schools where the latter is impractical, chemistry should be a corequisite course.

Recommendation: Both the AP and IB curricula should be updated to include topics of major current interest in biology, such as cell signaling, development, genomics, molecular systematics, and their evolutionary implications.

Recommendation: The AP curriculum should be better balanced, with more emphasis on molecular and cell biology. The IB core topics should include more evolutionary biology.

Recommendation: The College Board should seriously consider offering two different AP biology courses, one emphasizing MCD and the other EPO biology, with two corresponding exams. These courses should go into depth in one of these areas of emphasis and present the basics of the other. Both courses should include a strong emphasis on evolution.

Recommendation: More curricular flexibility should be built into the AP program so that students can study fewer areas in greater depth than is possible with the current overemphasis on breadth of coverage.

Recommendation: The AP program should place more emphasis on laboratory work by developing a new and larger set of innovative, inquiry-based laboratories that conform to the *National Science Education Standards* (NRC, 1996) and by including more laboratory-based questions on the exam. Enough laboratories should be available so that teachers have the opportunity to select among them according to their interests and those of their students, and the laboratory-related questions on the AP exam should be general enough so that teachers have real flexibility in deciding which laboratories to offer. In addition, the AP program should include a mandatory 1-week workshop on laboratory pedagogy for beginning teachers of AP biology and should provide more ongoing laboratory training for established teachers.

Recommendation: Assessments of schools and teachers should include determination of the amount and quality of the laboratory experience being provided. Scheduling of at least one 2-hour laboratory period per week should be strongly urged as a criterion for certification of an AP biology course.

Recommendation: The AP program should promote more interdisciplinary activities that relate AP biology to other academic work, as well as local and regional issues.

Assessment

Recommendation: The AP program should modify its assessment process to incorporate evaluation of laboratory portfolios and other samples of student work prior to the examination. There also should be more questions on the exam designed to test understanding of major concepts and the process of laboratory research, with less emphasis on rote memorization of facts.

Recommendation: To provide feedback, the AP program should make individual students' exam answers available to their teachers after the examinations have been evaluated.

The Secondary–Postsecondary Interface

Recommendation: More attention should be paid to the interface between advanced high school and college biology teaching. In particular, more communication and collaboration should be encouraged between college and university departments and high school teachers of biology. Colleges and universities are potential sources of enrichment and resources for high school courses, and college instructors can benefit from the teaching experience of high school teachers. The need for reform is systemic. Like the AP and IB programs, colleges and universities should revise or improve introductory biology courses as necessary to bring them into line with the recommendations made in this report for high school advanced study courses.

CHEMISTRY PANEL

Principal Findings

Finding: The AP and IB final examinations are formulaic and predictable in their approaches and question types from year to year. Thus, with sufficient practice on how to take such examinations and enough drill on major concepts that the examinations are likely to test, students can score well without actually understanding the major concepts associated with the topics being tested.

Finding: The AP and IB chemistry courses do not yet recognize the increasingly interdisciplinary nature of modern chemistry; its incorporation of important related fields, such as materials science and biochemistry; and the opportunities presented by such fields to teach related chemical concepts in a contextual manner.

Finding: The AP and IB examinations do not reflect recent developments in chemistry and in the teaching of chemistry at the college/university level.

Recommendations

Overall Recommendation: Advanced study options in high school chemistry should not necessarily be tied to the potential for earning college/university credit.

Overall Recommendation: Advanced study of chemistry at the high school level should provide students with a coherent, rigorous course that promotes further scientific literacy and prepares students to become part of a highly technological workforce, regardless of whether they continue studying chemistry at the college level.

Overall Recommendation: Advanced study in chemistry need not be based on AP or IB. Many top high schools for mathematics and science offer alternatives, which should continue to be explored. Where appropriate, college credit can be sought on the basis of passing the placement examination administered by many college or university departments.

Curriculum

Recommendation: Any high school course in chemistry that is labeled as advanced study, whether it is structured according to an established curriculum and assessment (such as AP or IB) or otherwise, should enable students to explore the chemistry concepts and laboratory practices introduced in the first-year high school course in greater depth and, where appropriate, to conduct some form of research or independent inquiry. Under the guidance of a qualified advanced study instructor, desirable features of such advanced study would include some combination of these characteristics: application of basic ideas regarding complex materials, systems, and phenomena; use of modern instrumentation, methods, and information resources; integration of concepts within and between subject areas, including extensions to other disciplines; use of appropriate mathematical and technological methods; extended use of inquiry-based experimentation; development of critical thinking skills and conceptual understanding; use of appropriate tools for assessment of student performance that reflect current best practices; and promotion of communication skills and teamwork.

Recommendation: With rare exceptions, students should not take advanced chemistry as their first chemistry course in high school.

Recommendation: To be effective, advanced courses in chemistry must reflect recommendations in the areas of content, pedagogy, and assessment embodied in the *National Science Education Standards* (NRC, 1996).

Instruction

Recommendation: Qualified AP or IB teachers should have a B.S. or B.A. degree in chemistry (which includes a two-semester physical chemistry course sequence with laboratories), and preferably an M.A. or M.S. degree in chemistry. The chemistry panel does not view a B.S. in science education as being adequate preparation for these teachers, nor does the College Board.

Recommendation: A qualified advanced study chemistry instructor should have experience with effective current and emerging approaches to teaching and assessment in the subject and their applications to the AP and IB chemistry courses.

Recommendation: AP or IB chemistry teachers should have a working familiarity with teaching technologies (e.g., Web, electronic media, laboratory instrumentation) and their appropriate uses.

Professional Development

Recommendation: Required periodic, funded professional development opportunities, including content instruction, research participation, and pedagogy workshops, should be provided for teachers of advanced courses in chemistry. This recommendation is consonant with the National Commission on Mathematics and Science Teaching for the 21st Century's description of professional development as "a planned, collaborative, educational process of continuous improvement for teachers that helps them to do five things: (1) deepen their knowledge of the subject(s) they are teaching; (2) sharpen their teaching skills in the classroom; (3) keep up with developments in their fields, and in education generally; (4) generate and contribute new knowledge to the profession; and (5) increase their ability to monitor students' work so they can provide constructive feedback to students and appropriately redirect their own teaching" (National Commission on Mathematics and Science Teaching for the 21st Century, 2000, p. 18).

Recommendation: Professional development opportunities, such as the experience of teaching courses or laboratories at colleges or universities and undertaking original research in industry, at government laboratories, or in collaboration with college faculty, would be particularly valuable for AP and IB chemistry teachers. High school–system personnel policies should encourage rather than inhibit such professional development activities during the academic year.

Recommendation: AP and IB chemistry teachers can profit from discussions with each other. School districts and schools should find ways to initiate and sustain such dialogue and to share it with a wider audience. Communication about areas of common interest between chemistry faculties in high schools and those teaching general chemistry in institutions of higher education would be extremely helpful for both communities (see also the recommendations under Vision 4 in *Transforming Undergraduate Education in Science, Mathematics, Engineering, and Technology* [NRC, 1999d]).

Recommendation: AP and IB chemistry teachers should be participating members of professional organizations such as the National Science Teachers Association and the American Chemical Society's Division of Chemical Education.

The Secondary–Postsecondary Interface

Recommendation: Institutions awarding AP examination–based course credit or advanced placement in chemistry should consider doing so only for a grade of 4 or 5, not for a grade of 3.

PHYSICS PANEL

Principal Findings

Overall Finding: The most important goals of advanced physics instruction are independent of the particular topics studied. Advanced physics instruction should be aimed at generating excitement and enthusiasm for further study in physics, at achieving deep conceptual understanding of the subject matter covered, and at instilling in students the scientific habits of mind that are important for their further education in science. Learning any particular physics subject matter is of lesser importance.

Overall Finding: There are far too few data on the long-term outcomes of physics education to allow important decisions about the physics education of large numbers of students to be made with confidence.

Curriculum

Finding: The study of Newtonian mechanics provides an ideal framework for developing the scientific habits of mind and deep conceptual understanding that are the primary goals of advanced physics instruction. Moreover, familiarity with Newtonian mechanics is universally expected of students who have completed an advanced high school physics program.

Finding: The AP Physics B curriculum is too broad for a 1-year course; it allows insufficient time to develop deep conceptual understanding. The IB Physics Higher Level (HL) course covers largely the same material over 2 years—an ideal pace.

Finding: The current AP physics curriculum does not encourage the inclusion of interdisciplinary content in AP physics programs. The IB physics program includes interdisciplinary content as an integral part of the IB program.

Instruction

Finding: More well-qualified teachers are desperately needed for advanced physics programs. With the continued growth of such programs across the nation, there is a severe shortage of qualified individuals to teach them.

Finding: The preparation and skill of the teacher are the principal factors that determine the ultimate success or failure of advanced physics instruction. Thorough understanding of the subject matter is a necessary but not sufficient condition for good physics teaching. Teachers must also be trained in the special pedagogy of physics.

Finding: Skilled physics teachers continuously diagnose the understanding of their students and change their objectives and strategies as that diagnosis indicates. It is impossible to assess the understanding of students without requiring them to explain their reasoning.

Finding: Thorough understanding of the subject matter is a necessary but not a sufficient condition for good physics teaching.

Finding: Traditional "cookbook" methods of laboratory instruction, in which students follow narrowly defined procedures to verify well-known principles, have little effect on students' conceptual understanding. In contrast, substantial improvements in understanding are possible through rigorous, interactive laboratory experiences.

Assessment

Finding: Current final assessments place too much emphasis on technical problem-solving skills and insufficient emphasis on deep conceptual understanding. For example, very rarely do the scoring rubrics of either AP or IB physics examinations provide for the deduction of credit for incorrect reasoning; correct final results nearly always receive full credit. Also, both AP and IB physics examinations contain too many multipart questions that lead students through the solution instead of requiring students to demonstrate their understanding by solving the problem on their own. On the whole, IB examinations are somewhat more conceptual in nature than their AP counterparts; recent AP examinations are much better in this regard than those of earlier years.

Finding: The scoring of written examinations must emphasize the evaluation of student understanding. Therefore, a rigid scoring rubric in which points are awarded for very specific correct responses to small parts of each question is not appropriate because it reduces the reader's ability to respond to a student's thinking (both correct and incorrect) not anticipated by the rubric.

Finding: The pace of IB physics final examinations is much more leisurely than that of their AP counterparts. In general, AP physics examinations require students to do too much in too short a time.

Recommendations

Overall Recommendation: Given the scarcity of data on the long-term outcomes of physics education, an effort should be made as soon as possible to follow the progress of physics students over a period of many years.

Student Preparation

Recommendation: Before enrolling in an advanced physics course in high school, students should have studied the physics that is suggested as a requirement for high school graduation in the *National Science Education Standards* (NRC, 1996). This requirement can be satisfied with the first year of a 2-year physics program (the approach adopted by the IB program).

Recommendation: Before taking advanced physics, students should be fluent in mathematics through the precalculus level. In particular, by the time they are ready to study advanced physics, students should be skilled in algebraic manipulation and have a firm grasp of basic trigonometry. Emphasis should also be placed on the use of proportions to solve problems, estimation skills, the use of international units, and scientific notation (powers of 10).

Curriculum

Recommendation: All advanced physics programs should aim to develop deep conceptual understanding of the topics studied. It is essential that whatever topics are chosen be addressed in depth, with an emphasis on conceptual understanding rather than on technical problem-solving skills. Students must learn that physics knowledge is built on general principles and gain the confidence to apply those principles to unfamiliar situations.

Recommendation: All students of advanced physics should study a nationally standardized one-semester unit in Newtonian mechanics. This unit should have the coverage of current AP Physics C Mechanics (including rotational dynamics), but should not require formal calculus. It should replace the multiple versions currently offered.

Recommendation: In a 1-year advanced physics program, students should study only one major area of physics in addition to Newtonian mechanics.

Recommendation: The AP Physics B program is too broad and should be eliminated as a 1-year course.

Recommendation: Meaningful real-world (laboratory) experiences should be included in all advanced physics programs. There is ample evidence that traditional "cookbook" laboratories do not meet this standard.

Recommendation: Advanced courses should have greater interdisciplinary content and make increasing use of cyberspace and information technology. Modern developments in both science and society as a whole indicate that physicists will be increasingly called upon to address problems that cross the boundaries between traditional disciplines. At the same time, the explosion of information technology provides a vast array of possibilities for improving advanced physics instruction. Teachers and administrators should be aware of these developments and help advanced physics programs expand their involvement in both areas over time.

Instruction and Professional Development

Recommendation: A concerted effort should be made throughout the physics community to contribute to the preparation and ongoing professional development of highly skilled physics teachers. Peer assessment programs should be implemented for certification and continuing assessment of physics teaching skill.

Recommendation: The panel strongly recommends that explanations of reasoning be required from the first day of an advanced course so that providing such explanations quickly becomes automatic for all students in whatever they do throughout the course.

Recommendation: Information technology should be used to create networks that will enable high school and college faculty and other professionals to share information useful for advanced physics teaching.

Assessment

Recommendation: The scoring of written examinations must emphasize the evaluation of student understanding. As noted above, a rigid scoring rubric in which points are awarded for very specific correct responses to small parts of each question is not appropriate; rather, the reader should evaluate the student's response as a whole. A maximum score should be given only for complete and clear physical reasoning leading to the correct conclusions. The recent trend toward increased emphasis on conceptual understanding should continue.

Recommendation: The standards for success on final assessments should be raised. The panel believes that if its recommended curriculum changes are implemented, successful students will know the material in the new, more manageable curricula thoroughly. Therefore, the panel recommends high standards of performance on the new final examinations.

Recommendation: The panel recommends that sufficient time be allowed for students to complete an entire examination. Final examinations must measure what students know, not how quickly they can recall and apply that knowledge.

MATHEMATICS PANEL

Principal Findings

Overall Finding: The AP and IB programs are both designed to meet the educational needs of highly motivated and well-prepared students, but the origins, goals, purposes, missions, organizations, and structures of the two programs are very different. These differences contribute to variations in the educational expectations, opportunities, and experiences of students and teachers participating in the two programs.

Curriculum

Finding: The AP calculus curricula are largely sound. The recently revised syllabi with more emphasis on conceptual understanding have significantly improved the program, although further change in this direction is desirable. The panel also finds the focus on reasoning to be less than is needed.

Finding: The IB mathematics curricula are largely sound. The portfolio requirement, with its emphasis on applications of mathematics, is likely to introduce a focus on modeling that will benefit IB students. However, the calculus section of the syllabi do not place enough emphasis on conceptual understanding. The panel also has some concern that the breadth of the curricula, although an attractive feature of the program, could lead to superficial learning.

Instruction and Professional Development

Finding: Neither the College Board nor the IBO explicitly articulates in its published materials what it considers to be excellent teaching in mathematics.

Finding: Adequate preparation of teachers for courses leading to calculus or other advanced study options is a critical factor in enabling students to succeed in the advanced courses.

Finding: The availability of high-quality professional development activities and the establishment of support networks for AP and IB mathematics teachers are crucial to promoting and maintaining excellence in these programs.

Finding: U.S. teachers have few opportunities to deepen their understanding of mathematics during the school year, and opportunities during the summer, while useful, tend to be disconnected from everyday teaching.

Assessment

Finding: AP and IB curricula are designed to prepare students for successful performance on end-of-course examinations. The content and structure of the examinations, therefore, have a profound effect on what is taught and how it is taught in AP and IB classrooms.

Finding: The AP examinations have improved under the current syllabi. The effort to promote conceptual understanding by asking nonstandard questions and requiring verbal explanations is excellent. For example, the fact that there is now a wider variety of applications of integration (and not from a prescribed list) encourages students to think about the meaning of an integral. The inclusion of graphing problems involving a parameter focuses attention on the behavior of a family of functions. The variety of representations of a function—by a graph and a table as well as by a formula—promotes better understanding of the concept of function. However, the exam is still predictable enough for many students to do respectably well by mastering question types rather than concepts. The exam does not include enough problems that focus on conceptual understanding. More problems are needed that involve multiple steps, test technical skills in the context of applied problems, ask for interpretation and explanation of results, include substantial realistic applications of calculus, and test reasoning or theoretical understanding.

Finding: The IB exam benefits from being more varied than the AP exams. However, a few exam questions are at too low a level as they ask students to perform algorithms specified in the problem. The exam should include more problems that focus on conceptual understanding, and does not include enough problems that test whether students know which algorithm to apply (e.g., integration by substitution), test technical skills in the context of applied problems, ask for interpretation and explanation of results, and include substantial realistic applications.

Finding: The problems on the AP and IB assessments are too predictable. This encourages teachers to focus on helping students recognize and solve particular problem types. A less predictable examination would encourage instruction focused on the development of students' critical thinking and problem-solving abilities.

Finding: Both AP and IB examinations lack good applications and connections to the real-world uses of mathematics. The IB examinations appear weaker than the AP examinations in this regard.

Finding: Students who do not take the examination at the conclusion of an AP or IB course miss the opportunity to pull the material together for themselves. They also have a negative effect on the experience of other students by making the course appear to be less serious.

Impact of Calculus

Finding: The adequacy of the preparation students receive before taking calculus has an effect on whether they can understand or merely do calculus. Without understanding, students cannot apply what they know and do not remember the calculus they have learned.

Finding: Many teachers and schools are under great pressure to compress algebra and trigonometry so they can prepare as many students as possible for calculus. Sometimes students spend too little time mastering the prerequisite knowledge and skills. The performance of many calculus students is undermined by the fact that they do not learn pre-calculus thoroughly or learn to solve problems and think mathematically. Thus, the rush to calculus may curtail their future options to pursue mathematics, science, and engineering. It is important to realize that it is not the structure or curriculum of AP calculus that causes this problem, but the ways in which the program are used.

Finding: There are not enough checks in the system to ensure that students have the prerequisite algebra, trigonometry, and precalculus skills necessary for success in calculus and courses beyond.

Finding: The courses that precede calculus are often designed to help students make a smooth transition to an AP course. The topics and speed of prerequisite courses are determined by what is needed for AP. Even schools that do not offer AP calculus usually teach from books and curricula that are used in other schools to prepare students for this course. Thus, the AP curriculum influences many more courses and many more students than those who take the AP examinations.

Finding: Most college and university placement and credit practices that are based on student performance on AP or IB calculus examinations are reasonable.

Finding: Data on the number of AP and IB courses offered by schools and the results of the examinations are sometimes used in ways for which they were not intended, thus creating situations that can be detrimental to student learning (see also Chapter 10, this volume).

Recommendations

Preparation of Students

Recommendation: All calculus taught in high school should be at a college level.

Recommendation: All students who enroll in AP calculus should have had at least 4 years of college preparatory mathematics prior to AP calculus.

The structure of IB mathematics courses is different, and this recommendation is not applicable to them.

Recommendation: Strategies must be developed to ensure that students who enroll in calculus have an adequate background in algebra and trigonometry for subsequent work in mathematics and science.

Instruction and Teacher Professional Development

Recommendation: On-going professional development opportunities should be improved, expanded, and made available to all AP and IB teachers.

Recommendation: Schools that choose to offer AP and IB programs must find ways to encourage all teachers to take part in professional development, perhaps by providing time during the school day rather than on nights and weekends.

Recommendation: The College Board should consider developing procedures to certify AP calculus teachers.

Assessment

Recommendation: The AP and IB examinations should vary more from year to year. If teachers expect that major ideas will be assessed rather than specific problem types, it is likely that instruction will encourage the development of students' critical thinking and problem-solving abilities. The AP and IB examinations must strike a balance between judging students' conceptual understanding by asking unfamiliar probing questions, and alarming teachers and students with a strange and unfamiliar test.

Recommendation: Both the AP and IB programs should maintain and increase their focus on conceptual understanding in their assessments.

Recommendation: To assess computational and procedural knowledge, students should be asked questions that demonstrate their ability to use these procedures in solving complex problems.

Recommendation: All students enrolled in AP and IB courses ordinarily should take the relevant external examinations as part of the course requirements.

Recommendation: Both AP and IB examinations should place more emphasis on realistic applications, including those in which students must set up the mathematical model.

ANNEX A-1
CHARGE TO THE CONTENT PANELS

Charge to the Parent Committee and Content Panels: The charge to the committee is to consider the effectiveness of, and potential improvements to, programs for advanced study of mathematics and science in American high schools. In response to the charge, the committee will consider the two most widely recognized programs for advanced study: the Advanced Placement (AP) and the International Baccalaureate (IB) programs. In addition, the committee will identify and examine other appropriate curricular and instructional alternatives to IB and AP. Emphasis will be placed on the biology, chemistry, physics, and mathematics programs of study.

Charge to Content Panels: The content panels are asked to evaluate the AP and IB curricular, instructional, and assessment materials for their specific disciplines.

Below is a list of questions that the content panels will use to examine the curriculum, laboratory experiences, and student assessments for their specific subject areas. The content panels will use these questions to issue a report to the committee about the effectiveness of the AP and IB programs for educating able high school students in their respective disciplines. In answering these questions, the content panels should keep in mind the committee's charge and study questions.

The panels should focus on the following specific issues in advising the committee:

I. CURRICULAR AND CONCEPTUAL FRAMEWORKS FOR LEARNING

Research on cognition suggests that learning and understanding are facilitated when students: (1) have a strong foundation of background knowledge, (2) are taught and understand facts and ideas in the context of a conceptual framework, and (3) learn how to organize information to facilitate retrieval and application in new contexts (see, for example, NRC, 2000b).

1. To what degree do the AP and IB programs incorporate current knowledge about cognition and learning in mathematics and science in their curricula, instructions, and assessments?

2. To what degree is the factual base of information that is provided by the AP and IB curricula and related laboratory experiences adequate for advanced high school study in your discipline?

3. Based on your evaluation of the materials that you received, to what extent do the AP and IB curricula and assessments balance breadth of cov-

erage with in-depth study of important topics in the subject area? In your opinion, is this balance an appropriate one for advanced high school learners?

4. Are there key concepts (big ideas) of your discipline around which factual information and ideas should be organized to promote conceptual understanding in advanced study courses (e.g., Newton's Laws in physics)? To what degree are the AP and IB curricula and related laboratory experiences organized around these identified key concepts?

5. To what degree do the AP and IB curricula and related laboratory experiences provide opportunities for students to apply their knowledge to a range of problems and in a variety of contexts?

6. To what extent do the AP and IB curricula and related laboratory experiences encourage students and teachers to make connections among the various disciplines in science and mathematics?

II. THE ROLE OF ASSESSMENT

Research and experience indicate that assessments of student learning play a key role in determining what and how teachers teach and what and how students learn.

1. Based on your evaluation of the IB and AP final assessments and accompanying scoring guides and rubrics, evaluate to what degree these assessments measure or emphasize:

   (a) students' mastery of content knowledge;

   (b) students' understanding and application of concepts; and

   (c) students' ability to apply what they have learned to other courses and in other situations.

2. To what degree do the AP and IB final assessments assess student mastery of your disciplinary subject at a level that is consistent with expectations for similar courses that are taught at the college level?

III. TEACHING

Research and experience indicate that learning is facilitated when teachers use a variety of techniques that are purposefully selected to achieve particular learning goals.

1. How effectively do the AP and IB curricula and assessments encourage teachers to use a variety of teaching techniques (e.g., lecture, discussion, laboratory experience and independent investigation)?

2. What preparation is needed to effectively teach advanced mathematics and science courses such as AP and IB?

IV. EMPHASES

The *National Science Education Standards* (NRC, 1996) and the NCTM Standards (NCTM, 2000) propose that the emphases of science and mathematics education should change in particular ways (see supplemental materials).

1. To what degree do the AP and IB programs reflect the recommendations in these documents?

V. PREPARATION FOR FURTHER STUDY

Advanced study at the high school level is often viewed as preparation for continued study at the college level or as a substitute for introductory-level college courses.

1. To what extent do the AP and IB curricula, assessments, and related laboratory experiences in your discipline serve as adequate and appropriate bases for success in college courses beyond the introductory level?

2. To what degree do the AP and IB programs in your discipline reflect changes in knowledge or approaches that are emerging (or have recently occurred) in your discipline?

3. How might coordination between secondary schools and institutions of higher education be enhanced to optimize student learning and continued interest in the discipline?

Appendix B

Biographical Sketches of Committee Members

JERRY P. GOLLUB *(Cochair)* is John and Barbara Bush Professor in the Natural Sciences (Physics) at Haverford College. He is a member of the National Academy of Sciences (NAS), a fellow of the American Academy of Arts and Sciences, and a recipient of a research award from the American Physical Society. His research focuses on nonlinear and nonequilibrium phenomena, including instabilities and pattern formation in fluids, chaotic dynamics and turbulence, and granular materials. He is coauthor of *Chaotic Dynamics: An Introduction*, an undergraduate textbook. Since 1981 he has also been affiliated with the University of Pennsylvania, where he is a member of the graduate groups in both physics and mechanical engineering. Dr. Gollub has served as Provost of Haverford College and currently chairs its Physics Department. He has served on the advisory board of the National Science Resources Center, curriculum developers for schools, and has been a member of the National Research Council's (NRC) Commission on Physical Sciences, Mathematics, and Applications. He received his Ph.D. in experimental condensed matter physics from Harvard University.

PHILIP C. CURTIS, JR. *(Cochair)* is Professor of Mathematics Emeritus at the University of California at Los Angeles, where he has taught mathematics since 1955. He has served as vice chair and chair of the University of California Board of Admissions and Relations with Schools, chairman of the faculty of the UCLA College of Letters and Science, chair of the UCLA Mathematics Department, director of the UCLA Teaching Interns Program in Mathematics, and chair of the Committee for Mathematics and Science Scholars. Dr. Curtis has served on the NRC's Study Group on Guidelines for Mathematics Assessment. He received his Ph.D. from Yale University.

CAMILLA BENBOW is Dean of the Peabody College of Education and Human Development at Vanderbilt University. Her field is educational psychology, and her research has focused on the optimal development of talent, strategies for teaching gifted and talented students, and academic achievement in math and science. She has also served as director of the Iowa Talent Search Program and as codirector for the Study of Mathematically Precocious Youth at The Johns Hopkins University, at Iowa State University, and now at Vanderbilt. In addition, she has directed other studies and programs for gifted and talented and mathematically precocious youth. Dr. Benbow received her M.A. in psychology and her M.S. and Ph.D. in education from The Johns Hopkins University.

HILDA BORKO is a professor in the School of Education at the University of Colorado at Boulder. Her field is educational psychology, and her research has focused on teacher cognition and teacher learning. Specific interests have included teachers' understanding of education reform, teacher preparation and professional development, and instruction and assessment. Dr. Borko has served on numerous professional committees. In addition to her service editing and reviewing for professional publications, she has published extensively on many aspects of teacher preparation and learning to teach. She received her M.A. in the philosophy of education and her Ph.D. in educational psychology from the University of California at Los Angeles.

WANDA BUSSEY is Mathematics Department chair and teacher of International Baccalaureate Higher Level Mathematics at Rufus King High School in Milwaukee, Wisconsin, where she has taught since 1979. She assisted the school in instituting and developing its IB program and is an IB Senior Teacher. She has also served as an assistant examiner for the IB Examinations Office. Her work in that capacity has entailed curriculum development, modeling of her school's program for others, and presentations at IB workshops around the country. Ms. Bussey has taught calculus at Marquette University and at the University of Wisconsin and is a recipient of the Tandy Technology Scholar Teacher of the Year award. She received her M.S. in mathematics from the University of Wisconsin, Milwaukee.

GLENN A. CROSBY is Professor of Chemistry and Materials Science Emeritus at Washington State University. His research has focused on investigation of the electronic excited states of metal complexes; design of materials for solar energy storage; investigation of photochemical reactions; and design of semiconducting, photoconducting, and paramagnetic solids. Dr. Crosby has received numerous awards for his teaching and has been active in the development of science programs for high school students and professional development programs for teachers. He received his Ph.D. in physical chemistry from the University of Washington.

JOHN A. DOSSEY is Distinguished University Professor of Mathematics Emeritus at Illinois State University. His research interests include evaluation in mathematics education, international mathematics education, and assessment in mathematics education. Dr. Dossey served as president of the National Council of Teachers of Mathematics during the writing of that organization's standards for school mathematics. He has also chaired the Conference Board of the Mathematical Sciences and the U.S. Commission on Mathematical Instruction at the NRC, as well as the College Board's Mathematical Sciences Advisory Committee. He has served on the NRC's Board on International Comparative Studies in Education, which has devoted considerable attention to the Third International Mathematics and Science Study. Dr. Dossey received his Ph.D. in mathematics education from the University of Illinois, Urbana-Champaign.

DAVID ELY is a teacher of Advanced Placement Biology at Champlain Valley Union High School in Hinesburg, Vermont. He has been an exam reader for the AP biology program for 7 years and has been involved in the development of Vermont's science framework and assessments. Mr. Ely has been named National Science Teachers Association/Shell Outstanding National Science Teacher of the Year and has received the Distinguished Teacher Award from the White House Commission on Scholars, as well as many other teaching awards. He received his B.A. and M.A.T. in zoology from the University of Vermont.

DEBORAH HUGHES HALLETT is a professor of mathematics at the University of Arizona; from 1991 to 1998 she was a professor of Practice in the Teaching of Mathematics at Harvard University. She was a principal investigator for the National Science Foundation (NSF)–funded Bridge Calculus Consortium. She has served on committees for the Graduate Record Examination and the Massachusetts state mathematics framework review process, and on the Mathematics and Science Teacher Education Program (MASTEP) Advisory Board, an NSF-funded program to improve teacher training in California. Dr. Hughes Hallett served on the NRC's Committee on Information Technology in Undergraduate Education. A Fulbright Scholar, she received M.A. degrees from both Harvard University and the University of Cambridge, England.

JOHN K. HAYNES is David Packard Professor of Science and chair of the Biology Department at Morehouse College. He is also an adjunct professor of Physiology at Brown University. He has served on a number of panels concerned with education issues, including that for the Undergraduate Biological Sciences Education Program of the Howard Hughes Medical Institute. Dr. Haynes served on the NRC's Committee on Undergraduate Science Education and has been a councilor in the Biology Division for the Council on Undergraduate Research. He serves as chair of the Minorities Affairs Committee of the American Society for Cell Biology. He received his Ph.D. in developmental biology from Brown University.

VALERIE E. LEE is a professor of education at the University of Michigan. Her research has focused on school size and the development of more personalized social relations in schools. She has also studied high school restructuring, factors that influence achievement, ability tracking, and academic behaviors. Some of her research has targeted the development of high-achieving minority students and gender differences in mathematics and science achievement. Dr. Lee received her Ed.D. from Harvard University.

STEPHANIE PACE MARSHALL is founding president of the Illinois Mathematics and Science Academy and has served in that capacity since 1986. A former Superintendent of Schools in Batavia, Illinois, she has also served as president of the Association for Supervision and Curriculum Development International, and was founding president of the National Consortium for Specialized Schools of Mathematics, Science, and Technology. Dr. Marshall received her M.A. in curriculum and philosophy from the University of Chicago and her Ph.D. in educational administration and industrial relations from Loyola University in Chicago.

MICHAEL E. MARTINEZ joined the NSF in September 2001 as a program officer in the Division of Research, Evaluation, and Communication. He is currently on leave from the University of California, Irvine, Department of Education, where he teaches courses in the psychology of learning and intelligence, evaluation and assessment, and research methods. A former high school science teacher, Dr. Martinez received his Ph.D. in Educational Psychology from Stanford University in 1987. He then joined the Division of Research at the Educational Testing Service in Princeton, New Jersey, where he developed new forms of computer-based testing for assessment in science, architecture, and engineering. This work led to two U.S. patents. In 1994–1995, Dr. Martinez was a Fulbright Scholar at the University of the South Pacific in the Fiji Islands. He now conducts research on the nature of proficiency in science and mathematics and on the nature and modifiability of intelligence. He has published in such journals as *Educational Psychologist*, the *Journal of Educational Measurement*, and the *Journal of the American Society for Information Science*. His first book, *Education as the Cultivation of Intelligence*, was published in 2000 by Lawrence Erlbaum Associates.

PATSY W. MUELLER taught science at Highland Park High School in Highland Park, Illinois, from 1966 until 2001, when she accepted a position teaching science at Regina Dominican High School in Wilmette, Illinois. For the past 24 years, Ms. Mueller has taught both Honors Chemistry and the Advanced Placement Chemistry course. She has conducted numerous AP summer institutes since 1991, including week-long sessions for other AP Chemistry teachers. Ms. Mueller has served as a member of the American Chemical Society's (ACS) Test Development Committee and the College Board's Chemistry Test Development Committee. She has received the Tandy Technology Award and been named a Siemens Scholar, both in recognition of her excellence in teaching. Ms. Mueller received her B.S. in chemical education from the University of Illinois and her M.S. in chemistry from Clarkson.

JOSEPH NOVAK is visiting senior research scientist at the Institute for Human and Machine Cognition at the University of West Florida. Previously he was professor of science education and Professor of Biological Sciences Emeritus at Cornell University, where he taught from 1969 to 1998. Dr. Novak has conducted research on teaching and learning in science and other areas. His research team developed the concept mapping tool now being used widely in schools and corporations. His recent books include *Learning, Creating and Using Knowledge*; *Teaching Science for Understanding*; and *Assessing Science Understanding* (with Joel Mintzes and James Wandersee). He has received numerous honors, including the first award for outstanding research contributions to science teaching from the Council of Scientific Society Presidents. Dr. Novak received an M.S. in science education and a Ph.D. degree in science education and biology from the University of Minnesota.

JEANNIE OAKES is Presidential Professor of Education in the Graduate School of Information Studies at the University of California at Los Angeles. She directs UCLA's Institute for Democracy, Education, and Access and the University of California's All Campus Collaborative on Research for Diversity. She has also served as a consultant and Senior Social Scientist for the Education and Human Resources Program at RAND in Santa Monica. Dr. Oakes's research has focused on resources and learning opportunities in U.S. schools, school reform, tracking, school organization, and curriculum. She received her M.A. in American studies from the California State University in Los Angeles and her Ph.D. in education from UCLA.

VERA RUBIN is an observational astronomer in the Department of Terrestrial Magnetism at the Carnegie Institution of Washington and a member of the National Academy of Sciences. She is a recipient of the National Medal of

Science and was honored at the Academy's first annual Women in Science and Engineering program. She is a former member of the Board on Physics and Astronomy and has served on many other NRC bodies. She earned her Ph.D. from Georgetown University.

ROBIN SPITAL is a teacher of Honors and Advanced Placement Physics at The Bolles School in Jacksonville, Florida. His career began at Illinois State University in Normal, where he was assistant professor of physics. He subsequently worked in the private sector as principal development engineer for the AAI Corporation in Hunt Valley, Maryland, and as principal scientist for Pfizer Medical Systems. Dr. Spital received his Ph.D. in theoretical high-energy physics from Cornell University.

CONRAD L. STANITSKI is professor of chemistry and chair of the Chemistry Department at the University of Central Arkansas. His principal focus is inorganic chemistry and general chemistry for science and nonscience majors. He is currently Chair of the ACS Division of Chemical Education, was a member of the ACS Committee on Education, has directed numerous ACS teacher-training workshops, is an NSF proposal reviewer, and has been an invited speaker and workshop leader in seven foreign countries. Dr. Stanitski has authored or coauthored several highly regarded textbooks in the field, including *Chemistry in Context: Applying Chemistry to Society*; *The Chemical World: Concepts and Applications*; *Chemical Principles*; *Chemistry in the Community*; and *Chemistry for Health-Related Sciences: Concepts and Applications*. He received his B.S. in science education from Bloomsburg State College, his M.A. in chemistry education from the University of Northern Iowa, and his Ph.D. in inorganic chemistry from the University of Connecticut.

WILLIAM B. WOOD is professor of Molecular, Cellular, and Developmental Biology at the University of Colorado, Boulder, where he formerly served as department Chair. He is a member of the NAS, a fellow of the American Academy of Arts and Sciences, and a recipient of the NAS Molecular Biology Award. His current research focuses on the mechanisms by which cell fates and patterns are determined during embryonic development of the nematode *C. elegans*, using techniques of genetics, cell biology, and molecular biology. Dr. Wood was lead author of the widely used textbook *Biochemistry: A Problems Approach*, which helped introduce problem-based learning to biochemistry; he subsequently spearheaded the development of a graduate core course in molecular, cellular, and developmental biology that served as a model for many departments around the country. He received his Ph.D. in biochemistry from Stanford University.

Appendix C

Statement of Task

The charge to the committee is to consider the effectiveness of, and potential improvements to, programs for advanced study of mathematics and science in American high schools. In response to the charge, the committee will consider the two most widely recognized programs for advanced study: the Advanced Placement (AP) and the International Baccalaureate (IB) programs. In addition, the committee will identify and examine other appropriate curricular and instructional alternatives to IB and AP. Emphasis will be placed on the mathematics, physics, chemistry, and biology programs of study.

I. LEARNING

1. What does research tell us about how high-school aged students learn science and mathematics? Does this process differ significantly for the most advanced students?

2. To what extent do the AP and IB or other programs for advanced students incorporate current knowledge about cognition and learning in mathematics and science in their curricula, instruction, and assessments? How could research on cognition and learning be used to improve these programs?

3. What is the impact of student assessment on the learning process in mathematics and science? How could student assessment be used to improve student learning in advanced courses?

II. TEACHING

1. What does research tell us about effective instructional practices for high-school aged students generally, and for advanced students in particular?

2. To what extent do AP and IB programs encourage teaching practices that are consistent with current research on effective instructional practices? Are there alternative programs that are more effective in this regard?

3. How do final assessments generally, and AP and IB assessments in particular, influence instructional practices?

4. What academic qualifications are needed to teach advanced science and mathematics courses, and how are teachers actually selected?

5. What does research tell us about how teachers learn to teach, and about effective professional development practices? What does this research imply about the nature and quality of professional development opportunities for teachers offered by programs of advanced study, including AP and IB?

III. CURRICULUM AND STANDARDS

1. To what extent do the IB and AP programs reflect the best in current thinking about content and curriculum for teaching mathematics and science? Are any alternative programs superior in some respects?

2. How do the content and performance standards of the AP and IB programs compare with one another and with the NRC *National Science Education Standards* or those of the Mathematical Association of America or the National Council of Teachers of Mathematics?

3. To what extent do programs such as AP and IB help to promote and elevate academic standards in high schools, both within individual subject areas and generally?

How do AP and IB standards compare with those used by other programs for advanced study in science and mathematics? How do AP and IB standards compare with those of other technologically advanced nations?

IV. CONTEXT AND CONSEQUENCES

1. How do the beliefs and values about the purpose of secondary schooling held by the American public influence what courses high schools offer, access to these courses, how the courses are taught, and what students learn in them, particularly in advanced courses in mathematics and science?

2. What constraints do the culture and resources of American high schools typically place on programs for advanced study?

3. How can the goal of equitable and broad access to programs for advanced study best be pursued?

4. How does the interface with higher education affect programs for advanced study in the secondary schools?

Index